Was the Good Samaritan a Bad Economist?

Was the Good Samaritan a Bad Economist?

Charles K. Wilber

LEXINGTON BOOKS
Lanham • Boulder • New York • London

Published by Lexington Books
An imprint of The Rowman & Littlefield Publishing Group, Inc.
4501 Forbes Boulevard, Suite 200, Lanham, Maryland 20706
www.rowman.com

6 Tinworth Street, London SE11 5AL, United Kingdom

British Library Cataloguing in Publication Information Available

Library of Congress Control Number: 2021931405

ISBN 978-1-7936-3700-0 (cloth)
ISBN 978-1-7936-3701-7 (electronic)

For my wife and partner of many years, Mary Ellen Wilber,
both for her steadfast support and for her participation in
the Catholic Action activities that have shaped our lives.

Contents

Acknowledgments

This book has been long in the making. It is my attempt to show how religious faith can be important in framing economic policy. Economics is enriched by recognizing that economic actors (consumers, workers, investors, et al.) are motivated by deeply embedded moral codes as well as self-interest. In this book I use Catholic Social Thought as the way to think through these issues. I have been fortunate to have had wonderful colleagues who taught me and inspired me along the way. Ken Jameson of the University of Utah and Jim Weaver of The American University have been especially close and important in my development both as a person and as an economist. For over 30 years we met every few years, three-four days at a time, to discuss and "solve" the problems of the world. Three other colleagues deserve special mention. Michael Baxter, a theologian and founder of a Catholic Worker house, urged me to write a book showing the role of faith in my economics. This may not be what he had in mind, but it is what it is. His approach to theology is apparent throughout the text. Denis Goulet, the founder of the field of development ethics, was both a collaborator and dear friend, who introduced me to a type of ethical reflection beyond the standard philosophic versions. Finally, my friend and colleague Amitava Dutt has reinforced my recognition that morality and goodness are not limited to Christians. They exist among all faiths and none. I emphasize my Christian faith because it is the way I know, and it has given meaning to my life and work. I need to acknowledge that several sections of this book are based on joint work with both Jameson and Dutt. I hereby thank them for their work as I do also in the text that follows.

Part I

FOUNDATIONS

Chapter One

The Good Samaritan and Catholic Social Thought

In this book I write as an economist and a Roman Catholic, but I hope it is useful to all Christians; and, of course, not only Christians, but all those of whatever faith who believe that their faith is important not only in their personal lives but also in their work. The Parable of the Good Samaritan has haunted me both in my personal life and as an economist. Was the Good Samaritan a bad economist?

> Just then a lawyer . . . asked Jesus, "And who is my neighbor?" Jesus replied, "A man was going down from Jerusalem to Jericho, and fell into the hands of robbers, who stripped him, beat him, and went away, leaving him half dead. Now by chance a priest was going down that road; and when he saw him, he passed by on the other side. So likewise a Levite, when he came to the place and saw him, passed by on the other side. But a Samaritan while travelling came near him; and when he saw him, he was moved with pity. He went to him and bandaged his wounds, having poured oil and wine on them. Then he put him on his own animal, brought him to an inn, and took care of him. The next day he took out two denarii, gave them to the innkeeper, and said, "Take care of him; and when I come back, I will repay you whatever more you spend." Which of these three, do you think, was a neighbor to the man who fell into the hands of the robbers?" He said, "The one who showed him mercy." Jesus said to him, "Go and do likewise." (Lk 10: 25, 29-37)

In the economics I studied, people are motivated primarily by self-interest and that behavior combined with free markets leads to optimal economic outcomes. The Catholic faith that I came to learn, and particularly the parable of the Good Samaritan, taught me that serving others comes before serving one's self. This contradiction has shaped both my economics and my personal life.

The traditional advice given to anyone preparing to give a speech is: "Tell them what you are going to say, say it, end by telling them what you said." This is also good advice for an author. I want to tell you three things: (1) the American economy has not only failed to overcome poverty, but it has also generated extreme inequality that in turn restricts social mobility and causes high levels of unhappiness; (2) economic theory and policy are inescapably value leaden with their focus on self-interest and bias for atomistic individualism; and (3) Christian values are one way to provide the needed values for an alternative social economics.

I do this in the context of how I learned the connection between economics and Christian values. This first chapter focuses on that context. My interest in economics was triggered after becoming involved in our parish social justice group. This requires some personal history.

FROM CATHOLIC ACTION TO ECONOMIC THEORY

After finishing my B.A. in accounting and philosophy at the University of Portland—the former to earn a living since I was married with two children when I graduated and the latter because I loved it—I worked in public accounting long enough to get my C.P.A. In 1958 we joined St. Cecilia's Catholic Church, Beaverton, Oregon, and became active in the Christian Family Movement (CFM). A concern with justice was instilled by our participation in CFM which utilized the observe-judge-act approach to bring Christian values to bear upon the problems of the social, economic, and political worlds in which we lived.

I worked in a small accounting firm doing the books and preparing tax returns for small businesses such as jewelry stores, sawmills, etc. My boss was asked for a suggestion of someone to teach accounting part time at Multnomah Junior College and he thought I might enjoy doing that in addition to working for him. I jumped at the chance and was required to teach economics (which I had only a couple of undergraduate courses in) and mathematics in addition to accounting. I became intrigued by economics because of my desire to attain a better understanding of the causes of poverty and how to overcome it. The national chaplain of CFM, Fr. Louie Putz, urged me to get a master's degree. As a result, I went back to school at the University of Portland and got a M.S. degree in social science. Then I quit the accounting firm and taught full time while doing the master's degree.

Our continued participation in CFM taught us that we are the hands and feet of Christ in the world. We are called to serve the poor and disadvantaged, seek justice and peace, and grow in faith wherever we found ourselves—in the home, at work, through church. Through our CFM group we lobbied for laws to protect migrant workers in the strawberry fields and helped set up and sponsor a program to bring in Dutch-Indonesian refugees to the Portland area. The idea spread to other CFM groups in the area and eventually 120 families were sponsored and brought into the area. But most of our actions were more modest and were home centered. Let me give one example. It is in families that children first learn to love their neighbors as themselves. One of the first times we taught our children this was at Christmas. After we opened our gifts, we suggested that each member of the family should select one of their gifts and give it to the local Catholic Worker house which in turn would see that the gifts went to those less fortunate than ourselves. We emphasized the obligation to share our riches with those who had none. Our oldest son, Kenny, who was four at the time, chose his most expensive present, a huge, beautiful fire engine that his grandmother had given him. We told him it wasn't necessary to give his biggest, most expensive gift. He insisted. We were rather red-faced when his grandmother asked where the fire engine was.

During this time that we were very involved in our local parish, particularly in its social ministry, our Christian faith became revitalized as we came to realize through study of the bible and Catholic social thought that we all are called to do God's work in this world. To love God is to love neighbor:

> Those who say, "I love God", and hate their brothers or sisters, are liars; for those who do not love a brother or sister- whom they have seen, cannot love God whom they have not seen. The commandment we have from him is this: those who love God must love their brothers and sisters- also. (1Jn: 4, 19-20)

The Biblical Tradition

I learned that the Old Testament prophets called for social justice and condemned excessive and irresponsible wealth. This changed my way of seeing the world. Central to the biblical view is that justice in a community is most directly tested by its treatment of the powerless in society, most often described as the widow, the orphan, the poor and the stranger (non-Israelite) in the land. The prophets continually call the king and the people back to commitment to justice for the powerless. They direct scathing attacks at the rich and powerful who "sell the just man for silver, and the poor man for a pair of sandals. They trample the heads of the weak into the dust of the earth and force the lowly out of the way" (Am 2:6-7). Isaiah pronounces God's judgment on those "who have devoured the vineyard; the loot wrested from the poor is in your houses" (Is 3:14). Jeremiah condemns the man "who builds his house on wrong, his terraces on injustice." He praises King Josiah because "he dispensed justice to the weak and the poor." Jeremiah then adds the startling statement: "Is this not true knowledge of me? Says the Lord" (Jer 22:16). He then adds, "your eyes and heart are set on nothing except on your own gain" (Jer 22:17). Thus, doing of justice is equated with knowledge of the Lord. The practice of justice is constitutive of true belief. And the pursuit of self-interest is seen as a stumbling block to knowing and serving God. At the beginning of Lent, a reading from Isaiah 58:5-7 proclaims:

> Is this the manner of fasting I would choose,/ a day to afflict oneself?/ To bow one's head like a reed,/ and lie upon sackcloth and ashes?/ Is this what you call a fast,/ a day acceptable to the LORD?
>
> Is this not, rather, the fast that I choose:/ releasing those bound unjustly,/ untying the thongs of the yoke;/ Setting free the oppressed,/ breaking off every yoke?/ Is it not sharing your bread with the hungry,/ bringing the afflicted and the homeless into your house;/ Clothing the naked when you see them,/ and not turning your back on your own flesh?

If Jesus is, as Christians claim, Lord, and the son of God, then he is Lord of every aspect of our lives, including the economic one, and his teaching and example must have some relevance to economics as well. In fact, Jesus followed in the prophetic tradition, taking the side of those who are powerless or on the margin of his society such as the tax collectors (Lk 15:12), the widow (Lk 7:11-17; Mk 12:41-44), the Samaritan (Lk 17:11-19), the sinful woman (Lk 7:36-50), and children (Mk 10:13-16). Jesus's description of the final judgment in Matthew 25 (31-46) still haunts me with its powerful message of what it means to be a Christian:

> When the Son of Man comes in his glory, and all the angels with him, he will sit upon his glorious throne, and all the nations will be assembled before him. And he will separate them one from another, as a shepherd separates the sheep from the goats. He will place the sheep on his right and the goats on his left. Then the king will say to those on his right, "Come, you who are blessed by my Father. Inherit the kingdom prepared for you from the foundation of the world. For I was hungry and you gave me food, I was thirsty and you gave me drink, a stranger and you welcomed me, naked and you clothed me, ill and you cared for me, in prison and you visited me." Then the righteous will answer him and say, "Lord, when did we see you hungry and feed you, or thirsty and give you drink? When did we see you a stranger and welcome you, or naked and clothe you? When did we see you ill or in prison, and visit you?" And the king will say to them in reply, "Amen, I say to you, whatever you did for one of these least brothers of mine, you did for me." Then he will say to those on his left, "Depart from me, you accursed, into the eternal fire prepared for the devil and his angels. For I was hungry and you gave me no food, I was thirsty and you gave me no drink, a stranger and you gave me no welcome, naked and you gave

me no clothing, ill and in prison, and you did not care for me." Then they will answer and say, "Lord, when did we see you hungry or thirsty or a stranger or naked or ill or in prison, and not minister to your needs?" He will answer them, "Amen, I say to you, what you did not do for one of these least ones, you did not do for me." And these will go off to eternal punishment, but the righteous to eternal life.

The Catholic Social Thought Tradition

My study of scripture was reinforced by the tradition of CST that I learned then and over the years since. It is rooted in a commitment to certain fundamental values—the right to human dignity, the need for human freedom and participation, the importance of community, and the nature of the common good. These values are drawn from the belief that each person is called to be a co-creator with God, participating in the redemption of the world and the furthering of the Kingdom. This requires social and human development where the religious and temporal aspects of life are not separated and opposed to each other.

As a result of these fundamental values two principles permeate CST. The first is a special concern for the poor and powerless which leads to a criticism of political and economic structures that oppress them. The second is a concern for certain human rights against the collectivist tendencies of the state and the neglect of the free market.

Ever since *Rerum Novarum*[1] in 1891, CST has taught that both state socialism and free market capitalism violate these principles. State socialism denies the right of private property, excites the envy of the poor against the rich leading to class struggle instead of cooperation, and violates the proper order of society by the state usurping the role of individuals and social groups.[2] Free market capitalism denies the concept of the common good and the "social and public character of the right of property,"[3] including the principle of the universal destination of the earth's goods;[4] and violates human dignity by treating labor merely as a commodity to be bought and sold in the marketplace.[5] Pope John Paul II summarizes the thrust of CST when he says:

> The individual today is often suffocated between two poles represented by the State and the marketplace. At times it seems as though he exists only as a producer and consumer of goods, or as an object of State administration. People lose sight of the fact that life in society has neither the market nor the State as its final purpose, since life itself has a unique value which the State and the market must serve.[6]

The concept of the common good in CST emphasizes both the dignity of the human person and the essentially social nature of that dignity. Both civil and political liberties on the one hand and social and economic needs on the other are essential components of the common good. The common good is not the aggregate of the welfare of all individuals. Rather it is a set of social conditions necessary for the realization of human dignity which transcend the arena of private exchange and contract. Such conditions or goods are essentially relational. To exist they must exist as shared. In short, individual persons have rights to those things necessary to realize their dignity as human beings. CST argues further that in pursuing the common good, special concern must be given to the economy's impact on the poor and powerless because they are particularly vulnerable and needy.[7]

Pope John XXIII, in his encyclical *Pacem in Terris*, set out in detail a full range of human rights that can only be realized and protected in solidarity with others.[8] These rights include the civil and political rights to freedom of speech, worship, and assembly. He also includes a number of economic rights concerning human welfare. First among these are the rights to life, food, clothing, shelter, rest, medical care, and basic education. In order to ensure these rights, everyone has the right to earn a living. Everyone also has a right to security in the event of illness, unemployment, or old age. The right to participate in the community requires the right of employment, as well as the right to healthful working conditions, wages, and other benefits sufficient to support families at a level in keeping with human dignity.

CST repudiates the position that the level of unemployment, the degree of poverty, the quantity of environmental destruction, and other such outcomes should be left to the dictates of the market. Emphasis on the common good means that the community has an obligation to ensure the right of employment to all persons, to help the disadvantaged overcome their poverty, and to safeguard the environment.[9]

Although CST defends the right to private ownership of productive property,[10] the common good sometimes demands that this right be limited by the community through state regulation, taxation, and even, under exceptional circumstances, public ownership.[11] The attainment and safeguarding of human rights sometimes require the overriding of market outcomes. Therefore, CST insists that "government has a moral function: protecting human rights and securing basic justice for all members of the commonwealth."[12] Pope John Paul II says society and the state have the duty of "defending the basic rights of workers," defending those "collective and qualitative needs which cannot be satisfied by market mechanisms," and "overseeing and directing the exercise of human rights in the economic sector."[13]

Catholic thought sees society as made up of a dense network of relations among individuals, families, churches, neighborhood associations, business firms, labor unions, and different levels of government. Thus, every level of society has a role to play in ensuring basic human rights and the common good. In CST this is expressed as the "principle of subsidiarity:"

> Just as it is gravely wrong to take from individuals what they can accomplish by their own initiative and industry and give it to the community, so also it is an injustice and at the same time a grave evil and disturbance of right order to assign to a greater and higher association what lesser and subordinate organizations can do. For every social activity ought of its very nature to furnish help (subsidium) to the members of the body social, and never destroy and absorb them.[14]

This principle provides for a pluralism of social actors. Each, from the individual person to the federal government, has obligations. Higher levels should not usurp the authority of lower levels except when necessary. However, the principle works both ways. When individuals, families, or local communities are unable to solve problems that undermine the common good, the state governments are obligated to intervene, and if their resources and abilities are inadequate, then the federal government assumes the responsibility. This principle also extends into the international economy. As Pope John Paul II says, "This increasing internationalization of the economy ought to be accompanied by effective international agencies which will oversee and direct the economy to the common good, something that an individual State, even if it were the most powerful on earth, would not be in a position to do."[15]

The right to private property and the principle of subsidiarity limit the role of the state while the principle of solidarity[16] requires that society and the state intervene in markets to protect human rights, particularly of the poorest. The thrust of CST, therefore, has been to repudiate both state socialism and free market capitalism.

Since the primary "signs of the times" that Pope John Paul II focused on in *Centesimus Annus* (1991) was the collapse of Communism in Eastern Europe, he emphasized the limits to the role of the state and the utility of markets in providing incentives for production. However, this was a highly qualified endorsement as when he says the efficiency of markets in fulfilling human needs is true only for those needs which are 'solvent,' insofar as they are endowed with purchasing power, and for those resources which are 'marketable,' insofar as they are capable of obtaining a satisfactory price. But there are many human needs which find no place on the market."[17] Thus, markets do not adequately fulfill the needs of those who have little income or provide for non-marketable goods such as a clean environment and participation in the workplace. He also registered his fears about the impact of markets on the "human environment" and their role in creating "consumerism."[18]

What actual economic system does CST endorse? Explicitly, none. As Pope John Paul II says: "The Church has no models to present"[19] of the best economic system; that is for history to decide in each individual case. However, he did carefully distinguish between free market capitalism, which he criticizes, and a socially regulated version he calls "the new capitalism." Free market capitalism fails to provide adequate housing, medical care, education, socio-economic security, and meaningful participation in economic life for all families, including the poorest. Its unrestrained profit motive results in environmental destruction, promotes a soulless consumerism, and destroys the human environment needed by a community of persons.[20] It is social regulation, guided by the principles of subsidiarity and solidarity, that can overcome the injustices of free market capitalism. The degree of regulation is not a matter of principle but rather a case of prudential judgment in particular cases.

Some argue that the U.S. economy comes closest to resembling the ideal of the new capitalism envisaged in *Centesimus Annus*.[21] It is true that the economic policies and social welfare measures enacted from the 1930s through the 1960s tamed the worst consequences of free market capitalism. Macroeconomic stabilization policies reduced average unemployment levels, Social Security enhanced the life of the elderly, and various income maintenance programs helped the very poor. However, this regulated market economy came under attack during the 1980s from a free market philosophy that was resurrected with the election of Ronald Reagan as president. Government programs established during the previous 45 years were attacked because they supposedly reduced incentives and thus productivity. Free up the economy and all would be well. Reduce welfare, minimum wages, and unemployment benefits so that the poor would have greater incentives to work. Lower taxes and remove regulations on business so that the resulting higher profits would encourage corporations and wealthy individuals to save and invest. Increased productivity and growth in GDP would result. Eventually, the benefits would trickle down so that even those on the bottom would be better off than before. This vision of the world—where free individuals pursue their self-interest to the greater good of all—is at odds both with the results of economic policies since the 1980s and with much of CST.

With this theological and philosophical background, and with a master's degree, I went, with my wife and children, to teach accounting, mathematics, and economics at the Catholic University in Ponce, Puerto Rico. It was the university vice-chancellor, Msgr. Ivan Illich, who invited me to teach in Puerto Rico. During our stay he became my mentor and convinced me that I needed to get a Ph.D. in economics before anyone would listen to what I had to say. I accepted an assistantship at the University of Maryland with the intention of concentrating on the problems of development in Third World countries.

ECONOMIC THEORY: FROM THE GOLDEN AGE TO A POST-PANDEMIC WORLD

At that time, the economics department at Maryland was dominated by Keynesians and even included courses in Institutionalism. However, they were all thoroughgoing secularists. As a Christian I wanted more. Two sources led me to see how my faith and economics could be reinforcing. The early 1960s issues of *The Review of Social Economy* are where I found many articles that connected economics and my Catholic faith. Articles critiquing the economic man idea in light of faith forced me to think creatively.[22] Other articles on Joseph Schumpeter's model of creative destruction opened new ways of seeing the economy in a more dynamic model.

A second important source for seeing connections between faith and economics was in the History of Economic Thought class I was required to take where we actually read Adam Smith's *The Wealth of Nations*[23] and the *Theory of Moral Sentiments*.[24] Doing so was a revelation. At that time most mainstream economists saw themselves following in his footsteps. However, I found that Smith had much in common with CST. I came to see that the popular version of Smith's theory that the so-called invisible hand of the free market converts the self-interest of individuals into the maximum social good is a caricature of the real Adam Smith. I have come to a fuller understanding of my original impressions through the work of others, particularly that of Professor Jerry Evensky.[25]

Smith's writings, especially his *Theory of Moral Sentiments*, suggest that he had a much more nuanced understanding of human beings than the one which assumes that individuals are driven solely by self-interest. Although Smith argued that self-interest has a strong influence on people's behavior, he had a pluralist view of human nature, in which empathy—the ability to perceive things from another person's perspective—also has an important role.

Moreover, his views on the role of self-interest leading to the common good are not so clear-cut either. He thought that "humanity, justice, generosity, and public spirit, are the qualities most useful to others,"[26] and believed that while self-interest is useful in certain situations, these virtues are useful in other cases.

Especially towards the end of his life Smith began to have doubts about the role of the invisible hand of competition and self-interest in yielding the common good. In his revision of the *Theory of Moral Sentiments* in 1789, he added a new sixth part containing a practical system of morality. He appeals to all people to place the well-being of society as a whole above that of their own factions, and stresses especially the role of statesmen in constructing such a moral society through their actions and by setting examples for others.

For Adam Smith virtue serves as "the fine polish to the wheels of society" while vice is "like the vile rust, which makes them jar and grate upon one another."[27] So Adam Smith, whose work was purely philosophical, would be quite comfortable reading in *Laudato Si*, Pope Francis's statement: "The economy accepts every advance in technology with a view to profit, without concern for its potentially negative impact on human beings. . . . Yet by itself the market cannot guarantee integral human development and social inclusion."[28] Rather we are called to control the unrestricted pursuit of profit by allowing ethics to guide us as citizens and consumers so that both the planet and all peoples can thrive.

The early 1960s, when I was in graduate school, appeared to be a propitious time for a Christian to be studying economics. Development economics was born after World War II with the acceptance of the inevitability of political, social, and economic change. In terms of developed countries such as the United States, Paul Samuelson's neo-classical synthesis version of Keynesian macroeconomic management was in high gear, and it did appear that the curse of unemployment with its attendant poverty would be overcome. But the history of the next four decades belied that complacency.

Faith in my newly acquired knowledge in economics was undermined over time by two realities: (1) the failure of the United States economy to overcome poverty and inequality after being guided by economics from 1960 to 2020; and (2) the stubborn reliance on the neo-classical model to the exclusion of all other approaches.

In the United States, after a golden age of economic prosperity, 1960 to 1973, guided by Washington economic policymakers, the American economy faced difficult times. Between 1974 and 1980 the New Deal-Keynesian economic consensus came apart at the seams. The simultaneous appearance of high unemployment and double-digit inflation—the clearest manifestation of an economic crisis—belied the ability of prevailing economic policy to confront these new challenges.

In 1980 Ronald Reagan represented an alternative social consensus—a return to less government and freer markets. In 1988 the American electorate decided to continue the same course for another four years with George Bush. Yet, when the 12-year Reagan-Bush record is examined closely, only in the case of inflation had the underlying problem been confronted. Unemployment remained high, productivity did not dramatically increase, and a host of other problems—huge budget and trade deficits, increased poverty, and in general a prosperity haunted by structural distortions in the economy and an underclass all too often hungry and homeless—grew despite blithe denials.

The 1992 election of Bill Clinton changed little. Recovery from the Bush recession reduced unemployment and the budget deficit, but most of the other problems remained. The George W. Bush administration pushed the economy further along the Reagan path. An examination of the data on income distribution and poverty since 1970 documents a deteriorating performance in these areas. There was a shift in the shares of income groups among quintiles, with a continual decline in the lowest and increases in the highest income groups since 1980. For example, the functional distribution of income shifted heavily in favor of profits and away from wages. After 1980 the share of wages declined by close to 4 percent by 2004, though it rose in 2005. The share of profits increased by 5.6 percentage points, and proprietors' income increased by 2 percentage points. Between 1980 and 2004, real wages in manufacturing decreased 1 percent, while during the same period the real income of the richest 1 percent increased 135 percent. These are large shifts. As the *New York Times* reported on August 28, 2006, "Wages and salaries now make up the lowest share of the nation's gross domestic product since the government began recording data in 1947, while corporate profits have climbed to their highest share since the 1960s."[29]

Starting in 2007-2008, the U.S. financial system imploded, followed by the collapse of the economy into a continuing recession with unemployment hovering around the 10 percent level. The recovery was slow but better than most other countries. Between 2008 and 2016 almost 19 million new jobs were created with unemployment sinking to near full employment levels and with little to no inflation. The downside has been the slow recovery of average wages. I would primarily attribute the recovery to President Obama's 2009 stimulus package. A host of other policies helped the recovery, including the extensions of unemployment insurance, payroll tax cuts, plus tax cuts for business investment and hiring. The auto industry bailout also contributed to the recovery. President Trump's 2017 tax cuts on corporate profits helped extend the recovery including lowering further the unemployment rate resulting in upward pressure on wages for the first time since 2008.

With the unemployment rate at 4 percent or below, 2018 appears to be the year when the economy finally became healthy again. But while low unemployment is good news, it does not tell the whole story of how typical families are faring in the current economy. Unfortunately, the fruits of economic growth are bypassing typical families and going straight into the hands of the already rich. People at the bottom of the pay scale lost their jobs during the crisis. The government's response to the crisis helped inflate the value of assets like stocks and real estate, which are more often owned by the wealthy. In addition, many of the lower-income homeowners are the ones who could not pay their mortgages and went bankrupt losing whatever equity they had.

In the United States, income inequality, or the gap between the rich and everyone else, has been growing markedly for some 30+ years and that trend has been magnified since the Great Recession of 2007-8. Income disparities have become so pronounced that America's top 10 percent now average more than nine times as much income as households in the bottom 90 percent. Americans in the top 1 percent average over 40 times more income than those in the bottom 90 percent. But that gap pales in comparison to the divide between the nation's top 0.1 percent and everyone else. Americans at this lofty level are taking in over 198 times the income of those in the bottom 90 percent. The top 1 percent of America's income earners have more than doubled their share of the nation's income since the middle of the 20th century. American top 1 percent incomes peaked in the late 1920s, right before the onset of the Great Depression and now are in the process of passing that record.

One result is that the top 1 percent owned 33.7% of all wealth in 2007 and 10 years later 38.7%; the next 9 percent owned 37.7% in 2007 and 38.5% 10 years later; the bottom 90 percent owned 28.6% in 2007 and 22.8% 10 years later.

This extreme inequality of income and wealth has had a powerful downward effect on economic opportunity, particularly for the poor, in the United States. Most people favor equality of opportunity, at least in principle. Few, however, believe equality of outcome is either possible or even desirable. While it is possible that attempts to force equality of opportunity by government intervention in the market might have the effect of reducing incentives which, in turn, reduces output; it is clearly the case that inequality itself distorts incentives and restricts opportunities. How does this apply in the United States?

Compare two groups of children: one group is born into wealthy families, with parents willing and able to provide books, museum visits, high-quality schooling including private universities. A second group has parents who struggle to put food on the table, who live in areas where the schools are run-down and under-staffed, and where expectations are low and hope for the future not re-enforced in home or school. We should expect that children from the first group almost invariably do better economically and they do. While some children from very disadvantaged backgrounds achieve success, most do not. The reality is that our vaunted social mobility is mostly a myth.

Ron Haskins and Isabel Sawhill of the Brookings Institution show in their book, *Creating an Opportunity Society*, how poorly the United States does. For example, 42 percent of those born in the bottom fifth of the income distribution remain there as adults. On the other hand, only 6 percent of those born into a family from the bottom fifth climb to the top fifth as adults.

Some claim that inequality is not a problem; in fact, policies that benefit the wealthy ultimately help everybody. It is the rich who invest and create jobs, so helping them helps everyone. However, there is little evidence for this claim over the past 40 years. Real median household income has actually declined over the last decade and has been stagnant since the 1970s. Wages for males with a high school education have fallen substantially over the same period. Most of the benefits of U.S. economic growth have gone to those in the top percentile of the income distribution. By 2007, just one out of 100 Americans received nearly a quarter of all personal income, more than the bottom 50 percent of households put together.

I am finishing this book just as the coronavirus epidemic has caused catastrophic damage in the United States. Over 225,000 people have lost their lives and the shut-down used to combat the virus resulted in near 15 percent unemployment, falling to 9 percent, and a shuttering of small businesses not seen since the Great Depression. In fighting the collapsing incomes of workers, businesses, and consumers, federal spending has added another $3 trillion to the national debt. The Federal Reserve Bank has had to drive down interest rates on long-term treasury bonds to near zero.

Growing Disillusionment

In addition to not overcoming poverty and inequality, the economist-led economy has seen growth of an economic philosophy dominated by an ideology fixated on competition and success as the measure of a person's worth. Many deny that this describes the essence of American economic philosophy.[30] And yet each day we are reminded of its accuracy: the down-sizing of corporations where the managers and stockholders get richer while the employees get fired, the exaltation of sports stars, the attitude of Congress and the business community toward welfare legislation, the whole philosophy of success which measures the value of people by their productivity.

The promotion of success and self-interest became epitomized in the 1980s by Wall Street stockbrokers and merger specialists and the goal of newly minted Harvard MBAs to make $1 million per year before their thirtieth birthday.

Government social programs established during the past 60 years have been attacked because they supposedly reduce incentives and thus productivity. Free up the economy and all will be well. Reduce welfare, minimum wages, and unemployment benefits so that the poor will have greater incentives to work. Lower taxes and remove regulations on business so that the resulting higher profits will encourage corporations and wealthy individuals to save and invest. Increased productivity and growth in GDP will result.

Eventually, the benefits will trickle down so that even those on the bottom will be better off than before.

However, this is more ideology than fact. We have been pursuing this goal since 1980. We have made the economy our master instead of using it as our servant. We close industrial plants, create unemployment, devastate whole communities, and call it an efficient reallocation of resources. We, who have prospered from free market policies, caution that nothing can be done because natural economic forces are at work. The poor, the unemployed and the underemployed bear the burden of this free market myopia.

The philosophy and set of values embodied in a society's institutions and policies help shape the character of the people in that society. It is most revealing to examine the character of the people in our society, such as big-time athletes, CEOs, and Wall Street brokers, who are considered successful. R. H. Tawney's[31] thoughts are illuminating:

> The types which it [the industrial system] carries to power tend to be not unlike those produced by war. They must have energy, self-control, foresight, a willingness to take risks. They must be undisturbed by pity for the weak, by doubts as to the value of the immediate ends at which they aim, by reverence for the finer and more delicate human qualities and achievements, by humility or consciousness of personal deficiencies. They are essentially a conquering race. Like other conquerors they leave a trail of wreckage, consisting of the weak, the exceptionally scrupulous and honourable, the unconventional, the merely gentle and kindly who "dare not have the lives of others on their conscience."[32]

If we believe that the natural order of society is one in which the strong win their way to power over the ruin of the weak, we will find nothing fundamentally wrong with business as usual. If we object, then we are driven to override market outcomes when they yield results that we regard as morally unacceptable. Then the hard work begins—how do you intervene in the market without creating more harm than good? This should be the issue we debate in the coming years of the 21st century.

TOWARD A NEW ECONOMICS

From 1964 to 1975 I was on the faculty at The American University. Since 1975 I have been at the University of Notre Dame. During this time, I became ever more disenchanted with traditional economic theory as the vehicle to develop adequate policies to overcome poverty in the Third World or in the United States. I found myself unable to accept the values embedded in economic theory, particularly the elevation of self-interest because it supposedly leads to efficiency, the neglect of income distribution, and the attempts to export these values into studies of the family, the role of the state and so on. But Christian thought and biblical tradition make self-interest a central aspect of *fallen* human nature which as Christian believers we are bound to strive to counter with prayer, good works, and the cultivation of virtue.

The Catholic tradition dissents from this materialist view of human welfare. In his 1968 encyclical, *Populorum Progressio*, Pope Paul VI wrote:

> Increased possession is not the ultimate goal of nations or of individuals. All growth is ambivalent. It is essential if man is to develop as a man, but in a way it imprisons man if he considers it the supreme good, and it restricts his vision. Then we see hearts harden and minds close, and men no longer gather together in friendship but out of self-interest, which soon leads to oppositions and disunity. The exclusive pursuit of possessions thus becomes an obstacle to individual fulfillment and to man's true greatness. Both for nations and for individual men, avarice is the most evident form of moral underdevelopment.[33]

On the twentieth anniversary (1987) of *Populorum Progressio*, Pope John Paul II wrote in *Sollicitudo Rei Socialis*: "All of us experience firsthand the sad effects of this blind submission to pure consumerism: in the first place a crass materialism, and at the same time a radical dissatisfaction because one quickly learns . . . that the more one possesses the more one wants, while deeper aspirations remain unsatisfied and perhaps even stifled."[34] In *Centesimus Annus*—marking the one hundredth anniversary of *Rerum Novarum*, Pope John Paul II writes: "It is not wrong to want to live better; what is wrong is a style of life which is presumed to be better when it is directed toward 'having' rather than 'being,' and which wants to have more, not in order to be more but in order to spend life in enjoyment as an end in itself."[35]

How has CST impacted my view of economics as a means of correcting social problems in the world? Ever since my CFM days I have grappled with the question: "Was the Good Samaritan a bad economist?" In Charles Dickens's novel, *Hard Times*, his character Thomas Gradgrind is "A man of realities. A man of facts and calculations. A man who proceeds upon the principle that two and two are four, and nothing over, and who is not to be talked into allowing for anything over."[36] Thus, he "sat writing in the room with the deadly statistical clock, proving something no doubt—probably, in the main, that the Good Samaritan was a Bad Economist."[37]

"'Some persons hold,' he pursued, still hesitating, 'that there is a wisdom of the Head, and that there is a wisdom of the Heart. I have not supposed so; but, as I have said, I mistrust myself now I have supposed the head to be all-sufficient. It may not be all-sufficient."[38] What is that wisdom of the heart and where is it found, certainly not in economics alone? To use Isaiah Berlin's words, we need to be foxes not hedgehogs.[39] Hedgehogs distill the world's complexity into a simple and universal theory. Foxes do the opposite and are skeptical of simple theories about complex systems such as national economies. Economics needs the humanities, particularly theology and religious belief, to be the fox that makes their theories more humane.

Morton Schapiro, professor of economics and president of Northwestern University highlights the limitations of economic theory by reflecting on his experiences of working in Egypt to "get prices right" in the 1980s. Under pressure from many economists and international agencies, the Egyptian government felt compelled to end their subsidies on bread and other goods for the poor. This allowed these goods to rise to market clearing levels, substantially higher than they were before. "Sitting with a 'thrilled' group of economists, Schapiro was haunted by reports indicating that this policy lead to riots, malnutrition, and death. Were these policies nevertheless justified? How does one properly weigh the value of life and death?"[40]

Let me give one more example about the head wisdom of economics and the lack of wisdom of the heart: " . . . onchocerciasis, also known as river blindness . . . is a parasitic disease that has cost millions of people their eyesight, and is endemic in large parts of sub-Saharan Africa. In 1974, seven West African nations got together, contacted donors, and set out to create the Onchocerciasis Control Program, overseen by the World Health Organization. The program was a huge success, in that it prevented hundreds of thousands of people from going blind, but there was a problem: the economists involved couldn't show that the venture was worth it. A cost-benefit analysis was "inconclusive": the people who were being helped were so poor that the benefit of saving their eyesight didn't have much monetary impact. 'There are humanitarian benefits associated with reducing the blindness and suffering caused by onchocerciasis,' the World Bank report allowed. But 'these benefits are inherently unmeasurable, and we will not account for them here.' In other words, the very thing that made the project so admirable—that it was improving the lives of the poorest people in the world—also made it, from an economic point of view, not really worth doing."[41]

We are faced with this same issue in balancing opening up the economy versus protecting the vulnerable from the coronavirus. A cost-benefit analysis could yield a similar result. The elderly and people with underlying health problems are the ones most at risk. Since their lost earnings from dying will be relatively low because they are retired or too sick to work, the economic rationale would tilt to opening up. The morality of doing so would get short shrift.

In this book I will try to be the fox that brings wisdom of the heart to economics. That is, the social science of economics needs to be leavened with the heart wisdom of the humanities including theology and religious faith. How do the humanities differ from economics as a social science?

Economists tend to be hedgehogs, forever on the search for a single, unifying explanation of complex phenomena. They take large, complicated issues involving human behavior and reduce it to an equation: supply-and-demand curves; the Phillips curve, which shows the relation between unemployment and inflation; or GDP, which measures total production and how rich we all are.

Economics has three systematic biases: "It ignores the role of culture, it ignores the fact that 'to understand people one must tell stories about them,' and it constantly touches on ethical questions beyond its ken. Culture, stories, and ethics are things that can't be reduced to equations, and economics accordingly has difficulty with them."[42] This is where the foxlike approach of the humanities is needed.

The fox's humanist approach is *holistic*. It is always concerned with a person's relationship to themselves but also to others, to social institutions, the physical world, God, history, as well as the economy itself. The obverse is also true: to the humanistic mind, things, incidents, even words are meaningless in isolation. Meaning is a function of tone, gesture, and situation as well as the denotation of words.

The fox believes in *mystery*. It believes in the unexpected, the unpredictable, the uncontrollable, the unknowable. It believes in that which is beyond logic, that which is too complex for rational understanding. It doubts the basic Aristotelian premise that "a" cannot be both "a" and "not-a." The process of reconciling opposites is indeed fundamental. Ambiguity, irony, paradox are essential categories. They do not represent challenges to be overcome so much as realities to be discovered and revealed.

The fox's mind analyzes life by *esthetic reasoning*. Basic to its forms of thought is a thinking process by which conflict and contradiction are discovered in unity, and unity is revealed in contradiction.

The fox's humanistic mind believes in *subjectivity*. It takes emotions seriously. It believes as much in knowing experientially what it feels like to hold a certain conviction as in knowing rationally an idea's logical implications or practical consequences. It believes that a person is more than the sum of his/her behavior, age, sex, socio-economic status, etc. It does not deny their importance but believes there must be room for intuition and insight; and, I might add, room for God's grace.

The fox is concerned with the *concrete*. It imagines how an individual will behave under a particular set of circumstances. It approaches understanding by narrating about one person rather than generalizing about many, by metaphor rather than by principle. Its interest in abstractions is less in their truth or logic than in how people act who believe them. Like a golfer, the fox succeeds not by memorizing rules but by imagining the precise line the ball must follow to land in the cup.

The fox's mind tends to be *apocalyptic*. It is concerned with first things and last and with such ultimate states of being as life, death, and freedom. Loss, suffering, failure, defeat are not merely unsolved problems, but part of the ultimate comedy/tragedy called life. A poor, homeless, unwed mother is more than a symbol for social reform; she, too, is a child of God. Solutions to social problems as often involve changes in human perception as they do changes in external conditions.

Obviously, I will try and get the fox and the hedgehog to work together in the coming chapters. As a result of the above, I started researching and writing on the philosophy of science as it applied to economics. This work led me to two important conclusions. First is the conviction that economic theory is not value free as is so often claimed but, rather, it presupposes a set of value judgments upon which economic analysis is erected. Second is the realization that the economy itself requires that the self-interest of economic actors be morally constrained. Chapters 2-5 explain in detail the role and importance of ethics in economics.

Over time I came to see myself as a social economist who questioned the free market model with its emphasis on fulfilling consumer preferences as the primary criterion of human welfare and as the engine of economic growth and development. The fundamental premises of this social economics, in contrast to mainstream economics and complementary to CST, are fourfold:

First, economic actors as persons are the basic unit of the economy. Second, they act freely but within certain limits, self-interestedly but often with regard for others, and calculatedly but at times impulsively, whimsically, or altruistically, in a self-regulating economy which from time to time must be constrained deliberately in order to serve the common good[43] and to protect the weak and the needy. Third, their economic behavior is grounded in reason and in faith,[44] changing as economic conditions change but at times reflecting moral rules and principles, predictable and unforeseeable, and knowable with mathematical certainty and empirical precision but sometimes mysterious and beyond human understanding. Fourth, their worth at times may be construed instrumentally but finally is not reducible to economic calculus because it rests squarely on the conviction that humans have a worth and dignity beyond measure.[45]

These premises explain why social economics sees the economic world differently and approaches policy questions differently than mainstream economics. To social economists:

> Economic acts are both moral and economic. They are economic in that they are necessary means for persons to act and survive. At the same time the acts are moral or immoral insofar as they relate to dealing justly with other people and in using material things as means to their ultimate good and purpose. Thus economics is both a praxis and a science . . . As a science it . . . may be correct or incorrect but not morally right or wrong. As a praxis, however, . . . economic acts or economic conduct . . . can also be judged unjust, imprudent, intemperate, and in general moral or immoral.[46]

Instead of the neo-classical *homo economicus*, social economists focus on the whole person, sometimes labeled *homo socio-economics*.[47] This enables us to utilize concepts usually excluded from mainstream economics: needs, power, equity, gender, culture, family, institutional context, among others. This focus requires social economists to incorporate value frameworks that include the use of terms such as fairness, human dignity, human rights, and the common good.

Clearly the view of human behavior in social economics is much richer than in neo-classical economics but that very richness of detail causes problems for economic research and policy making. The power of the rational actor model is that its simplicity lends itself to formal modeling and empirical research in a way impossible for the more complex models of social economics. But is there really an advantage? This is an issue we will explore in the following chapters.

CONCLUSION

Part I of this book focuses on how my Catholic faith has shaped my view of economics as a means of correcting social problems in the world; while grappling with the question: "Was the Good Samaritan a bad economist?" In Chapter 2 I argue that economics is permeated with ethical values and any economics must be so; in Chapter 3 that human behavior is more complex than the standard economic man theory; in Chapter 4 that markets require intervention to create equity; in Chapters 5 and 6 that a moral theory is required, with philosophical moral theories covered in Chapter 5 and in Chapter 6, CST as a theological moral theory that provides a perspective to develop a social economics.

Part II takes that modified economics and uses it to deal with specific social problems: labor markets in Chapter 7, poverty in Chapter 8, inequality in Chapter 9, financial crisis in Chapter 10, and development in Chapter 11. An observant reader might ask, Why no chapter on the environment? After a lot of starts and stops I decided that it is too important to be relegated to a single chapter. The reader will find that it is an important factor in a number of the chapters.

In Part III, Chapter 12 focuses on what we as individuals and as members of families and other mediating institutions can do to carry out our Christian duty to love our neighbor. Then in Chapter 13 I look at the Catholic Worker movement and Distributism as an example of CST in practice. I conclude, in Chapter 14, "Wisdom and the Christian Economist," by returning to the question, Was the Good Samaritan a Bad Economist?

NOTES

1. Leo XIII, *Rerum Novarum*, encyclical letter, Vatican website, May 15, 1891. In most CST documents the paragraphs are numbered. Thus, the numbers refer to paragraphs not pages. http://www.vatican.va/content/leo-xiii/en/encyclicals/documents/hf_l-xiii_enc_15051891_rerum-novarum.html
2. Leo XIII, *Rerum*, para. 7-8; John Paul II, *Centesimus Annus*, encyclical letter, Vatican website, 1991, para. 13-14. http://www.vatican.va/content/john-paul-ii/en/encyclicals/documents/hf_jp-ii_enc_01051991_centesimus-annus.html
3. Pius XI, *Quadragesimo Anno*, encyclical letter, Vatican website, 1931, para. 46. http://www.vatican.va/content/pius-xi/en/encyclicals/documents/hf_p-xi_enc_19310515_quadragesimo-anno.html
4. Leo XIII, *Rerum*, para. 14; John Paul, *Centesimus*, para. 6.
5. Leo XIII, *Rerum*, para. 31; Pius XI, *Quadragesimo*, para. 83; John Paul II, *Centesimus*, para. 33-35.
6. John Paul II, *Centesimus*, para. 39.
7. John Paul II, *Centesimus*, para. 11.
8. John XXIII, *Pacem in Terris*, encyclical letter, Vatican website, April 11, 1963, para. 8-27. http://www.vatican.va/content/john-xxiii/en/encyclicals/documents/hf_j-xxiii_enc_11041963_pacem.html; John Paul II, *Centesimus*, para. 8, 15.
9. John Paul II, *Centesimus*, para. 15, 19, 37, 40.
10. Leo XIII, *Rerum*, para. 10, 15, 36.
11. Paul VI, *Populorum Progressio*, encyclical letter, Vatican website, March 26, 1967, para. 23. http://www.vatican.va/content/paul-vi/en/encyclicals/documents/hf_p-vi_enc_26031967_populorum.html
12. John XXIII, *Pacem*, para. 60-62.
13. John Paul II, *Centesimus*, para. 40, 48.
14. Pius XI, *Quadragesimo*, para. 79; John Paul II, *Centesimus*, para. 15.
15. John Paul II, *Centesimus*, para. 58.
16. John Paul II, *Centesimus*, para. 15.
17. John Paul II, *Centesimus*, para. 34.
18. John Paul II, *Centesimus*, para. 36-39.
19. John Paul II, *Centesimus*, para. 43.

20. John Paul II, *Centesimus*, para. 33-38.

21. See Michael Novak, *The Spirit of Democratic Capitalism* (New York: Simon & Schuster, 1982), and Richard John Neuhaus, *Doing Well and Doing Good: The Challenge to the Christian Capitalist* (New York: Doubleday Religious Publishing Group, 1992).

22. See F. Knox, "The Doctrine of Consumer Sovereignty," *Review of Social Economy* 18, no. 2 (1960): 138-149.

23. Adam Smith, *An Inquiry into the Nature and Causes of the Wealth of Nations*, ed. W. B. Todd, Vol. 2 of *The Glasgow Edition of the Works and Correspondences of Adam Smith*, general editors, D. D. Raphael and A. Skinner (Oxford: Clarendon Press, 1976).

24. Adam Smith, *The Theory of Moral Sentiments*, ed. D. D. Raphael and A. L. Macfie, Vol. 1 of *The Glasgow Edition of the Works and Correspondences of Adam Smith*, general editors, D. D. Raphael and A. Skinner (Oxford: Clarendon Press, 1976).

25. Jerry Evensky, "Ethics and the Invisible Hand," *Journal of Economic Perspectives* 7, Vol. 2 (Spring 1993): 197-205.

26. Smith, *Theory*, 190.

27. Smith, *Theory*, 244.

28. Francis, *Laudato Si*, encyclical letter, Vatican website, para. 109, 123. http://w2.vatican.va/content/francesco/en/encyclicals/documents/papa-francesco_20150524_enciclica-laudato-si.html

29. This and the above material are drawn from the *Economic Report of the President 2005* (Washington, D.C.: United States Government Printing Office, 2005) and the Census Bureau's online 2005 report on poverty (released August 29, 2006). https://www.census.gov/library/publications/2006/acs/acs-02.html

30. See Novak, *Democratic Capitalism*, Neuhaus, *Doing Well*, and almost any introductory textbook in economics.

31. The late Richard Henry Tawney, Christian, socialist, Professor of Economic History at the London School of Economics, was the author of *Religion and the Rise of Capitalism*, *The Acquisitive Society*, *Equality*, and many other works on the origins, nature, and reform of modern industrial economies.

32. Richard Tawney, *R.H. Tawney's Commonplace Book* (Cambridge University Press, 1972, 2006.

33. Paul V1, *Populorum*, para. 19.

34. John Paul II, *Sollicitudo Rei Socialis*, encyclical letter, Vatican website, 1987, para. 36. http://www.vatican.va/content/john-paul-ii/en/encyclicals/documents/hf_jp-ii_enc_30121987_sollicitudo-rei-socialis.html

35. John Paul II, *Centesimus*, para. 28.

36. Charles Dickens, *Hard Times* (New York: Random House, 2001), Book 1, Chapter 2.

37. Dickens, *Hard Times*, Book 2, Chapter 12.

38. Dickens, *Hard Times*, Book 3, Chapter 1.

39. See Isaiah Berlin, "The Hedgehog and the Fox: An Essay of Tolstoy's View of History," in *Russian Thinkers*, ed. H. Hardy (Princeton, NJ: Princeton University Press, 2013).

40. Gary Saul Morson and Morton Schapiro. *Cents and Sensibility: What Economics Can Learn from the Humanities* (Princeton, NJ: Princeton University Press, 2017). Cited by Jeffrey R. Bloem in a review in *Faith & Economics*, No. 71 (Spring 2018), 75.

41. Cited in John Lanchester, "Can Economists and Humanists Ever Be Friends?" *New Yorker,* July 16, 2018. https://www.newyorker.com/magazine/2018/07/23/can-economists-and-humanists-ever-be-friends

42. Lanchester, "Ever Be Friends?"

43. The common good is defined by Dempsey (pp. 272-273) as the fulfillment of the needs of human beings which arise from their living together, as in the case of public health, instead of each one living alone. Two characteristics set these needs off: (1) they are common to all, and (2) they can be met only through the united efforts of all members of the community acting together. The fulfillment of these common needs depends critically on each person contributing to the community because the community by itself has nothing to contribute to its members apart from what its various members contribute to it (Dempsey, pp. 219-220). Thus, the common good is dependent on contributive justice. See B. Dempsey, *The Functional Economy: The Bases of Economic Organization* (Prentice-Hall, Inc., Englewood Cliffs, NJ).

44. Reason discovers truth from direct, personal experience; faith accepts truth on the word of another.

45. Edward O'Boyle, "Requiem for Homo Economicus," *Markets and Morality* 10, no. 2 (2007): 321-338.

46. P. Danner, *The Economic Person* (London: Rowman and Littlefield Publishers, 2002): 44.

47. However, of late, O'Boyle has been using instead "the acting person" and "the person in action." See his "Requiem" article in *Markets and Morality,* 2007. The reasons are to underscore the difference between the individual and the person and to highlight *acting* as critical to *being* more. Also see Danner's *The Economic Person.*

Chapter Two

Economic Theory Requires Moral Values

Economics strives to be a value free science. In this chapter I will show that this is impossible. The failure to recognize that values are embedded in the very act of theorizing continues to mislead economic policy. CST recognizes that economic relations are part and parcel with social and political relations.

> The Church's social doctrine holds that authentically human social relationships of friendship, solidarity and reciprocity can also be conducted within economic activity, and not only outside it or "after" it. The economic sphere is neither ethically neutral, nor inherently inhuman and opposed to society. It is part and parcel of human activity and precisely because it is human, it must be structured and governed in an ethical manner. (Pope Benedict XVI, *Caritas In Veritate*, para. 36.)

Economists, for the most part, failed to foresee the Great Recession of 2007-2008, the worst financial and economic crisis since the 1930s. Now they cannot reach a consensus on what caused it. James Galbraith, an economist at University of Texas, says that "it's an enormous blot on the reputation of the profession. There are thousands of economists. Most of them teach. And most of them teach a theoretical framework that has been shown to be fundamentally useless."[1] Richard Posner, with no trace of irony, wrote on the Chicago School–based Becker-Posner Blog, in response to the question, Why were the warnings about a looming crisis ignored rather than investigated? : "Many economists and political leaders are heavily invested in a free market ideology which teaches that markets are robust and self-regulating."[2] A reasonable question might be: Why listen to economists?

THE FAILURE OF ECONOMICS AND THE FREE MARKET MODEL

Economics is a lot like theology despite its claim to be a science. Traditional theology establishes first principles (which are taken as axiomatic) from revelation or natural law and then with the use of intermediate principles and judgment evaluates real-world issues.

Economics uses an abstract model constructed from axiomatic assumptions about how the world works—people are motivated by self-interest, wants exceed resources, resources are mobile and fungible. Then with appropriate regard for real-world deviations from the model, economists derive economic policies.

The problem, for both theologians and economists, lies in going from the general to the specific. I cannot speak for theologians, but economists are seldom trained in the specifics of how the real world works. Rather a graduate student in economics spends all his or her time learning mathematics, statistics, and general theory. These then are used to do policy by finding a data set somewhere and applying the given tools to yield an answer. For example, the theory says that inter-personal wage differences are the result of different amounts of human capital embodied in workers. How is human capital measured? There is no thing called "human capital" out there to measure. Rather a proxy must be constructed, such as years of schooling. One result of this is that if a statistical test appears to falsify the theory, the test is rejected, and the proxy re-specified until the test comes out the way expected. That is, economists believe their theory the way theologians believe the core tenets of their faith.[3]

How do people become economists? As David Colander says in his delightful book, *The Making of an Economist, Redux*,[4] "were an undergraduate student to ask an economist how to become an economist, he would tell her to go to graduate school. She might demur, asking, 'Wouldn't it make more sense to go to Wall Street and learn how markets work?' Getting firsthand experience may sound like a good idea to her, but most economists would briskly dismiss the suggestion. 'Well, maybe I should get a job in a real business—say, turning out automobiles.' The answer will be 'no' again: 'That's not how you learn economics.' She might try one more time. 'Well, how about if I read all the top economists of the past—John Stuart Mill, David Ricardo, Adam Smith?' Most economists would say, 'It wouldn't hurt, but it probably won't help.' Instead, he would most likely tell her, 'To become an economist who is considered an economist by other economists, you have to go to graduate school in economics.' So, the reality is that, to economists, an economist is someone who has a graduate degree (doctorates strongly preferred) in economics. This means that what defines an economist is what he or she learns in graduate school."[5]

Over the past 30 years or so the graduate economics curriculum has become ever more like a program in applied mathematics with a corresponding reduction in economic history, history of economic thought, industry studies, and industrial relations. This narrowing of focus gets reinforced as the student finishes the PhD and gets a job in the academy. The greatest rewards go to those making advances in theory and publishing in the half dozen top general journals. Few articles will be accepted by these journals that do not start with the standard abstract model and then derive some new "interesting" result. Publishing in policy journals receives much less prestige and can even count against one as showing you are not a serious economist. And of course, after receiving tenure, this is what one knows how to do.

I tried to build a different type of economics program at Notre Dame, but ultimately it was unsuccessful. I was hired in 1975 to build a department that used CST as the base from which to fashion a unique program. The graduate PhD program was restructured to create a distinctive program marked by its focus on socioeconomic issues such as economic development, its openness to alternative methodologies such as political economy, its concern for social justice, and its reaffirmation of standard economic theory and quantitative methods. By redirecting its energies, the program not only reflected the goals and objectives of the economics profession but also those of the University of Notre Dame, as specified by Father Ted Hesburgh, C.S.C., president of the university: "Notre Dame as a Catholic university, must be all of this and something more. . . . Its concern touches the moral as well as the intellectual dimensions of all the questions it asks itself and its students." Doing economics differently was not prized by the profession, and low department rankings according to the disciplines criteria eventually led the university to abandon the experiment and pursue the traditional academic route with the result that standard criteria taken over from the secular academic world came to be the only criteria that mattered.

The microeconomic model that is the core of traditional economic theory is a beautiful mathematical construct. With the assumptions of self-interest of economic actors, perfect mobility of resources, perfect competition, no externalities, etc., the model yields a so-called Pareto Optimal outcome where no one can be made better off without making someone worse off. Since economists rule out interpersonal comparisons of utility, there is nothing more to be said. The result is that economists learn to believe that this is the way the world works, and students drawn to study economics are frequently those who already believe this. In addition, behavioral economics research indicates that as undergraduate students study economics, they demonstrate ever more self-interested behavior with each class taken.[6]

Until the mid-1930s, most economists believed a "free market" economy would solve whatever problems arose. If goods and services and inputs into production were bought and sold in markets, the economy would function as well as possible. Thus, they called on public authorities for a *laissez-faire* policy of "hands-off" of markets.

However, with the breakdown of the economy in the 1930s, *laissez-faire* economics seemed discredited, and the activist policies of Keynesian economics dominated until the stagflation of the late 1970s. One of the cornerstones of Keynes's theory was his treatment of investment. He argued forcefully that investment decisions were closely linked with what he called "animal spirits." The term suggested fragility and instability, even when it was, in large measure, narrowed to refer to profit expectations or business optimism. Keynes had ample evidence for his case in the Depression, for even though investment was sorely needed, and the interest rate had fallen below 1 percent, there was still minimal investment. No sane business would invest, regardless of the interest rate, if convinced that the project would incur losses in the future. Thus, the psychological basis of profit expectations makes economics more of an art than a science.

In addition, Keynes rejected the neoclassical notion that wage reductions would restore full employment equilibrium by leading employers to hire more labor because of lower costs. Instead, he argued that wages are also a part of aggregate demand, in addition to being production costs. If wages fall, aggregate demand and sales will fall. If sales fall, profits will decline, and firms will demand less labor. The Depression experience made these points convincing to all who were not wedded to neoclassical economics.

However, a small band of economists never accepted the Keynesian notion that markets were not self-regulating and that government could play an important role in stabilizing the economy. Almost from the beginning there were efforts to re-interpret Keynes to make his macroeconomics compatible with neo-classical microeconomics. Eventually this work developed the idea of micro foundations where any macroeconomics had to be derived from individual behavior that was rational and informed. In this theory of rational expectations, where actors have perfect knowledge, they act in such a way that any governmental policy will be offset unless it is a complete surprise. Thus, Keynesian policy is seen as ineffective at best and most probably harmful.

In the 1980s this renewed version of *laissez-faire* economics regained ascendency with the election of Ronald Reagan in the United States and Margaret Thatcher in Great Britain. At the heart of this position is the belief that markets are self-correcting. Financial economists developed this into the "efficient market hypothesis" which argues that markets quickly and correctly incorporate all publicly available information into prices. Under the strong version of this theory, the only reason prices of assets like stocks move is because new information becomes available; thus, financial markets could not consistently mis-price assets and therefore needed little regulation.

Between their narrow technical training and their bias in favor of free markets, most economists failed to see the coming perfect storm of economic recession and financial crisis. In fact, they paved the way by urging the deregulation of financial markets which in turn allowed the creation of all kinds of dubious new debt instruments, wildly increasing leverage of bank capital, and even huge Ponzi schemes to go undetected. Add to this the extremely low interest rates set by the Federal Reserve and the "bubble" created in the housing industry was a natural outcome and its spread to the financial sector through these new instruments was catastrophic.

The most astonishing admission of failure of the free market model was that of former Federal Reserve chairman Alan Greenspan in autumn 2008 that the Fed's regime of monetary management had been based on a "flaw." The "whole intellectual edifice," he said, "collapsed in the summer of last year."[7]

Robert Schiller, an economist at Yale, thinks the failure to foresee the financial collapse is the result of fearing to deviate from the consensus of the profession. And he doesn't see economists learning enough to change their basic paradigm: "The rational expectations models will be tweaked to account for the current crisis. The basic curriculum will not change."[8] Dani Rodrick, an economist at Harvard, said, "The problem wasn't with the economics but with the economists. . . . We have fixated on one of the possible hundreds of models and elevated that above the others,"[9] referring to the free market model.

John Kay, a financial columnist for *Financial Times*, wrote that Max Planck, the physicist, said he had abandoned economics because it was too difficult. John Maynard Keynes explained that economic understanding required a mixture of logic and intuition and a wide knowledge of facts, most of which are not precise. The mathematically inclined find this frustrating and unscientific. "On this, as on much else, Keynes was right."[10] The hedgehog needs the fox as the social sciences need the humanities.

I must also say some positive things about economics and economists. There is much new work, even though still seldom included in the core, that is exciting and holds out varying degrees of hope for a regeneration of economics. Behavioral economics, evolutionary economics, happiness economics, economics of social capital, and social norms, the economics of asymmetric information, and Big Data economics all hold out hope of breaking through the twin constraints of methodological formalism and competitive equilibrium. Also, behavioral finance theory should provide a sounder basis than the efficient market hypothesis for future analyses of financial markets.

Even more encouraging is a growing recognition that economies require ethical behavior in addition to self-interest. As we saw in Chapter 1, modern economics has selectively adopted Adam Smith's invisible hand metaphor, focusing on the economically wondrous effects of the butcher and baker trading out of their self-interest and ignoring his prior description of the same deistic hand's propelling the creation of a virtuous society. Virtue serves as "the fine polish to the wheels of society" while vice is "like the vile rust, which makes them jar and grate upon one another."[11] Indeed, Smith sought to distance his thesis from that of Mandeville and the implication that individual greed could be the basis for social good. Smith's understanding that virtue is a prerequisite for a desirable market society remains an important lesson. As Jerry Evensky, an economist at Syracuse, argues, for Smith "ethics is the hero—not self-interest or greed—for it is ethics that defend the social intercourse from the Hobbesian chaos."[12]

The heavy reliance on mathematics has contributed to the widening separation of economics and ethics. Economics is about human behavior, not the action and reaction of inanimate objects. It is closer to psychology or sociology than astronomy or physics. Economics and ethics are, in fact, interrelated because both economists (theorists and policy advisers) and economic actors (sellers, consumers, workers, investors) hold ethical values that help shape their behavior. In the first case economists must try to understand how their own values affect both economic theory and policy and that is the task in the remainder of this chapter. In the second case this means economic analysis must broaden its conception of consumer, worker, and investor behavior. This is the task of Chapter 3. Ethics enters economics in a third way—since economic policies and institutions impact people in differential ways, questions of efficiency cannot be separated from the ethical issues involved. That is a topic I will treat in Chapters 4 and 5. By the end of these four chapters we should have no trouble agreeing with Pope Benedict XVI when he rejects "the conviction that the economy . . . must be shielded from 'influences' of a moral character."[13]

THE ETHICAL FOUNDATIONS OF SCIENTIFIC INQUIRY

Many economists argue that while values might have a place in what is termed normative economics, they should be kept out of the everyday scientific business of the profession—the development and testing of falsifiable propositions—which is often referred to as positive economics. This separation, as this chapter shows, is problematic. Value-free science is a laudable but impossible goal in the social sciences, including economics. Economists, as persons, necessarily work from a viewpoint that structures the questions asked, the methods, the evidence, the answers deemed acceptable. The following demonstrates how normative values play an important role in the conduct of everyday science.

The 1996 American Economic Association Presidential address was given by health economist Victor Fuchs.[14] After quoting a 1965 article by George Stigler that "the age of quantification is now full upon us" and that it will be "a scientific revolution of the very first magnitude,"[15] Fuchs goes on to note that the revolution is still in the future: "the shallow and inconclusive debate over health policy in 1993-94 contradicts (Stigler's) expectation that this research would narrow the range of partisan disputes and make a significant contribution to the reconciliation of policy differences."[16] The debate over health care reform continues unabated over 25 years later, highlighted by the arguments over Obamacare and even more recently the claims and counterclaims over the feasibility of Medicare for All.

There are many other examples of contemporary social issues, and the policies to address them, whose resolution seems immune to the insights claimed by the social sciences: environmental disputes ranging from the northwest salmon to the Utah wilderness, welfare reform, in particular the treatment of teenage welfare mothers, or even the inheritability of intelligence with all of its racial and social Darwinist implications. Does the continued intransigence of social issues and the stubborn intractability of social policy imply that all of the developments in data collection, data storage, and data analysis have come to naught, that the age of quantification is a bust and that the future should see social science move in a different direction? I do not see that as the appropriate conclusion,[17] though I see the problem as a real one.

I believe that social science and empirical investigation can make important contributions to our understanding and resolution of policy issues, but only if we are clear on the nature of social science and the role of theory and quantification. In particular we must recognize the limits of our truth claims, and the possibility of their being utilized to serve vested interests. Finally, I think that we must find ways of making our basic data and analyses more understandable, so the public is better able to join the policy debates.

I suggest that there is a way of understanding the very real problem that Fuchs highlights. It starts from an understanding of the nature of economic science. There is a substantial literature on methodological issues in economics, much of it calling into question its supposed scientific character. Part of that literature deals explicitly with the impact of ethical value judgments on economics as a science. Of this literature a greater amount argues the value-permeation thesis than defends the idea of value-neutrality.

Value Permeation vs. Value Neutrality

The value permeation position argues that while science is driven by a search for truth, it is not interested in just any truth. The relevant truth must be both "interesting" and "valuable," and thus all science is goal-directed activity. Further, the criteria for a "good" or "acceptable" scientific theory cannot be ranked in terms of their intrinsic importance, but only in relation to the degree they serve goals of the scientific community.

Theory choice is not, therefore, based objectively on non-controversial criteria (e.g., degree of verification or corroboration), but on criteria that are inevitably value-laden (i.e. the extent to which each theory serves specific ends). The scientists" search for "valuable truth" is directed by what they think society (and science) ought to do. No amount of evidence ever completely confirms or disconfirms any empirical hypothesis but only renders it more or less probable.

Another line of reasoning is even more convincing. Thomas Kuhn introduces the concept of paradigms, characterized by the shared values of a given scientific community.[18] It is Kuhn's rejection of the second tenet—that we have objective access to the empirical world through our sense experience—that is important for rejecting the value-neutrality position. He argues that the empirical world can be known only through the filter of a theory; thus, facts, of necessity, are theory laden. The major argument of those who build on Kuhn's approach runs as follows: A world view greatly influences the scientific paradigm out of which one works; value judgments are closely associated with the world view; theories must remain coherent with the world view; facts themselves are theory-laden; therefore, the whole scientific venture is permeated by value judgments from the start. This world view, or *Weltanschauung*, shapes the interests of the scientist and determines the questions asked, the problems considered important, the answers deemed acceptable, the axioms of the theory, the choice of relevant facts, the hypotheses proposed to account for such facts, the criteria used to assess the fruitfulness of competing theories, the language in which results are to be formulated, and so on.

The Neo-Classical World View: A Case in Point

I illustrate the world view argument by applying it to mainstream neo-classical economics.[19] The world view of mainstream neo-classical economics is closely associated with the notion of the good embedded in its scientific paradigm. Neo-classical economics is founded on a world view made up of the following propositions:

1. Human nature is such that humans are:
   a. Self-interested.
   b. Rational. That is, they know their own interest and choose from among a variety of means in order to maximize that interest.
2. The purpose of human life is for individuals to pursue happiness as they themselves define it. Therefore, it is essential that they be left free to do so.
3. The ideal social world is a gathering of free individuals who compete with each other under conditions of scarcity to achieve self-interested ends. As in the natural world with physical entities, in the social world too there are forces at work which move economic agents toward equilibrium positions (equilibrium simply means a price and quantity bought and sold position that buyers and sellers have no incentive to move from).

Neo-classical economists either accept the preceding empirically unverifiable and unfalsifiable statements or, barring overt acceptance, conduct scientific inquiry with methods based thereon.

To state it simply, neo-classical economists believe that humans are rational maximizers of their own self-interest and that humans act in a rational world characterized by forces which move things toward equilibrium.[20] The first two propositions contain the motivating force in economic life (satisfaction of self-interest) and the third proposition spells out the context in which that force works itself out.

It seems clear that judgments of value, of a particular notion of the good, are directly implied by propositions one and two of this world view. If the purpose of life is that individuals pursue happiness, and if they do so self-interestedly, then it certainly would be good for individuals to receive what they want. Here is the basic notion of the good permeating all neo-classical economics: individuals should be free to get as much as possible of what they want. Other value judgments of the neo-classical paradigm either qualify what types of individual wants will be considered or are derivative from this basic value judgment. That this basic position is, in fact, a judgment of value, or of the good, is a point willingly granted by many economists.[21]

Thus, any use of economic theory, such as cost-benefit analysis, is founded on two basic value judgments. The first of these is that *individual preferences should count*. The second value judgment derives from elements one and three of the neo-classical world view and from the basic value judgment that individual preferences should count. If one takes the core ideas of individualism, rationality and the social context of harmony among diverse and conflicting interests, along with a number of limiting assumptions, it can be shown that *competitive equilibrium maximizes the value of consumption and is therefore the best of all possible economic situations*. The second value judgment is thus a different sort than the first, because it is conditional on the first. It does not stand alone. Competitive market equilibrium is good, in part, because it allows the greatest number of individual preferences to be satisfied. Moreover, this value judgment is also determined by the world view. Without the third proposition such a judgment could not be made, for then some other economic condition could be found to satisfy individual preferences. Competitive market equilibrium is good because the world view insists that only this condition can be ideal.

The notion of competitive equilibrium carries out two basic functions: it serves as an ideal and as a standard by which to measure the real value of current economic conditions. Because it serves as an ideal for which we strive, it leads directly to the auxiliary value judgment that wherever competitive markets do not exist or are weak, they should be instituted or promoted. Wherever markets do not exist, the natural competitiveness of human beings will be channeled into other nonproductive directions. It is better to establish markets where this competitiveness and self-interest–seeking behavior can be channeled into mutually satisfying activities. Wherever markets are weak and distorted due to monopoly power or government interference there is sure to be a reduction in actual consumption. Therefore, perfectly competitive markets should be promoted so that the ideal competitive equilibrium can be achieved.

There are two other auxiliary value judgments, but these do not spring directly from the world view. Instead, they make the neo-classical paradigm operational. These are: (1) means and ends should be bifurcated into two mutually exclusive categories and (2) means and ends should be measured quantitatively.

The separation of means and ends is not strictly required by the world view itself, but is an operational requirement, without which the paradigm could generate no meaningful research or study. If means and ends were not mutually exclusive, then neo-classical economics would be nothing more than a simple statement that humans do what they do because they wish to do it. There could be, for example, no inquiry into how satisfaction is maximized by choosing among various alternatives. If some activity (e.g., production or consumption) could be both means and end, then one could not determine which part is which. As Jerome Rothenberg concedes, the intermixing of means and ends "does violence to our paradigm."[22] This results in the value judgment that consumption is the end or "good" to be achieved. In so doing, any good inherent in the process or means for obtaining higher consumption is ignored. For example, if the production activity of human labor were more than just a means—if work was good in and of itself[23] regardless of the final product—then it would be impossible for the neo-classical economist to discover how much individual wants are satisfied by the activity. The ends and the means would be all mixed together and it would be impossible to speak of the value of the product and the cost of the resources independently.

The splitting of economic activities into means and ends by its very nature promotes a notion of the good. It may be an operational necessity, but it is also a judgment of value. With means and ends separated, it becomes convenient to measure the satisfaction given by particular ends and the dissatisfaction (costs) resulting from employing various means. It becomes possible to measure how much better one situation is than another, by comparing numbers instead of concepts or ideas. Things that are apparently incommensurable thus become commensurable. This is evident in many branches of neo-classical analysis; when money values are unavailable or inappropriate, quantified units, such as years of schooling for a proxy for human capital, are used in their place. The case from the first chapter that showed a cost-benefit analysis concluded the costs of fighting river blindness exceeded the benefits of the saved lives is a sad example of this incommensurability. The actual monetary cost of producing and delivering the medicine is the means and saving lives is the end and to make them commensurable the human lives are priced out at what their income earnings would be if they lived.

The emphasis on quantification in neoclassical economics adds another element to its particular notion of the good. The second auxiliary value judgment tells us to focus on means and ends that can be quantified. One practical outcome of this is a heavy emphasis on things over interpersonal relationships, education, cultural affairs, family, workplace organization, etc. Things are countable while the quality of these other spheres of human life is not. In the area of economic policy especially, such concerns are treated often as obstacles to be removed or overcome.[24] To the extent that this occurs, the notion of the good which focuses on quantifiable inputs and outputs is embedded in the paradigm. Again, the river blindness example applies. All kinds of ways are used to make "non-things" quantifiable.

Within neo-classical economics there are thus judgments of value which are rooted in a fundamental world view. There are also judgments of auxiliary value which operate in concert with the world view and which allow the neo-classical approach to be operational. Together these judgments make up the neo-classical position on the character of the good, and when an economic policy is planned, implemented, and evaluated, it is done based on these clearly defined standards.

Thus, in summary, economic theory focuses on people as hedonists who want to maximize pleasure and minimize pain.[25] It assumes that pleasure comes primarily from the consumption of goods and services; and that pain comes primarily from work and from parting with your income. Thus, given resource constraints, the goal of the economy should be to maximize the production of goods and services. In short, more is better.

In modern industrial economies such as ours, it is perfectly rational for people to accept a philosophy of consumerism. People have little opportunity to choose meaningful work because the nature of jobs is determined by competitive pressures. The demand for labor mobility as firms hire and fire disrupts a satisfying sense of community. And the enjoyment of nature is attenuated by urbanization and the degradation of nature resulting from industrial and consumption practices. Thus, the only thing left under the individual's control is consumption. And it is true that consumption can substitute, however inadequately, for the loss of meaningful work, community, and a decent environment. With enough income people can buy bottled water, place their children in private schools, buy a mountain cabin, and obtain the education necessary to get a more interesting job.

However, when people are surveyed about their views on what the economy should do, some surprising results emerge. For example, a study by Scitovsky[26] found that the simple increase in the amount of consumption in the U.S. has not increased people's happiness.[27] Richard Easterlin[28] discovered that a crucial component of such an evaluation was the perception of one's relative situation. Thus, it would seem to be exceptionally difficult for an economy to improve its performance, for every relative gain would imply a relative loss, or no net gain! This reality and the confusion in our society between growth, which we place as a preeminent goal, and affluence, which by all standards we have clearly obtained, suggests that one of the problems of our society is to deal with "the poverty of affluence."[29]

To conclude this discussion, the paradigm or research program of *any* scientific community is circumscribed by boundaries laid out in a world view which, while not perhaps individually subjective, is nevertheless empirically untestable, or metaphysical as Boland would say.[30] How then do value judgments about the good, the just and the right, enter into scientific analysis? Such value judgments are themselves entailed by the same world view which gives rise to theoretical and factual analysis. "What is" and "what ought to be" are thus inextricably commingled in the data, the facts, the theories, the descriptions, the explanations, the prescriptions, and so on. All are permeated by the a priori world view.[31]

In a "fox"-like article, Professor D. McCloskey[32] argued that economics is best understood as a form of argumentation or persuasion rather than a value-free scientific endeavor. The effort does allow economists and other social scientists to "make knowledge," but it is a contingent knowledge which depends greatly on factors such as operation of the scientific community of economists, the times, the biases or ideologies of researchers, the historical development and context of the issues, and the technical capacities of the scientists. Richard Rorty[33] describes this as "pragmatism" and suggests that the aspiration of scientists should be to find mechanisms to bring about "unforced agreement" among themselves, rather than to reach *Truth*. However, this methodological perspective remains controversial,[34] and, for the most part, economists are minimally introspective about their methodology.

Within the "fox"-like approach of rhetoric, data-based empirical analysis is only one among many ways to persuasion/knowledge. For the Greeks the intrinsic components of an argument are the proofs and the canons or principles.[35] For Aristotle, data are "extrinsic" to making an argument, i.e. not an inherent part of the process. As Sharon Crowley notes:

> Ancient philosophers seem to have had a clearer understanding of the limited usefulness of empirical facts than moderns do. . . . Perhaps because of their skepticism about the nature of facts, ancient rhetoricians were equally skeptical about the persuasive potential of facts. Aristotle wrote that facts and testimony were not truly within the art of rhetoric. . . . He considered extrinsic proofs to be outside of the art of rhetoric because a rhetor only had to pick them up and display them to an audience.[36]

Making a convincing argument on any economic policy becomes much more complex in this framework. Data and quantitative analysis can play a role, but many other elements enter into the research, influence what is accepted as true, and determine what is persuasive in policy. Indeed, much of McCloskey's original article is concerned with illustrating how metaphors, appeals to authority, analogies, etc. are immanent in good economic argument.

The personalist tradition within social economics, which was noted in the previous chapter, sees the economic world differently and approaches policy questions differently than mainstream economics. To them:

> persons are moral agents which means that by virtue of intelligence and free will they are capable of making moral choices. In economic affairs, the moral choices they make are governed by justice and caring or charity. Their behavior, therefore, reflects those kinds of choices and must be judged according to the principles of economic justice and caring or charity.[37]

Economists need to recognize that there is no alternative to working from a world view, whether it be economic individualism, Christian communalism, or whatever. Making explicit the values embodied in that world view will help keep economics more honest and useful. Furthermore, it is not sufficient to simply reject the neo-classical position that satisfying individual preferences, as expressed in the market, is the only measure of economic welfare. Alternatives must be proposed and developed.

Scripture will be a major source of ethical guidelines for any attempt at an economic theory informed by Christian belief. But the relationship of Scripture to ethics is a tremendously complex one. The Bible originated in a completely different culture and historical setting than our own. Economies in the ancient world were largely agricultural, rather than industrial; religion and society were much more closely linked; and a communal anthropology prevailed, in contrast to modern individualism. It is questionable to assert that specific Scriptural rules can be transported directly into the modern world. God's will was mediated to the Israelites in their concrete historical situation, and can only be mediated to us in our historical situation. We should certainly attempt to discern basic ethical principles in Scripture and apply them to our economic analysis, but this is different from finding exact blueprints. CST is such an attempt to use Scripture and Tradition to address the problems of the modern economy, as we will see in Chapter 6.

NOTES

1. James K. Galbraith, " Interview, *The Populist*, by Debra Solomon, Oct. 31, 2008, *New York Times Magazine* (November 2, 2008). https://www.nytimes.com/2008/11/02/magazine/02wwln-Q4-t.html?partner=permalink&exprod=permalink

2. Richard Posner, "The Financial Crisis: Why Were Warnings Ignored?" *The Becker-Posner Blog*, October 12, 2008. https://www.becker-posner-blog.com/2008/10/the-financial-crisis-why-were-warnings-ignored—posner.html

3. See Charles K. Wilber, "Empirical Verification and Theory Selection: The Keynesian-Monetarist Debate," *Journal of Economic Issues* XIII, no. 4 (December 1979): 973-982.

4. David Colander, *The Making of an Economist, Redux* (Princeton University Press, 2007).

5. Colander, *The Making*, 2.

6. See Robert H. Frank, Thomas Gilovich, and Dennis T. Regan, "Does Studying Economics Inhibit Cooperation," *Journal of Economic Perspectives* 7, no. 2 (Spring 1993): 159-171.

7. Greenspan's testimony before the U.S. House of Representatives' Committee on Oversight and Government Reform in late October. https://www.congress.gov/congressional-report/110th-congress/house-report/930/1

8. Quoted in Patricia Cohen, "Ivory Tower Unswayed by Crashing Economy," *New York Times*, March 4, 2009.

9. Quoted in Cohen, "Ivory Tower."

10. John Kay, "How Economics Lost Sight of Real World," *Financial Times*, April 21, 2009. https://www.ft.com/content/35301d06-2eaa-11de-b7d3-00144feabdc0

11. Smith, *Theory of Moral Sentiments*, 244.

12. Jerry Evensky, "Ethics and the Invisible Hand," *Journal of Economic Perspectives* 7, no. 2 (Spring 1993): 197-205.

13. Benedict XVI, *Caritas in Veritate*, encyclical letter, Vatican website, para. 34. http://www.vatican.va/content/benedict-xvi/en/encyclicals/documents/hf_ben-xvi_enc_20090629_caritas-in-veritate.html

14. I owe reference to this article and to the analysis that follows to Ken Jameson, "Data and Social Science Rhetoric: Policy and Instruction." Presented at joint IASSIST/Computing in the Social Sciences Conference, Minneapolis, MN, May 15, 1996.

15. Victor Fuchs, "Economics, Values, and Health Care Reform," *The American Economic Review* 86, no. 1 (March 1996): 1-24.

16. Fuchs, *Health Care*, 6.

17. See *Using Big Data to Solve Economic and Social Problems*, https://opportunityinsights.org/course/ This website presents the new Introductory Economics course taught at Harvard by Prof. Raj Chetty.

18. Thomas S. Kuhn, *The Structure of Scientific Revolutions*, 2nd ed. (Chicago: University of Chicago Press, 1970); Thomas S. Kuhn, "Reflections on My Critics," in *Criticism and the Growth of Knowledge*, ed. Imre Lakatos and Alan Musgrave (Cambridge: Cambridge University Press, 1970).

19. This section is based on Charles K. Wilber and Roland Hoksbergen, "Ethical Values and Economic Theory: A Survey," *Religious Studies Review* 12, no. 3/4 (July/October 1986): 211-212.

20. It is interesting that experimental studies by psychologists indicate that people are concerned about cooperating with others and with being fair, not just preoccupied with their own self-interest. Ironically, these same studies indicate that those people attracted into economics are more self-interested and taking economics makes people even more self-interested. Thus, economic theory creates a self-fulfilling prophecy. See Robert H. Frank, Thomas Gilovich, and Dennis T. Regan, "Does Studying Economics Inhibit Cooperation," *Journal of Economic Perspectives* 7, no. 2 (Spring 1993): 159-171.

21. D. W. Pearce and C. A. Nash, *The Social Appraisal of Projects* (New York: John Wiley & Sons, 1981).

22. Jerome Rothenberg, "Cost-Benefit Analysis: A Methodological Exposition," in *Handbook of Evaluation Research*, Vol. II, ed. M. Guttentag and S. Strueninge, (Beverly Hills: Sage Publications, 1975), 57.

23. See John Paul II, *Laborem Exercens* and Benedict XVI, *Caritas In Veritate* and Chapter 8 in this book for CST's position on the dignity of labor.

24. A classic example is the construction of public housing for the poor. Square footage per household is the key variable, not such intangibles as neighborhood, community, or access to services. Another example is welfare policy that concentrates on levels of support and ignores the psychological impact of means testing or the prohibition of able-bodied males in the household.

25. This is not quite accurate. Many economists would say that in maximizing their self-interest people might choose to help others because it makes them feel good. But in practice economists focus on people wanting more goods and services.

26. Tibor Scitovsky, *The Joyless Economy: An Inquiry into Human Satisfaction and Consumer Dissatisfaction* (New York: Oxford University Press, 1976).

27. However, for a dissenting view see Stanley Lebergott, *Pursuing Happiness: American Consumers in the Twentieth Century* (Princeton, NJ: Princeton University Press, 1993).

28. Richard A. Easterlin, "Does Economic Growth Improve the Human Lot? Some Empirical Evidence," in *Nations and Households in Economic Growth: Essays in Honor of Moses Abramovitz*, ed., Paul A. David and Melvin W. Reder (New York: Academic Press, 1974), 89-126.

29. Paul L. Wachtel, *The Poverty of Affluence: A Psychological Portrait of the American Way of Life* (New York: Free Press, 1983).

30. See Lawrence Boland, "On the Futility of Criticizing the Neo-classical Maximization Hypothesis," *American Economic Review* 71, no. 5 (December 1981): 1031-1036, and his *The Foundations of Economic Method* (London: Allen & Unwin, 1982). The recent literature on "rhetoric" takes the argument another step—economic theory is a conversation, and different groups of economists (neo-classicals, marxists, institutionalists, et al.) have their own conversations which are different. See discussion below.

31. An in-depth survey of academic economists found a clear correlation between conservative political beliefs and support for the free market and between liberal political beliefs and support for market regulations. See Anthony Randazzo and Jonathan Haidi, "The Moral Narratives of Economists," *Economic Journal Watch* 12, no. 1 (January 2015): 49-57.

32. Donald McCloskey, "The Rhetoric of Economics," *The Journal of Economic Literature* 21 (June 1983): 481-517.

33. Richard Rorty, "Science as Solidarity," in *The Rhetoric of the Human Sciences: Language and Argument in Scholarship in Public Affairs*, ed. John Nelson et al. (Madison: The University of Wisconsin Press, 1987).

34. Uskali Maki. "Diagnosing McCloskey," *The Journal of Economic Literature* 33 (September 1995): 1300-18.

35. William Covino and D. Jolliffe, *Rhetoric: Concepts, Definitions, Boundaries* (Boston: Allyn and Bacon, 1995).

36. Sharon Crowley, *Ancient Rhetorics for Contemporary Students* (New York: MacMillan College Publishing Company, 1994): 6.

37. Edward J. O'Boyle, *Personalist Economics: Unorthodox and Counter-Cultural*, Presidential Address, Association for Social Economics, January 6, 2001, New Orleans, Louisiana. Revised. August 15, 2001.

Chapter Three

Individual Actors Have Moral Values

Economic theory, with its focus on self-interest, obscures the fact that people's preferences are formed not only by material self-interest but also by other factors such as habit, ignorance, and my major concern in this chapter, ethical values. Writing in the fourth century, Macarius of Egypt, an Egyptian Christian monk and hermit, said:

> The heart itself is but a small vessel, yet dragons are there, and there are also lions; there are poisonous beasts and all the treasures of evil. But there too is God, the angels, the life and the kingdom, the light and the apostles, the heavenly cities and the treasures of grace—all things are there.

We will see in Chapter 5 that market economies require that ethical behavior for efficient functioning.

Economic theory focuses on people as hedonists who want to maximize pleasure and minimize pain. It assumes that pleasure comes primarily from the consumption of goods and services; and that pain comes primarily from work and from parting with your income. Thus, given resource constraints, the goal of the economy should be to maximize the production of goods and services. In short, more is better.

INDIVIDUAL PREFERENCE FORMATION

Mainstream economics' rational actor theory is more than an empirical theory of behavior. This is perhaps most clear when economists try to gauge the relative efficiency of alternative economic arrangements, and, therefore, the desirability of policies. Since the definition of welfare is individual preference satisfaction, an individual's utility function becomes a normative benchmark. To provide empirical measurement, economists utilize cost-benefit analysis (CBA). In this practice, the merit of projects or policies is determined by adding up their costs and benefits. The benefits are usually measured in terms of the willingness of the affected parties to pay for them; with willingness-to-pay the normatively relevant piece of data because it reflects preferences. Thus, when applying CBA, economists rely on the notion that welfare amounts to the satisfaction of observed individual preferences.

One problem[1] with the use of preference-satisfaction as a yardstick for policy choice is not that it gives the wrong policy recommendations, but that in some cases it fails to issue in any coherent recommendations at all. This argument is analogous to a problem raised by Tibor Scitovsky. Incomes depend in some cases on which policy is chosen, and, in turn, partly determine the measured benefit of any particular policy. Thus, the valuation of benefits, which is the basis for policy choice, itself depends on the policy chosen; thus, the economist's logic is circular.

The argument I make here is based on this paradox. Preferences, and not just income, shift in response to policy. Thus, there is a second potential source of circularity in the use of preferences to guide policy. An example will serve to illustrate the point. Suppose that liberal education instills in students liberal values and a tendency to favor government support for liberal education; at the same time, those educated in a more authoritarian system tend to support authoritarian educational policies. In this situation, the preference sovereignty standard fails to provide any consistent advice to the policy maker. Which policy satisfies preferences best depends upon which policy is implemented in the first place. Thus, "preference sovereignty" as a criterion for policy selection is not only incorrect; it is incoherent.

These problems are compounded when considering the problem of how to count the welfare of future generations. The shape (and existence!) of future individuals' preferences are determined in part by the policies adopted today, so again one is faced with the question of which preferences to count.[2]

A related problem arises when we deal with the problem of imperfectly informed preferences. It has been empirically documented that in the real world, preferences are affected by all kinds of irrational influences. Advertising shapes our preferences and addiction overrides our desire to quit smoking, gambling, or using drugs. How, then, can one justify relying on those preferences to guide policy? This problem leads to efforts by some theorists to save the preference-sovereignty criterion by using preferences that are "cleansed" of malign influences such as imperfect information. But this only introduces new problems. For example, people often value things or not—such as a surprise birthday present—because of the very uncertainly surrounding them. In such situations, the "cleansing" process may not just cleanse but also distort preferences. Thus, the supporter of preference sovereignty has a dilemma. Either he or she must accept "bad" preferences or tolerate an alien version of preferences, which may lack the moral appeal of more authentic, but ill-informed, ones. The preference sovereignty standard thus fails even when modified to take account of imperfect information.

Amitai Etzioni[3] suggests a way in which deontological considerations might be used to augment neo-classical economics. The essence of the deontological,[4] or Kantian, approach, he says, is that while the utilitarian views the person as a unified bundle of preferences, the Kantian sees the self as bifurcated. Each person has a set of desires as well as a separate aspect of the self that judges those preferences in light of moral considerations. The ultimate choices of the individual are the product of both aspects of the self. This notion, as Etzioni points out, is consistent with the work of those economists such as Amartya Sen who have introduced "meta-preferences"—a secondary set of preferences over the domain of all possible preferences. For example, if my faith commitments lead me to support farm workers, I may choose to not buy grapes, which I dearly love. My meta-preference for justice overrides my preference for grapes. In addition to the fact that preferences have this dual nature, Etzioni points out that preferences respond to experience, and thus are endogenous in an important way.

Etzioni argues for the incorporation of the moral aspects of the individual into economic theory and he argues against seeing the moral aspects of the world as a limited and distinct area in which special rules apply. Morality interpenetrates all of economic life; its implications are sweeping and do not apply only to certain areas. For example, in considering work life, the moral value of work, and not just preferences, Etzioni says, must be considered.[5] Moreover, moral behavior undergirds all of the economy, which would quickly disintegrate if large numbers of people attempted to cheat one another or failed to honor their contracts. Thus, moral considerations demand a radical rethinking of all of economics.

Virtue theory[6] also can add insight into the role of ethics in economics. All evidence indicates that people as economic actors (consumers, workers, investors) act out of more than calculated self-interest. People's behavior is influenced by many things including ethical norms.

The most recent evidence on people acting out of more than self-interest comes from a large three-year study, 2015-2018, carried out in 40 countries.[7] The study examined the trade-off between honesty and self-interest in 355 cities by having researchers turn in over 17,000 "lost" wallets with varying amounts of money to public and private institutions such as banks and then seeing if the recipients (employees or managers) contacted the owner to return the wallets. In virtually all countries people were more likely to return wallets that contained money; and the more money, the better the chances of being returned. Additional data from the study suggest these findings can be explained by a combination of altruistic concerns and an aversion to viewing oneself as a thief, which increases with the material benefits of dishonesty.

What impact does this have upon the ability of economic theory to predict outcomes of economic actions? To the extent that economics is used as an empirical science, a faulty theory of human behavior will lead to an inability to predict and control. For example, how should government encourage people to behave in socially beneficial ways, say, to donate blood? If people are self-interested maximizers, government can best achieve its ends by providing a proper set of economic incentives for such behavior. But if economics misconceives the way people are motivated, material incentives might fail to work. In fact, there is some evidence that blood donations decline when a system of cash payments is introduced. How can this be?

It is not totally clear how to account for the decline in blood contributions, but one possible answer relates to a second, *generative,* role for economic theory. By this is meant its role in generating behavior as opposed to merely predicting or controlling it. Economics can play this role in several possible ways. First, as an article by Frank, Gilovich and Regan[8] suggests, economics can become a sort of philosophy of life for those who study it, leading them to behave in economically rational ways. Economists bring certain values to their interpretation of the facts, for example, by imposing a neoclassical template on the world they observe. Frank et al. go a step further. They experimentally demonstrate that economists' values can affect the "real world" itself—and not just economists' interpretations of it. This happens when economists "export" values in the classroom by teaching the economic theory of rationality. The authors report several experiments, in one of which they put students in a prisoners' dilemma situation, with actual cash at stake. In a regression model of the resulting data, with the decision to defect as the dependent variable, an economics-major variable was significantly positive; those who had studied economics the most were more likely to take the most self-interested action. If this kind of effect is common, then even clearly self-interested behavior may not constitute an independent verification of the theory of rational self-interest, but instead may be a *product* of that theory.

Dawes and Thaler attempt to empirically document and catalog moral behavior as it has been observed in experiments. They recount evidence that in experimental situations people will contribute money toward a public good, contrary to the predictions of rational actor theory. And, reminiscent of the paper by Frank, Gilovich and Regan, they show that groups that have studied economics contribute much less to the public good than others—an illustration of the generative role of social science. They show that groups that can have discussions before they decide how to play have much lower rates of defection, which to them suggests a role for "impure altruism"—obtaining utility from doing the right thing. Finally, people seem to be more inclined to cooperate when they have been given an opportunity to develop a sense of common identity with the beneficiaries of their cooperation.

Second, economically rational ways of behavior can be taught by exposure to social policies and practices that presuppose economic rationality. Thus, for example, even those who initially behave according to social norms about giving blood may come to view blood donation as just another economic transaction, once they see people being paid for their donations. Thus, their non-economic motives are undercut by an economic policy based solely on self-interest; what was a priceless gift becoming merely a $50 one.

Robert Goodin[9] describes a "Gresham's Law of Sentiments" that seems to operate when a reward system (such as monetary incentives) is introduced to encourage an activity that individuals already find intrinsically valuable. Citing experiments in which the introduction of money rewards results in a reduction of individuals' volunteering to perform the same task, Goodin argues that, with respect to moral motives and altruistic behavior, we see real evidence of "base motives driving out noble ones." The introduction of material incentives does not, as economists would predict, necessarily complement altruistic or beneficent impulses, but rather may have the contrary effect of contaminating and making profane the very impulses that they were designed to foster.

The Example of Blood Collection Systems

I want to illustrate the problem of relying solely on self-interest by pursuing further a comparison of the system of blood collection for medical purposes in the United States and in England. In his 1970 book, *The Gift Relationship*, Richard Titmuss questions the efficiency of market relationships based on purely monetary self-interest principles.[10] Instead he hypothesizes that in some instances, such as blood giving, relying on internalized moral values (in this case, altruistic behavior) results in a more efficient supply and better quality of blood. Kenneth Arrow's response[11] to Titmuss questions the extent to which altruism or other internalized moral values may be counted upon as an organizing principle yet acknowledges that there may, indeed, be a role for altruistic giving.

This claim can be stated in economists' jargon as: "Material incentives crowd-out moral incentives." But what is the empirical evidence? The original claim by Titmuss about blood donations was never tested empirically until much later. An exception to this is the questionnaire data collected by Ireland and Koch.[12] They asked a class of economics students if they would be willing to provide blood at various prices. Consistent with the crowding-out hypothesis there was a reduction in the supply of blood donors at the first positive price.

In a much later study, "Crowding Out in Blood Donation: Was Titmuss Right?" Carl Mellstrom and Magnus Johannesson[13] test Titmuss's argument that monetary compensation for donating blood might crowd out the supply of blood donors. To test this claim they carried out a field experiment in Sweden with three different options. In the first one, subjects were given the opportunity to become blood donors without any compensation. In the second, subjects received a payment of approximately $7 for becoming blood donors, and in the third, subjects could choose between a $7 payment and donating the $7 to charity. The results differ markedly between men and women. For men the supply of blood donors is not significantly different among the three experimental groups. For women there is a significant crowding-out effect. The supply of blood donors decreases by almost half when a monetary payment is introduced. There is also a significant effect of allowing individuals to donate the payment to charity, and this effect fully counteracts the crowding-out effect.

Moving beyond the blood donation case, the general idea that economic incentives may sometimes backfire has received substantial empirical support in recent years. Building on work in social psychology, Frey and Oberholzer[14] argued that the introduction of monetary payments may reduce the intrinsic motivation to behave altruistically or perform one's civic duty. They illustrated this with questionnaire data about the location of a nuclear waste repository facility, showing that individuals were less willing to accept locating the facility in their community if they were offered monetary compensation.

A growing experimental literature testing monetary incentives also suggests that financial incentives can be counterproductive. Gneezy and Rustichini[15] found that subjects answered fewer questions correctly on an IQ test if they were paid a small fee per correct answer, and that high school students in Israel collected less money towards charity if they were offered a small monetary incentive. In a field experiment on day-care centers in Israel, Gneezy and Rustichini[16] furthermore found that introducing a fine increased the number of late-coming parents. Consistent with this finding, several recent laboratory experiments suggest that the introduction of fines or minimum performance requirements can reduce performance.[17]

This research illustrates that a person is not born with a set of ready-made values; rather the individual's values are socially constructed through his or her being a part of a family, a church, a school, and a particular society. If these groups expect and urge people to give their blood as an obligation of being members of the group that obligation becomes internalized as a moral value. Blood drives held in schools, churches, and in Red Cross facilities reinforce that sense of obligation. As commercial blood increases, the need for blood drives declines. Thus, the traditional reinforcement of that sense of obligation declines with the result that the embodied moral value atrophies. There is also an information problem. As blood drives decline it is rational for an individual to assume that there is no need for donated blood. The outcome is that a typical person must overcome imperfect information and a lack of social approbation to be able to choose to donate blood.

This suggests that the type of policy recommended will have implications for the type of society that will develop. Inherent in the type of policy suggested is a preference as to the motivational attitudes that are appropriate and should be encouraged.

In South Asia several countries have worked at setting up a volunteer blood donor system. They have found that:

> The most satisfactory way to attract and retain blood donors is to appeal to their altruistic motivation. Donors who give blood because they really desire to help their community need little by way of physical rewards. The downside of such a recruitment drive is that it requires additional financial input and considerable effort by all concerned to present a campaign that will appeal to the hearts and intellects of the population. For this reason, there has been considerable reluctance on the part of authorities in some countries to have the courage to rely on the goodwill of a community to provide blood. Countries such as Korea, Hong Kong, Singapore, Macau and Thailand and others have faced this problem successfully, with the result that each has now good functioning voluntary blood services. The pathway to success in this area of health services is reasonably clear. . . . Volunteer donors eventually can provide the safest and surest supply of blood, but for such a program to be successful, good regional and national planning in all aspects of blood transfusion service is required to ensure that all needs of the donor are met.[18]

One implication of these examples is that the motivations on which the results are based are also important, that is, *how* we achieve these results needs to be addressed. This problem arises because economists take preferences as given—they neither change over time nor are affected by the preferences of other individuals or society. Consequently, the process of preference formation and the nature of the preferences that people have are ignored. That the distribution of beliefs and behaviors at time t influences individual beliefs and behaviors at time $t+1$ is, however, the single most basic finding of the voluminous research within sociology on the behavior of groups.[19]

Even though economists are seldom interested in why people behave the way they do, society usually places a high value on motivations. This is readily evident if one looks at the legal system. Consider a situation in which a person shoots and kills someone else. The result is the same but depending on the motivation the act may be judged to be murder, justifiable homicide, or even just an accident.

In short, three conclusions can be derived from our discussion of the blood supply issue. First, economic policies have a direct effect on both market outcomes and individual values. Second, economists should drop their narrow approach to human behavior and join the rest of society in giving attention to the effect that policies have upon values. How we achieve results *is* important. Finally, economists must recognize that the policy impact upon values exerts its own influence on future market activity. Thus, over time the type of values promoted by public action has significance even within the "efficiency" realm of traditional economic analysis.

WHAT NEEDS TO BE DONE?

Can anything be done to reduce the reliance on self-interest and the emphasis on consumption while, at the same time, increasing the possibilities for meaningful work and the restoration of community? I am not optimistic, but as a Christian and as an economist I would argue we need to develop habits of morally constrained behavior, reinforced by cultural practices, so that short-run rewards become less important. We need values that transcend the narrow self-interest of the economic model as the guide for individual behavior. Is it possible to rebuild a moral consensus wherein we re-learn habits of morally constrained behavior? Yes, this is a major point of Catholic Social Thought which we will explore in Chapter 6. Economists need to re-think their view of people as simply self-interested maximizers. They have made a major mistake in treating love, benevolence, and particularly public spirit as scarce resources that must be economized lest they be depleted. This is a faulty analogy because, unlike material factors of production, the supply of love, benevolence, and public spirit is not fixed or limited. As Hirschman[20] says: "First of all, these are resources whose supply may well increase rather than decrease through use; second, these resources do not remain intact if they stay unused." These moral resources respond positively to practice, in a learning-by-doing manner, and negatively to non-practice. Obviously, there are limits; if overused they become ineffective.

I do not want to leave the impression that ethically based behavior and self-interest are always mutually exclusive. Proximity to self-interest alone does not defile morality. Moral values are often necessary counterparts in a system based on self-interest. Not only is there a "vast amount of irregular and informal help given in times of need"[21]; there is also a consistent dependence on moral values upon which market mechanisms rely. Without a basic trust and socialized morality, the economy would be much more inefficient.

Peter Berger reminds us that "no society, modern or otherwise, can survive without what Durkheim called a 'collective conscience,' that is without moral values that have general authority."[22] Fred Hirsch reintroduces the idea of moral law into economic analysis:

> Truth, trust, acceptance, restraint, obligation—these are among the social virtues grounded in religious belief which . . . play a central role in the functioning of an individualistic, contractual economy. . . . The point is that conventional, mutual standards of honesty and trust are public goods that are necessary inputs for much of economic output.[23]

Hirsch argues that there has been an erosion of this internalized moral code as religious belief has declined. This has "freed" economic actors of the old religious and moral constraints; but the self-interest led growth process has not provided any ready substitute social morality. Thus, the previously effective inhibitions on lying, cheating, and stealing have lost their effectiveness and the functioning of both the public and private economy has suffered. The legacy is an upper class bent upon immediate gains and conspicuous consumption and an underclass frequently hungry, homeless, and incapacitated by drug dependency.

Attempts to rely solely on material incentives in the private sector, and more particularly in the public sector, suffer from two defects. In the first place, stationing a policeman on every corner to prevent cheating simply does not work. Regulators have a disadvantage in relevant information compared to those whose behavior they are trying to regulate. In addition, who regulates the regulators? Thus, there is no substitute for an internalized moral law that directs persons to seek their self-interest only in "fair" ways. The second shortcoming of relying on external sanctions alone is that such reliance can further undermine the remaining aspects of an internalized moral law. As discussed above, by promoting solely self-interest, society encourages that type of behavior rather than ethical behavior. The argument is not that there is no role for self-interest, but rather that there is a large sphere for morally constrained behavior. To distinguish in which sphere self-interest should be used and in which sphere altruism should be promoted is very important and sends signals to society as to what we value.

The coronavirus pandemic of 2020 highlights this issue. People are asked to wear masks to protect others, but many resist, saying, "You are taking away my freedom." Our emphasis on individualism does not serve us well in this situation.

In summary, the erosion of society's religious-based moral code has important practical results. As Hirsch says:

> Religious obligation performed a secular function that, with the development of modern society, became more rather than less important. It helped to reconcile the conflict between private and social needs at the individual level and did it by internalizing norms of behavior. It thereby provided the necessary social binding for an individualistic, nonaltruistic market economy. This was the non-Marxist social function of religion. Without it, the claims on altruistic feelings, or on explicit social cooperation, would greatly increase, as was foreseen, and to some extent welcomed, by a long line of humanists and secular moralists. Less love of God necessitates more love of Man.[24]

Values can be changed. In fact, a principal objective of publicly proclaimed laws and regulations is to stigmatize certain types of behavior and to reward others, thereby influencing individual values and behavior codes. Aristotle understood this: "Lawgivers make the citizen good by inculcating habits in them, and this is the aim of every lawgiver; if he does not succeed in doing that, his legislation is a failure. It is in this that a good constitution differs from a bad one."[25] While families, churches and schools play the most important role in shaping behavior and inculcating values, public laws have a role to play. For example, while law cannot make people stop holding racist beliefs, it can make them stop engaging in certain types of racist behavior. With time that behavior, say refusing service in a restaurant, becomes delegitimized in public opinion.

The churches have an important role to play in this regard. Stanley Hauerwas argues that:

> Christian enthusiasm for the political involvement offered by our secular polity has made us forget the church's more profound political task. In the interest of securing more equitable forms of justice possible in our society, Christians have failed to challenge the moral presuppositions of our polity and society. Nowhere is the effect of this seen more powerfully than in the Christian acquiescence to the liberal assumption that a just polity is possible without the people being just. We simply accepted the assumptions that politics is about the distribution

of desires, irrespective of the content of those desires, and any consideration of the development of virtuous people as a political issue seems an inexcusable intrusion into our personal liberty.[26]

CONCLUSION

There are other differences between economic theory and Christian beliefs. Economic theory abstracts man/woman into a rational calculator of pleasures and pains. Christianity teaches us the stories of the Good Samaritan and the Sermon on the Mount. Meaning and dignity come from being participating members of the faith community. And a faith community is neither created nor maintained by rational self-interest alone. We would do well to heed Ken Boulding's caution of almost 50 years ago:

> There is a danger . . . in a predominately commercial society, that people will take economic behavior as the measure to all things and will confine their relationships to those which can be conducted on the level of the commercial abstraction. To do this is to lose almost all richness or purpose in human life. He who has never loved, has never felt the call of a heroic ethic to give and not to count the cost, to labor and not to ask for any reward has lived far below the peak levels of human experience. Economic man dwells in Limbo—he is not good enough for Heaven or bad enough for Hell. His virtues are minor virtues: he is punctual, courteous, honest, truthful, painstaking, thrifty, hardworking. His vices are minor vices: niggardliness, parsimoniousness, chicanery. Even the covetousness of which he is often accused is a playful and innocent thing compared with the dreadful covetousness of the proud. On the whole he escapes the deadly sins, for his very vulgarity saves him from pride (how much better, for instance, is the commercial vulgarity of Coca Cola than the heroic diabolism of Hitler). But he misses the Great Virtue, and in that he is less than Man, for God has made man for himself, and he has an ineradicable hunger for the Divine, the heroic, the sanctified and uneconomic.[27]

NOTES

1. Tyler Cowan, "The Scope and Limits of Preference Sovereignty," *Economics and Philosophy* 9, no. 2 (1993): 253-269.
2. See Chapter 6 for additional discussion.
3. Amitai Etzioni, "Toward a Kantian Socio-Economics," *Review of Social Economics* 45, no. 1 (April 1987): 37-47.
4. See Chapter 5 for a complete discussion of ethical theories.
5. See John Paul II, *Sollicitudo Rei Socialis*. Also see more in Chapter 8.
6. See Chapter 5.

7. Alain Cohn et al. "Civic Honesty around the Globe," *Science* 20 (June 2019). https://science.sciencemag.org/content/early/2019/06/19/science.aau8712

8. Robert H. Frank, Thomas Gilovich, and Dennis T. Regan, "Does Studying Economics Inhibit Cooperation," *Journal of Economic Perspectives* 7, no. 2 (Spring 1993): 159-71.

9. Robert E. Goodin, "Making Moral Incentives Pay," *Policy Sciences* XII (1980): 131-145.

10. Richard M. Titmuss, *The Gift Relationship: From Human Blood to Social Policy* (London: Allen and Unwin, 1970).

11. Kenneth Arrow, "Gifts and Exchange," *Philosophy and Public Affairs* 14, no. 4 (Summer 1972): 343-362.

12. Thomas R. Ireland and James V. Koch, "Blood and American Social Attitudes," in *The Economics of Charity* (London: Institute of Economic Affairs, 1973): 145-155.

13. Carl Mellstrom and Magnus Johannesson, "Crowding Out in Blood Donation: Was Titmuss Right?" Working Papers in Economics #180, Department of Economics (Goteborg University, 2005).

14. Bruno S. Frey and Felix Oberholzer–Gee, "The Cost of Price Incentives: An Empirical Analysis of Motivation Crowding-Out," *American Economic Review* 87, no. 4 (1987): 746-755.

15. Uri Gneezy and Aldo Rustichini, "Pay Enough or Don't Pay at All." *Quarterly Journal of Economics* 115, no. 2 (2000): 791-810.

16. Uri Gneezy and Aldo Rustichini, "A Fine Is a Price," *Journal of Legal Studies* 29, no. 1 (2000): 1-17.

17. See Ernst Fehr and John A. List, "The Hidden Costs and Returns of Incentives: Trust and Trustworthiness Among CEOs," *Journal of the European Economic Association* 2, no. 5 (2004): 743-771; Ernst Fehr, and Bettina Rockenbach, "Detrimental Effects of Sanctions on Human Altruism," *Nature* 422, no. 137-140 (2003); Ernst Fehr and Simon Gächter, "Do Incentive Contracts Undermine Voluntary Cooperation?" Working Paper No. 34, 2002, Institute for Empirical Research in Economics, University of Zurich; Armin Falk and Michael Kosfeld, "The Hidden Costs of Control." Working Paper No. 250, 2005, Institute for Empirical Research in Economics, University of Zurich.

18. G. Woodfield, "Road Blocks in Achieving a 100% Voluntary Blood Donation Rate in the South Asian Region", *Asian J Transfus Sci,* serial online, 1:33-38 (2007). Cited Mar 23, 2007. Available from: http://www.ajts.org/article.asp?issn=0973-6247;year=2007;volume=1;issue=1;spage=33;epage=38;aulast=Woodfield

19. Steven Kelman, *What Price Incentives? Economists and the Environment* (Boston, MA: Auburn House Publishing Company, 1981): 31.

20. Albert Hirschman, *Rival Views of Market Society* (New York: Viking Press, 1986): 155.

21. Kenneth Arrow, "Gifts and Exchange," *Philosophy and Public Affairs* 14, no. 4 (Summer 1972): 343.

22. Peter Berger, "In Praise of Particularity: The Concept of Mediating Structures," *Review of Politics* 38, no. 3 (July 1976): 134.

23. Fred Hirsch, *Social Limits to Growth* (Cambridge, MA: Harvard University Press, 1978): 141.
24. Hirsch, *Social Limits*, 141.
25. Aristotle, *The Politics*, trans. Carnes Lord (Chicago: University of Chicago Press, 1984).
26. Stanley Hauerwas, *A Community of Character* (Notre Dame, IN: University of Notre Dame Press, 1981).
27. Kenneth E. Boulding, *The Economy of Love and Fear* (Belmont, CA: Wadsworth Publishing Co., 1973): 215.

Chapter Four

Markets Require Intervention

In this chapter I will explain why I believe our market economy and, for that matter, any market economy, requires intervention to channel its positive results so they benefit everyone and why its negative results need to be constrained by countermeasures. To quote Pope Francis:

> The need to resolve the structural causes of poverty cannot be delayed. . . . As long as the problems of the poor are not radically resolved by rejecting the absolute autonomy of markets and financial speculation and by attacking the structural causes of inequality, no solution will be found for the world's problems, or, for that matter, to any problems.
>
> Pope Francis, *The Joy of the Gospel*, para. 202

First, I will focus on the origins and history of market economies to show intervention was and is a necessary part of their evolution. Second, I will discuss moral limits to the use of markets and of market-oriented policies in the allocation of resources. The first objection is based on the belief that not all market exchanges are truly voluntary but rather contain an element of *coercion*. The second objection is based on the concept of *corruption*. It focuses on the degrading effect that market allocation can have on certain types of goods and services. Finally, I will discuss duty- and virtue-based objections.

THE EVOLUTION OF THE SELF-REGULATING MARKET SYSTEM

The market economy is an evolving system of self-regulating markets that had a beginning in historical time and has been in the process of transformation ever since. Let me develop this argument in some detail, building on the original work of Karl Polanyi.[1]

Most historians, whether their orientation is political, cultural, or economic, clearly recognize that the eighteenth century was a turning point in the nature of the Western world which saw momentous movements and events intellectual, political, military, social, cultural and economic. The enlightenment, with its emphasis on reason, natural law, and progress, and its avant-garde philosophes and physiocrats opened new vistas, although most of the population of Europe and the remainder of the world scarcely glimpsed those vistas. The writings of the philosophes, Rousseau, Montesquieu, and Voltaire in particular, infected the rising bourgeoisie of France and, together with the maladministrations of Louis XV and XVI, brought on the French Revolution, the second momentous event of the eighteenth century.

In economic affairs, the eighteenth century began with Francois Quesnay's campaign against mercantilism and ended with the completion of the campaign by Adam Smith. In the process, the classical school of economics, a new social science, came into being. Finally, in the course of the century, the agricultural and commercial revolutions of the previous two centuries initiated the Industrial Revolution in England in four key industries: mining, metallurgy, munitions, and textiles.

It was England of the later eighteenth century which provided the fertile ground in which the self-regulating market could and initially did take root and mature. Not only had the Industrial Revolution begun in the four industries cited above; of equal or greater importance, it began in a period in English history when poverty and its tragic result, pauperism, showed an alarming increase. Even more to the point the poor laws were modified to throw a great mass of English paupers upon the mercy of market wage levels.

Now that the self-regulated market had arrived, what were its characteristics? A capitalist market economy is controlled, regulated, and directed by markets alone. Order in the production and distribution of goods is entrusted to this self-regulating mechanism, based on the expectation that human beings behave to achieve money gains. It assumes markets in which the supply of goods, including services available at a definite price, will equal the demand at that price. A market economy assumes the presence of money, which functions as purchasing power in the hands of its owners. Production will then be controlled by prices, for the profits of those who direct production will depend upon them; the distribution of the goods also will depend upon prices, since prices form incomes and it is with the help of these incomes that the produced goods are distributed among the members of society. Thus, order in the production and distribution of goods is ensured by prices alone.

In contrast, during preceding historical periods, markets were never more than accessories of economic life. Generally, the economic system was embedded in the social system. In Babylonia and even Greece, the local markets (trading centers) were compatible with the established social way of life; markets did not expand at the expense of the society. Even under the mercantile system of the previous two centuries, where markets had expanded to involve a large part of the nation, they were not free markets as described above but were subjected to centralized administration. In Karl Mannheim's words, the market was transformed from a regulatory mechanism utilized by society into the very organizing principle of society itself.

On the eve of the Industrial Revolution, the English economy could be characterized as follows: (1) Although the new national markets were in some degree competitive, the overriding feature of these markets was regulation; (2) The self-sufficing household of the peasant remained the basis of the economic system and was being integrated into large national units through the formation of an internal market; and (3) Agriculture was supplemented by internal commerce, although at the beginning of the eighteenth century the system of internal commerce was one of relatively isolated markets.

This new phenomenon, the self-regulating market, would include some additional ingredients: (1) Self-regulation implied that all production was for sale on the market and that all incomes derived from such sales; (2) there were markets for all elements of industry including goods, labor, land, and money, whose prices were respectively commodity prices, wages, rent, and interest; (3) The state would do nothing to inhibit the formation of markets, and incomes would be formed only through sales; and (4) there would be no interference in adjustment of prices to changed market conditions.

The self-regulating market, which came into existence during the latter part of the eighteenth century and became fully operative with the creation of a true labor market in 1834, and the repeal of the Speenhamland system, was an economic utopia along the lines envisaged by free market advocates. The transition from regulated to self-regulating markets represented a complete transformation in the structure of society. A self-regulating market demanded nothing less than the institutional separation of society into an economic and a political sphere, a singular departure from previous societies whose economies were embedded in the social system and "economic" decision making was determined by larger needs and values.

Moreover, such an institutional pattern could not function unless society was subordinated to its requirements. A market economy could only exist in a market society, as the following examination of the institutional nature of a market economy will serve to illustrate.

Labor, land, and money, as well as commodities, form a vital part of the economic system. They are, in fact, just like commodities, to be bought and sold on the market. However, labor, land, and money are obviously not commodities since they are not "produced" primarily for sale. Labor is only another name for a human activity which is part of life itself, and which is not "produced" for sale but occurs for entirely different reasons. In addition, that human activity cannot be separated from the rest of life. Land is only another name for nature, which is not produced either. Actual money is merely a token of purchasing power that is not produced but comes into existence through the mechanism of banking or state finance. None of the three is produced for sale, so the commodity description of labor, land, and money is purely fictitious. Never in history had there been true self-regulating markets in labor, land, and money. As Polanyi notes, however:

> It is with the help of this fiction that the actual markets for labor, land, and money are organized; they are being actually bought and sold on the market; their demand and supply are real magnitudes; and any measures or policies that would inhibit the formation of such markets would ipso facto endanger the self-regulation of the system. The commodity fiction, therefore, supplies a vital organizing principle in regard to the whole of society affecting almost all its institutions in the most varied way, namely, the principle according to which no arrangement or behavior should be allowed to exist that might prevent the actual functioning of the market mechanism on the lines of the commodity fiction.[2]

This meant that the self-regulating market mechanism became, in fact, the sole director of the fate of human beings and of their natural environment. Polanyi observed that:

> . . . the alleged commodity "labor power" cannot be shoved about, used indiscriminately, or even unused, without affecting also the human individual who happens to be the bearer of this peculiar commodity. In disposing of a man's labor power the system would, incidentally, dispose of the physical, psychological, and moral entity "man" attached to that tag. Robbed of the protective covering of cultural institutions, human beings would perish from the effects of social exposure; they would die as the victims of acute social dislocation through vice, perversion, crime, and starvation. Nature would be reduced to its elements, neighborhoods and landscapes defiled, rivers polluted, military safety jeopardized, the power to produce food and raw materials destroyed. . . . But no society could stand the effects of such a system of crude fictions even for the shortest stretch of time unless its human and natural substance as well as its business organization was protected against the ravages of this satanic mill.[3]

This was, indeed, a creative-destructive process which would have annihilated society but for protective countermoves. Accordingly, no sooner had the utopia of the self-regulating market been established than it was challenged in order that society itself might survive. Polanyi observed: "Accordingly, the countermove consisted in checking the action of the market in respect to the factors of production, labor and land. This was the main function of interventionism."[4]

Interventionism, of course, did not occur simultaneously both on the national scene and in international affairs. On the national scene it did not become a potent force until after midcentury while the international market system was not placed in jeopardy until the last quarter of the nineteenth century. The forces of intervention gathered only slowly; as they accelerated, all was swept before them.

By 1820, in England at least, three tenets of classical laissez-faire economics had been clearly identified: that commodities (including labor) find their price on the market; that the creation of money should be subject to an automatic mechanism; that goods should be free to flow from country to country without hindrance or preference. Policy called for a free labor market, the gold standard, and free international trade. Between 1820 and 1850 economic laissez-faire was fully implemented in England, France, and the Low Countries.

In England, the Poor Law Amendment Bill terminating the Speenhamland system became effective in 1834, thereby ending the system of poor relief and creating a free labor market. Given the assurances that the market knows best, economists and their followers in the nineteenth century thought indifference to the condition of the poor served the best interest of society. This peculiar moral system embodied in the economics of the day was quite evident to Charles Dickens, who, as we saw earlier, devoted *Hard Times* to attacking it.[5] "In the novel, the doctrines of classical political economy are taught in a proprietary school owned by one Thomas Gradgrind. Dickens sarcastically dismisses the writings of his character Gradgrind as "proving . . . that the Good Samaritan was a Bad Economist"—or, as the modern economics-text writers might say, irrational. Dickens thus warned that the moral precepts of the parable and of economics were poles apart.[6]

By 1825, despite inflation and a business slump following the Napoleonic Wars, it was clear that Parliament intended to adhere to the classical principle of a sound currency; its method was to support and defend the gold standard. However, the gold standard implied deflation and monetary stringency in the face of depression. The chief supporter of laissez-faire and the self-regulated market, the manufacturer, had therefore to be protected. Wages had to fall at least in proportion to the general fall in prices to allow the exploitation of an ever-expanding market. Thus, the repeal of the Corn Laws in 1846, a corollary of Peel's Bank Act of 1844, was undertaken to bring laissez-faire to world trade, to allow the free flow of grain into Britain, and to ensure that wages and prices would tend to a free market equilibrium. By 1850 in England, therefore, it appeared that the self-regulating market was triumphant as these three elements, a true labor market, the gold standard, and free trade now formed a coherent whole.

The utilitarians, including Bentham, however, had long since reflected on the shortcomings and contradictions inherent in this classical utopia and were more than mildly distressed at the sacrifices such a system exacted from the people. The utilitarian critiques and the excesses of the market system in general sparked a revolt among not only the working class but more significantly among the rising middle class. Polanyi termed this revolt the collectivist movement. In England, the collectivists, led by the utilitarians, looked to the government for redress. On the Continent, after the unifications of Germany and Italy and the creation of the Third Republic in France, the governments of these countries followed the utilitarian lead. Scarcely more than a decade after the self-regulating market appeared to be triumphant, it was already in retreat, however grudgingly.

Then on the Continent and in England, particularly after the English Parliamentary Reform Act of 1867 which gave the working class the right to vote, a series of "protectionist" legislation was enacted. Factory laws, social insurance, municipal trading, health service, and public utility laws were passed in close succession. New tariffs, embargoes on immigration, national subsidies, formation of cartels and trusts, and curtailment of capital movements were also enacted, all of which inhibited the self-regulating mechanism of the market. German, Japanese, and American growth in the late nineteenth and early twentieth centuries took place behind high tariff walls; and in the first two countries, government intervention was pervasive.

The countermove against economic liberalism and laissez-faire possessed all the unmistakable characteristics of a spontaneous action. At innumerable disconnected points it set in without any traceable links between the interests directly affected or any ideological conformity between them. Even in the settlement of one and the same problem, as in the case of workmen's compensation, solutions switched from individualist to collectivist merely as a result of the increasing realization of the nature of the problem in question. The change took place in several countries at a similar stage in their industrial development. Finally, even free-market liberals were forced to support government intervention to prevent monopoly and so secure the preconditions of the self-regulating market. Indeed, such a market, in all its manifestations, threatened society—which undertook measures to protect itself.

Despite ample evidence that the self-regulating market, and with it nineteenth-century market society, had broken down, efforts were made during the post–World War I years to rehabilitate both. The chief instigators of this effort, of course, were the laissez-faire economists.

The root problems of market society, interventionism and currency, reappeared after Versailles and these issues became the center of politics in the 1920s. A singular effort was made in Geneva during the 1920s, particularly by Britain, France and the United States, to reestablish stable exchanges through a return to gold. Increasingly the responsibility for carrying this burden fell on the United States; and when the Depression struck in 1929, the effort dissolved with the stock market. The effort, however noble, to re-create free trade, a free labor market, and a freely functioning gold standard went the way of the inflated stock. The self-regulating market had succumbed to its own nemeses.

The response to this collapse was Fascism in some countries and the expansion of the welfare state in others. The conclusion I draw is that the free market economy, in the sense of a self-regulating system, is a utopian vision in the minds of economists and was at best a temporary aberration in the history of humankind. Individual markets may have always existed (at least for commodities), but an economy run by free markets was anything but natural and required specific actions of government to come into existence. The mercantilist controls over the economy that laissez-faire economics fought against were merely that era's way of embedding the economy into the social system. The attempt to "free" markets (particularly for the fictitious commodities of labor, land, and money) from societal control was a failure. Society was not willing to live with the creative-destructive process and the uneven development results of a pure market system. In practice, few would accept the notion that everything and everyone's worth was measured by a market determined price. Workers formed trade unions to eliminate competition in the labor market, business firms merged or sought government regulation to eliminate competition. Farmers sought government price supports. And consumers sought government protection from the free market in the form of pure food and drug acts. Professionals convinced government that the public welfare demanded the licensing of lawyers and physicians.

If anything is "natural," it is social control of the economy as a way of embedding it in the total social system; and, if anything is "unnatural," it is a laissez-faire system of self-regulating markets. Government may interfere with our private lives; an unregulated market system with its creative-destructive processes and uneven development has an even greater negative effect in most lives. Therefore, CST argues that the burden of proof should lie with the free market devotees. History and common sense make the real issue, "What type of policies will harness the creative side of the capitalist market economy to achieve our economic goals without allowing the destructive side to override our social and political values and needs?"

This historical analysis casts serious doubt on the long-term success of free market policies in the United States. The attempts to dismantle the protective devices created by previous generations by the Reagan, Bush and Trump administrations are fraught with danger. "Freeing-up" labor markets and creating an enterprise culture will release the destructive forces of the market system upon individual lives and society itself. "Freeing-up" land use and an emphasis on unfettered economic growth threaten the environmental system within which we all must live.

In brief, it is incorrect to assume that the problem is too much government intervention. Rather the problem is the specific structure of government intervention. This implies that more, and different, government intervention might be necessary to overcome our current economic problems. The analysis above implies that government interventions are constitutive of a market economy—without them capitalist society could not exist. Thus, it does not make sense to speak of a contradiction between government intervention and the internal logic of a market economy. Some economic policies are more effective than others and an explanation for the difference will be found at a more concrete level of analysis than the general incompatibility theses propounded by free markets devotees.

Of course, government cannot have an unlimited range of action either. The problems of the communist economies and their move to greater use of markets attest to this. It must be limited to actions that clearly enhance the goals of the economy. I understand, using David Brook's thoughtful words, "that capitalism is really good at doing the one thing socialism is really bad at: creating a learning process to help people figure stuff out. If you want to run a rental car company, capitalism has a whole bevy of market and price signals and feedback loops that tell you what kind of cars people want to rent, where to put your locations, how many cars to order. It has a competitive profit-driven process to motivate you to learn and innovate, every single day."[7]

Chapter 6 will use CST to argue that there must be a balance of government and the market, a mixed economy which must be guided to serve human needs of life-sustenance, fellowship, and freedom. Also, in Chapter 12 I will argue that mediating institutions must be encouraged as an important means of carrying out needed policy.

MARKETS REQUIRE MORAL VALUES

In this section, I will reinforce the historical analysis above (that people try to re-embed the market into the total social system) by focusing on ethical issues involved in using markets as not only the primary but almost the sole means of determining usage of economic resources including that of labor.[8] This term labor, of course, hides the reality that it is the lives of individual human beings that are being talked about.

To discuss moral limits to the use of markets and of market-oriented policies in the allocation of resources, we need to distinguish between two objections to extending the reach of market valuation and exchange.

The first objection is based on the belief that not all market exchanges are truly voluntary but rather contain an element of *coercion*. When people buy and sell things under conditions of severe inequality or out of extreme economic necessity, calling it voluntary seems misplaced. Rather there is more than a little coercion involved and is thus unjust. A poor person may agree to sell a kidney or cornea in order to feed their starving family, but this agreement is not truly voluntary. They are coerced, in effect, by the necessities of the situation.

The second objection is based on the concept of *corruption*. It focuses on the degrading effect that market allocation can have on certain types of goods and services. Moral and civic goods can be damaged or corrupted if bought and sold for money. If, for example, the sale of human body parts, such as kidneys, is intrinsically degrading as a violation of the sanctity of the human body, then kidney sales would be morally wrong for rich and poor alike. Thus, this objection is valid even without the coercive effect of economic necessity.

Each objection is based on a different moral ideal. The objection from coercion draws on the ideal of consent exercised within a fair context, i.e., a more or less level playing field. It is not an objection to markets *per se*, but rather to markets that operate within a context of income and wealth inequality that is so extreme that market bargaining conditions can only be described as coercive. The objection based upon coercion provides no basis for rejecting market allocation of goods where the income and wealth context is just.

The objection based on corruption appeals not to the voluntary nature of consent but to the moral importance of the goods and services being exchanged. The argument from corruption is more basic in the sense that it applies under conditions of equality and extreme inequality alike.

To illustrate the difference between the two objections, Sandel says:

> Consider two familiar objections to prostitution. Some object to prostitution on the grounds that it is rarely, if ever, truly voluntary. According to this argument, those who sell their bodies for sex are typically coerced, whether by poverty, drug addiction, or other unfortunate life circumstances. Others object that prostitution is intrinsically degrading, a corruption of the moral worth of human sexuality. The degradation objection does not depend on tainted consent. It would condemn prostitution even in a society without poverty and despair, even in cases of wealthy prostitutes who like the work and freely choose it.[9]

The point is not to argue for or against prostitution, but rather to show the difference between the two objections and to illustrate the further part of the claim, which is that the second objection is not reducible to the first. Even when there are no unjust differences in income and wealth, there will still be goods and services that should not be bought and sold through markets.

I need to emphasize an important distinction. There may be situations where the sale of a good through markets is morally objectionable and yet the practice should not be legally banned. As Sandel says: "Prohibition may carry moral and practical costs that outweigh the good of preventing the practice."[10] And there may be other, better ways of discouraging it. For example, a tax on cigarettes instead of outright banning. The moral status of a good or service should count as one consideration among others in determining its legal permissibility.

No one defends the out-right purchase and sale of votes.[11] But why is it objectionable? The answer lies in our understanding of what it means to be a citizen. If that means to be a participating member of a community with the obligation to help decide the issues facing the community, then selling your vote abdicates your responsibility. If on the other hand, your understanding of the purpose of democracy is simply a mechanism to aggregate people's interests and preferences and translate them into policy, then there is no good reason to prohibit the buying and selling of votes. In this understanding of democracy "citizens are consumers and politics is economics by other means."[12]

Coercion-Based Objections

It is possible to provide general reasons for using the market to allocate goods and services—it is efficient, except where there is market failure due to externalities, public goods, monopoly, or imperfect information. The objection based on coercion is like the efficiency argument for the use of markets in that it points to a single reason—the lack of consent. The form of the objection is always the same. What appears to be a free exchange of goods or services for money is not truly voluntary, because economic coercion, or economic necessity, is operating to vitiate consent.

During the 2020 Coronavirus pandemic, meat packer workers were ordered to return to work while the virus was still active or lose their jobs and thus be unable to support their families. The choice to get the virus or to go hungry is not a free choice. And it was made worse by the employer reporting that the employee quit and therefore was ineligible for unemployment insurance payments.

Another example of moral limit on markets, based on coercion, is illustrated by considering what we owe the interests of future generations in making decisions.[13] Of course, the market in most cases is blind to such considerations, since it is oriented to the purchasing power of those who are alive today. If it is determined that future generations indeed should have some sort of moral standing in our deliberations, then we have a failure of the market and intervention on their behalf may be needed. In instances when government intervention is already taken for granted, as in cases in which cost-benefit analysis is being used to evaluate a project, the interests or needs of the future represent at least an additional factor to be added to the analysis.

If it is decided to consider the interests of future generations and to do so in a quantified, utilitarian way, one question that arises is whether and by how much costs and benefits in the future should be discounted. What this means is that interest rates that are determined by the existing population decide what future costs and benefits are worth. For example, benefits received 12 years in the future, if discounted at 6 percent, are worth half as much as a dollar today, and in 25 years less than a fourth as much. This is the crux of the problem in attempting to solve environmental issues where the costs are born now, and the benefits reaped in the future. In effect, future generations are coerced—that is, their preferences do not count. The future generations' vital, and only, voice is the conscience of the present generation. As Pope Francis said in *Laudato Si*:

> If we approach nature and the environment without this openness to awe and wonder, if we no longer speak the language of fraternity and beauty in our relationship with the world, our attitude will be that of masters, consumers, ruthless exploiters, unable to set limits on their immediate needs. By contrast, if we feel intimately united with all that exists, then sobriety and care will well up spontaneously.[14]

Corruption-Based Objections

The objection based on corruption must be made in a different way, case by case. It must be shown how, in each case, market valuation and exchange degrade or corrupt important values or ends that non-market practices may embody. An example is the voting issue mentioned above. Our conception of citizenship requires us to exercise our duty to help decide issues. Selling our vote vitiates that understanding of democracy.

Elizabeth Anderson suggests one generalized approach to showing how market valuation and exchange degrade or corrupt important values or ends that non-market practices may protect. She argues that when we distribute a good in a certain institution such as the market, we treat it in accordance with the norms of that institution. Those norms may allow us to realize some values but fail to realize—or even undermine—others. Thus, a good is properly traded on the market if its value is successfully realized by the norms of the market. Also, an institution like the market, together with its associated norms, embodies certain interpretations of ideals, while possibly denying or ignoring other ideals. To determine whether a good is appropriately distributed by the market, we can examine the rival ideals at stake. The way we value things when they are on the market is what Anderson calls *use*. When we *use* something, we treat it in accordance with certain norms of the market.

First, market relations are impersonal ones. Second, the market is understood to be a sphere in which one is free, within the bounds of the law, to pursue one's personal advantage unrestrained by any consideration of the advantage of others. Third, the goods traded on the market are exclusive and rivals in consumption. Fourth, the market is purely want-regarding: from its standpoint all matters of value are simply matters of personal taste. Finally, dissatisfaction with a commodity or market relation is expressed primarily by "exit," not "voice."[15] To determine whether a good should be traded on the market, according to Anderson, we should consult this list of market norms to see if they are compatible with the full realization of its values.

To illustrate the application of this theory, consider Anderson's treatment of the good of personal relationships. Anderson says that the practice of modern relationships is informed by the ideals of intimacy and commitment, as opposed to the ideal of market freedom embodied in the market. This means that the goods of personal relationships are, to a significant extent, shared ones. So, each partner enjoys those goods and knows that the other also enjoys them. And the goods at stake must be provided in the spirit of a gift, rather than out of narrow self-interest, meaning for Anderson that they must express a cognizance of and appreciation for the personal characteristics of the recipient.

All this conflicts with the market norm of impersonality, which requires that goods be provided without regard to any characteristics of the buyer other than his or her willingness to pay. Also, the goods of personal relationships cannot be attained if they are given for base motives, like economic gain. Thus, Anderson argues, we can see that sexuality is not appropriately traded on the market. For a prostitute is motivated by monetary gain and, in providing her sexual "services," does not respond to the personal qualities of his or her customer. Furthermore, the goods of personal relationships can be seen as "higher" than those of the market. By implicitly equating the personal goods of the prostitute with the money of the client, a lower good, prostitution degrades the prostitute. For these and other reasons cited by Anderson, prostitution does not realize the goods of love; thus, we should not distribute sex on the market.

For another example, let us apply Anderson's theory of what goods are properly traded on the market to the case of commercial surrogate mothering. This is where a couple, through a broker, hires a woman to carry a child conceived through artificial insemination. Should such a contract be enforceable in law? To answer this, Anderson asks if the goods of women's labor are best realized when they are treated as commodities. She argues that they are not, for two sets of reasons, one relating to the commodification of the mother's "services" and another centering on the commodification of the children themselves.

I focus here on the argument regarding the commodification of children. At issue once again in this case are several rival modes of valuation. Anderson argues that the values involved are best served when children are valued according to the norms of parental love, rather than those of the market. These norms require that parents act in the interests of children, or in the family's shared interests; on the other hand, surrogate mothers must give up the children involved for private gain, without considering the interests of the child. The norms of parental love dictate that parents love their child unconditionally and not based on any particular characteristics of the child. The parents who acquire the child from a surrogate mother violate this norm, because they choose the mother based partly on IQ and other characteristics, to ensure the "quality of the product." Finally, like the surrogate mother, the surrogacy agency acts solely in the interests of the couple who pay the fee, for example, by doing everything in its power to pry the child free from the birth mother. All these violations of parental norms amount to treating the child as a commodity, which is degrading to the child. It is easy to dismiss such effects as merely symbolic, but children in general may be hurt by the degradation, if, for example, they come to fear being sold themselves.

Art Okun has provided another example in his book *Equality and Efficiency*,[16] where he says you can defend minimum wage laws by arguing that no one should be forced to sell their labor for less than a living wage. A fundamental human right, at least in a prosperous society like ours, is the right to earn a minimum livelihood. If markets do not yield minimum wages that provide for this living wage, then society has a moral right to intervene and enact minimum wage laws. Without these laws human life is corrupted in the sense that life itself is threatened. It is a similar argument to the one against indentured servitude. We do not allow someone to sell themselves into servitude for a set period. This was a common phenomenon at the time the country was founded. By some estimates some one third of the population in the early 1700s had arrived here as indentured servants.

Although the goods and services involved will vary, it is still possible to identify one general feature of objections based on corruption that are leveled against market allocation: all call into question an assumption that informs market theory. This is the assumption that all goods are commensurable, that all goods can be translated without loss into a single measure or unit of value—a monetary value.

Other coercion- or corruption-based objections can be leveled at an all-volunteer army versus a citizen army utilizing a system of drafting everyone within a certain age cohort; a market in human organs; a market for child pornography; etc.

Duty- and Virtue-Based Objections

Financial issues, including usury, profit maximization, and insider trading, provide additional examples of potential moral limits to markets. Amartya Sen considers both deontological and consequentialist perspectives on these issues.[17] As described in Chapter 5, by duty-based, or deontological, ethical approaches, we mean those that claim certain actions have ethical value in themselves and independent of their consequences. This contrasts with the consequentialist view that rules or actions can only be justified by their consequences. It might be wondered how anything other than consequences could possibly matter, but consider an example. Suppose we have a business opportunity that involves cheating a customer, but we know that if we do not take the opportunity, someone else will. The consequences are the same regardless of our action because the customer is cheated no matter what we choose to do; only the identity of the cheater depends on our action. A duty-based ethic, unlike a simple consequentialist one, may hold that we are obligated not to cheat in this scenario because we have a duty not to deceive that holds regardless of the consequences for us or others. Consider a second example, first noted in Chapter 4. In the mid-1980s many colleges and universities were considering divesting their portfolios of securities of companies that did business in South Africa. Some economists argued that this well-intentioned effort would be ineffectual since other investors from around the world would provide any needed capital. This argument clearly neglected the possible relevance of agent-centered restrictions.

As one more example, I want to briefly look at profit-making and financial responsibility. Here the question becomes: Should firms maximize profits without regard to moral considerations? Amartya Sen rejects both the consequentialist argument that profit maximization leads to a Paretian optimum and the deontological one that firms are bound by their fiduciary responsibility to shareholders to maximize profits. As a member of an ongoing community firms have responsibilities to other *stakeholders*—employees, customers, suppliers, and the community in which they operate.

The above examples do not exhaust what can be said about the moral limitations of markets. In virtue ethics, the main criterion to judge the market mechanism is whether the market contributes to the well-being of individual and community life. Since the attainment of the good life depends on the development of virtues and the restraint of vices, the market should be evaluated by considering its impact on virtues and vices.

An analysis of the impact of markets upon virtues is also relevant from a consequentialist or purely economic point of view. As discussed in Chapter 4, ethically embodied behavior such as altruism and trust are important to sustain efficient market operations. Therefore, economists need to be interested in how this ethically embodied behavior comes about and what are the cultural effects of market operations.

Markets and other economic institutions do more than allocate goods and services. They also influence the evolution of values, preferences, and personalities. There is considerable empirical evidence that market-type policies can crowd out social virtues. For example, there are several studies that show that market policies can crowd out the intrinsic motivation to contribute to the social good. As we saw in Chapter 4, Frey and Oberholzer tested the "base motives driving out noble ones" hypothesis by analyzing the preparedness of citizens to accept a nuclear waste repository in their hometown.[18] They found that if citizens were offered financial compensation, the acceptance rate declined from 51 percent to 25 percent. Detailed statistical analyses showed that civic-mindedness and care for the broader social costs had a significant positive impact on the willingness to accept the waste repository. When compensation was offered, the positive impact of these social factors on the willingness to accept the repository disappeared. Frey and Oberholzer conclude that where public spirit prevails, the use of price incentives tends to crowd out civic duty and therefore needs to be reconsidered as an instrument of social policy. Fehr and Gachter[19] present an experiment in which an increase in monitoring of workers and the imposition of fines in case of verified shirking significantly reduces workers' efforts. This indicates that explicit incentives may destroy embodied ethical motivations. Finally, it should be noted that crowding out of intrinsic motivation may not only result from market incentives, but also from government regulations that reduce the freedom of agents. For example, volunteer work has been found to be lower in state welfare countries than in countries where there is less government intervention with the social economy.[20]

I conclude this discussion with a specific example of the possible role of virtue in the economy. In an opinion piece on inner-city poverty in *The Wall Street Journal*, Glenn Loury[21] argues that policy makers must recognize that creating incentives based solely on the assumption of rational self-interest is doomed to failure. He says liberals, like the sociologist William Julius Wilson, now acknowledge that behavioral problems are fundamental, but they still insist that these problems derive ultimately from a lack of economic opportunities and will abate once "good jobs at good wages" are at hand. Conservatives, such as the political scientist Charles Murray, see the tragic developments in the inner cities as the unintended legacy of a misconceived welfare state. If the government would stop underwriting irresponsible behavior, they argue, poor people would be forced to discover the virtues of self-restraint.

Loury argues these polar positions have something in common. They both implicitly assume that economic factors lie behind the behavioral problems, even behaviors involving sexuality, marriage, childbearing, and parenting. Both points of view suggest that behavioral problems can be cured from without, by changing government policy or by getting the incentives right. As he says, "Both smack of a mechanistic determinism, wherein the mysteries of human motivation are susceptible to calculated intervention." He goes on to say:

> Ultimately, such sterile debates over policy fail to engage the fundamental questions of personal morality, of character and values. We do not give public voice to the judgments that it is wrong to abuse drugs, to be sexually promiscuous, to be indolent and without discipline, to be disrespectful of legitimate authority, to be unreliable, untruthful, unfaithful.

Social scientists need to understand that a conception of virtuous living needs to be revived in the public debate over workable policies. More surprising, coming from an economist, is his argument that virtuous living requires a spiritual motivation that is learned in the home and church. "No economist can devise an incentive scheme for eliciting parental involvement in a child's development that is as effective as the motivations of conscience deriving from the parents' understanding that they are God's stewards in the lives of their children." He urges that future policy debates need to bear these behavioral issues in mind. And, of course, to evoke the issue of spirituality is not to deny the relevance of public action.

To be healthy every economy needs some degree of market competition, which stimulates efficiency and development. But there are limits as Pope Pius XI wrote in *Quadragesimo Anno*: "The right ordering of economic life cannot be left to a free competition of forces."[22]

In the next chapter I will examine moral theories and theories of justice as guides to how and when the market requires intervention. Then in Chapter 6 I will present modern Catholic social thought, focusing on the United States

Catholic bishops' 1986 pastoral letter, *Economic Justice for All*, and the papal encyclicals from Leo XIII's *Rerum Novarum* in 1892 to Pope Francis' *Laudato Si* in 2015 and *Fratelle Tutti* in 2020.

NOTES

1. See Karl Polanyi, *The Great Transformation* (New York: Farrar and Rinehart, 1944).
2. Polanyi, *The Great*, 72-73.
3. Polanyi, *The Great*, 73.
4. Polanyi, *The Great*, 134.
5. Charles Dickens, *Hard Times*, Book II, chap. 12 (Oxford: Oxford University Press, 2008).
6. Donald E. Frey, "The Good Samaritan as Bad Economist," *Cross Currents* 46, no. 3 (Fall 1996).
7. David Brooks, "I Was Once a Socialist. That Changed," *New York Times*, December 6, 2019.
8. This chapter relies heavily on the following sources: Elizabeth Anderson, "The Ethical Limitations of the Market," *Economics and Philosophy* 6, no. 2 (1990): 179-205; Michael J. Sandel, "What Money Can't Buy: The Moral Limits of Markets," *The Tanner Lectures on Human Values*, delivered at Brasenose College, Oxford, May 11 and 12, 1998, 89-122; Paul Streeten, "What Do We Owe the Future?" *Resources Policy* (March 1986): 4-16; Amartya Sen, "The Moral Standing of the Market," in *Ethics and Economics*, ed. Ellen Frankel Paul, Fred D. Miller Jr., and Jeffrey Paul (Oxford: Blackwell, 1985): 1-20.
9. The quote is from Sandel, "Moral Limits," 95.
10. Sandel, "Moral Limits," 96.
11. However, the Dallas oilman, H. L. Hunt, once thought the richest man in America, published a novel, *Alpaca*, that advocated "graduated suffrage." Votes are apportioned by age and income. In Alpaca, every citizen 18 and older may vote. Voters between 22 and 65 automatically get two votes apiece; young and elderly voters get one vote. Beyond that, citizens may earn "premium votes," up to seven more, based on how much they pay in taxes. H. L. Hunt, *Alpaca* (Dallas, TX: H. L. Hunt Press, 1960).
12. Hunt, *Alpaca*, 118.
13. See Streeten, "The Future."
14. Francis, *Laudato Si*, para. 11.
15. Anderson, "Ethical Limitations," 184.
16. Arthur M. Okun, *Equality and Efficiency: The Big Tradeoff* (Washington D.C.: The Brookings Institution, 1975).
17. Amartya K. Sen, "Money and Value: On the Economics and Ethics of Finance," *Economics and Philosophy* 9, no. 2 (1993): 203-227.

18. Bruno S. Frey and Felix Oberholzer–Gee, "The Cost of Price Incentives: An Empirical Analysis of Motivation Crowding-Out." *American Economic Review* 87, no. 4 (1997): 746-755.

19. Ernst Fehr and Simon Gachter, *Fairness in the Labour Market: A Survey of Experimental Results* (Working paper No. 114: Institute for Empirical Research in Economics; University of Zurich, 2002).

20. In fact, Frey finds that a regulatory approach generates more crowding-out effects on intrinsic motivations than price incentives, used for the same purpose. See Bruno S. Frey, "Institutions and Morale: The Crowding-out Effect," in *Economics, Values and Organizations*, ed. Avner Ben-Ner and Louis Putterman (Cambridge: Cambridge University Press,1998): 437-460.

21. Glenn C. Loury, "God and the Ghetto, *Wall Street Journal*, February 25, 1993.

22. Pius XI, *Quadragesimo Anno*, para. 88.

Chapter Five

Moral Theories and Justice

In this chapter I will analyze the need for people, both as individual economic actors and together in communities, to make the moral decisions required for an economy to be judged moral. As the United States Catholic Bishops said:

> Christians, like all people, must be concerned about how the concrete outcomes of their economic activity serve human dignity; they must assess the extent to which the structures and practices of the economy support or undermine their moral vision.
>
> *Economic Justice for All*, para. 127

I will first discuss ethics at the individual level and then turn to a discussion of ethics for society as a whole. It is meaningful and relevant to examine separately both what is intrinsically good at the individual level—for instance, who is a good person, or what are good actions of individuals—and what is intrinsically good at the social level—that is, what is a good society. Moreover, ethics at the individual level and at the societal level are related in various ways. First, it may be instructive to examine analogies between individual and societal ethics, since such an examination can increase our understanding of both. In the *Republic*, for instance, Plato compared the virtuous individual to the virtuous society to understand what it means for individuals to have virtue, but he was also concerned intrinsically with virtuous states or societies. Second, individuals collectively comprise societies, and societies affect individuals and their actions so that goodness at the individual level and at the social level may be instrumental for each other. The consequences of individual actions will depend on what others in society do, social rules and norms can limit or otherwise affect what individuals can do, and the nature of society can have an influence on the kinds of people who live within it. Moreover, individual ethics is likely to affect societal ethics both in the sense of what kinds of ethical considerations will actually be adopted in social arrangements and how society as a whole evaluates the goodness of collective actions and their consequences.

MORAL THEORIES

A moral theory is needed to provide a framework for responding to the ethical questions that arise in the course of economic activity.[1] For example, if one decides that value-free economics is impossible, which moral values should inform the discipline? If people do not behave simply as self-interested rational maximizers, what moral theories might guide their actions? What moral theory should be used to answer applied policy questions? And finally, if individual preference sovereignty is not accepted as the overriding goal of the economic system, what moral benchmarks or objectives should take its place? None of these issues can be understood, much less resolved, without some sort of a moral theory as a guide.

In addition, moral theory may be of help in answering some questions that we have only hinted at so far. First, in a market society such as ours, in which firms have strong incentives to act in their own interests, is there a place for morality, or a kind of business ethics? Do firms have any obligations other than to earn money for their stockholders? Consider a recent regulatory case. It was discovered that a particular model of automobile was susceptible to catching on fire in an accident, leading to unnecessary deaths and injuries. The costs of recalling all the vehicles involved and fixing each one would have been high. Finally, the producers of the car agreed to a settlement with regulators in which they would not be forced to fix the defect but promised to undertake other safety measures that would save as many lives, but at lower cost.

What moral issues are at stake here? If the company knew of the problem before it sold the cars, did it act improperly in selling them? Once the problem became apparent, did the firm have a duty to fix the defect at any reasonable expense? Did the firm relieve itself of any such responsibility when it agreed to alternative actions that would save as many lives? Trying to answer such questions without a moral theory is like trying to send a rocket into space without physical theory. I will examine several of the philosophic candidates for this theoretical role in this chapter and then examine a religious approach using modern CST in Chapter 7.

Types of Moral Theories

In philosophy ethical theories are usually classified into three basic types: virtue theories, deontological theories, and consequentialist theories. I examine these three types of normative theory with the aim of exploring their distinctive features. As will become clear, these categories, while useful, have limitations. In practice, all three may be appealed to for guidance.

As Solomon points out,[2] the basis for distinguishing the three types of normative theory lies in three universal features of human actions. Every human action involves (1) an agent who performs (2) some action that has (3) consequences. These three features may be set out as follows:

AGENT >>>>> ACTION >>>>> CONSEQUENCES

If Jones tells a lie to Smith that causes Smith to fire White, a good reliable worker, then Jones is the agent, his telling a lie is the action, and White losing his job is one of the consequences of the action.

Ethical or broadly evaluative judgments can also be classified using a taxonomy drawing on these features of human action. Some ethical judgments are primarily evaluations of agents, such as "Smith is a compassionate and understanding supervisor" or "White is a conscientious worker." In these cases, the object evaluated is a particular person, and he or she is evaluated as a possible or actual agent of an action. Some other ethical judgments are primarily about actions in the narrow sense, such as "Jones has a duty to tell the supervisor the truth about the accident" or, at a higher level of generality, "The direct killing of the innocent is always wrong." In these cases, the primary object of ethical evaluation is an action—the thing done or to be done. This action may be characterized either as required ("X must be done") or as permitted ("X would be right to do) or as forbidden ("A would be wrong to do"). In all the cases the action is the primary object of evaluation.

A third class of ethical judgments is primarily about states of affairs or objects that are neither agents nor actions, such as "Being fired unfairly is wrong" or more generally "Health is more important than money" or "Human suffering is a terrible thing." Ethical judgments like these do not, directly at least, evaluate either agents or actions. However, the objects evaluated in them may be, and frequently are, the possible consequences of actions. Thus, this last class of judgments can also be matched to one of the three basic features of human action.

Normative theories may have any of three basic structures, and the differences among these structures are determined by which of the three kinds of practical judgments is taken as basic by a theory. Virtue theories take judgments of agents or persons as most basic; deontological theories take judgments of actions as most basic; and consequentialist theories take judgments of the possible consequences of an action as more basic. The sense in which a theory takes a judgment of a certain kind as most basic will become clear in the discussion of each type of theory.

I will discuss these three theories in reverse order and in accord with their current popularity: consequentialist, deontological, and virtue ethics.

Consequentialist Theories

Consequentialist ethical theories take the value of the consequences of actions as most basic. According to these theories, one's crucial ethical task is to act so that one will bring about as much as possible of whatever the theory designates as most valuable. If a particular consequentialist theory designates, for example, that pleasure is the only thing valuable in itself, then one should act so as to bring about as much pleasure as possible. The goals of a consequentialist theory itself are threefold: (1) to specify and to defend some thing or list of things that are good in themselves; (2) to provide some technique for measuring and comparing quantities of these intrinsically good things; and (3) to defend some practical policy for those cases where one is unable to determine which of several alternative actions will maximize the good thing or things.

For consequentialists, the distinction between *instrumentally* good things and *intrinsically* good things is of special importance. Instrumentally good things are good only insofar as they play some role in bringing about intrinsically good things. Its goodness is merely dependent. Intrinsically good things, on the contrary, are good not because of any relation in which they may stand to other things. Their goodness is independent because it is constituted by the kind of thing the good thing is. Thus, a consequentialist theory may hold that only pleasure is intrinsically good, but that other things, including types of action and states of character, are instrumentally good. The virtue of honesty, for example, might be regarded as instrumentally good by such a theory since honesty is likely to contribute to maximizing human happiness. Even if honesty is typically instrumentally good, however, situations may arise in which one could maximize pleasure by acting deviously rather than honestly. In such cases, a consequentialist theory (complications about rule versions of the theory aside) would hold that one should perform the devious action. According to this view, there is nothing about honesty in itself that is good.

Consequentialist theories find their fullest expression in modern thought, especially in the thought of British utilitarian's Jeremy Bentham, John Stuart

Mill, and Henry Sidgwick. Drawing on earlier work in the British empiricist tradition, the classic utilitarian claimed that the only intrinsically good thing is human happiness, which they understood as constituted by pleasure and the absence of pain. The utilitarian maxim, "Act always in such a way as to promote the greatest happiness to the greatest number," has been the paradigmatic consequentialist moral principle and has inspired many more recent consequentialists.

There was much disagreement among classical utilitarians, however, about the details of their view. Can pleasures be distinguished qualitatively as well as quantitatively? What role should rules and virtues play within the practical thought of a utilitarian? How can the flavor of the absolute prohibitions associated with justice and the inviolability of the person be preserved within a utilitarian framework? These questions, along with other similar ones, were answered differently by different utilitarians. They were at one, however, in aspiring to formulate and defend a particular version of consequentialism.

Implementing utilitarianism presents certain problems. How does one measure welfare or preference satisfaction, particularly when different individuals must be compared? Do consequences count if they are not expected in advance? Does the welfare of future generations matter? What of animals? How does one compare two different states of affairs in which population levels differ? How does an individual make ethical decisions when quantifying utility is difficult if not impossible?

Despite these difficulties, it is argued by many that utility is the only intrinsically good thing. Others argue that utilitarianism is justified on the basis of equal respect among persons. There has been a recent resurgence in the popularity of consequentialism and many economists find it appealing because of its apparent compatibility with neo-classical economic theory.

Deontological Theories

Deontological normative theories take moral judgments of action as basic, and they regard the fundamental ethical task for persons as one of doing the right thing—or, perhaps more commonly, of avoiding doing the wrong thing. While virtue theories guide action by producing a picture of ideal human character and a list of virtues constitutive of that character, deontological theories characteristically guide action with a set of moral principles or moral rules. These rules may refer to particular circumstances and have the following form:

Actions of type T are never (always) to be performed in circumstance C. Or they may be absolute in that they forbid certain actions in all circumstances and have the following form: Actions of type T are never to be performed.

The essential task of a deontological theory, then, is twofold: (1) to formulate and to defend a particular set of moral rules and (2) to develop and defend some method of determining what to do when the relevant moral rules come into conflict.

Just as a virtue theory subordinates judgment of actions and consequences in a characteristic way, a deontological theory subordinates judgments of character and consequence. The state of character ethically most important in a deontological view is conscientiousness—that state of character that disposes persons to follow rules punctiliously, whatever the temptations may be to make an exception in a particular case. Conscientiousness does not have value in itself, but it has value derivatively because it is the most important state of character for ensuring that persons follow rules and, hence, that they do what is right. In a similar way, the consequences of actions that deontologists are most concerned with are the consequences of particular rule-followings.

The most profound attempt to defend this view was anticipated in ancient moral philosophy by the Stoics and was developed in its most persuasive form by the modern German philosopher Immanuel Kant. The Stoics claimed that moral rules are expressions in the human realm of laws of nature and that rational creatures are required to follow these rules because, as creatures, they are part of nature and, as such, obligated to bring their action in line with natural forces. Human beings differ from other objects of nature by possessing both freedom and reason. Since they are free, they may act against nature; since they have reason, however, they can understand natural laws and choose to bring their action in line with such forces. Kant's view agrees with the Stoic view in broad outline, but he develops the notions of freedom and reason far beyond the Stoic view. Kant's ultimate answer to questions about how we discover the correct set of moral rules is that only by following the dictates of reason can we be genuinely free.

Hausman and McPherson[3] demonstrate that the deontological position is intuitively appealing by means of an example: a situation in which a person must choose between killing one innocent person himself or allowing two others to be murdered by another person. The consequences, in terms of the number of lives lost, are not as bad if the person commits the murder. But to do so violates the duty not to kill. This may seem to be an obvious point and perhaps beyond the scope of economics but consider a second example. In the mid-1980s many colleges and universities were considering divesting their portfolios of securities of companies that did business in South Africa. Economists argued that this well-intentioned effort would be ineffectual since other investors from around the world would provide any needed capital. This argument clearly neglected the relevance of agent-centered restrictions;

to many people, support for companies operating under apartheid conditions was morally unacceptable.

Amitai Etzioni,[4] as we saw in Chapter 3, suggests a way in which deontological considerations might be used to augment neoclassical economics. The essence of the deontological, or Kantian, approach, he says, is that while the utilitarian views the person as a unified bundle of preferences, the Kantian sees the self as bifurcated. The person has a set of desires as well as a separate aspect of the self that judges those preferences in light of moral considerations. The ultimate choices of the individual are the product of both aspects of the self. This notion, as Etzioni points out, is consistent with the work of those economists who have introduced "metapreferences"—a secondary set of preferences over the domain of all possible preferences. For example, we like to buy our clothes cheaply but our moral commitment to justice keeps us from buying those made in sweatshops.

Virtue Theories

Normative theories that regard judgments of agents or of character as most basic are called virtue theories because of the central role played in them by the notion of a virtue. In the context of these theories, a virtue is understood as a state of a thing "in virtue of which" it performs well or appropriately.

A virtue theory takes judgments of character or of agents as basic in that it regards the fundamental task of normative theory as depicting an ideal of human character. Those features of human beings on which virtue theories concentrate in depicting the ideal human being are states of character. Such theories typically issue in a list of virtues for human beings. These virtues are states of character that human beings must possess to be successful as human beings. Typically, a virtue theory has three goals:

1. to develop and to defend some conception of the ideal person
2. to develop and to defend some list of virtues necessary for being a person of that type
3. to defend some view of how persons can come to possess the appropriate virtues.

Virtually all ancient moral philosophers developed normative ethical theories of this sort. The ethical theories of Plato and Aristotle provide models of this kind of normative ethical theory. Much of the discussion of ethics in ancient Greece centered on a particular short list of virtues—justice, temperance, courage, and wisdom—that came to be called the *cardinal virtues*. After the introduction of Christianity into Europe, these four virtues were joined by faith, hope, and charity—the so-called *Christian virtues*—to form the seven virtues; these, together with the seven deadly vices, dominated medieval thinking about ethics.

One can also see how questions of human character are basic according to virtue theories by seeing how questions about (1) which actions one ought to perform and (2) which consequences one ought to bring about are subordinated to questions of human character. For a virtue theory the question "Which actions ought one to perform?" receives the response "Those actions that would be performed by a perfectly virtuous agent." Similarly, those states of affairs one is required to bring about in the world because of one's actions are those states of affairs valued by a perfectly virtuous person. Of course, particular actions may also be required by one's particular virtues. For example, someone who possesses the virtue of honesty may be required by the virtue itself to tell the truth in certain cases. Or someone may be required to pursue certain consequences by certain virtues. For example, an agent who has the virtue of benevolence may be required to pursue the happiness or well-being of others. But these requirements are derivative from the virtues, and the fundamental ethical question thus remains a question about the correct set of virtues for human beings.

Happiness plays a central role in virtue theory, but virtue theorists mean something different than what is usually thought when they refer to happiness. Aristotle used the term to refer to activity in accordance with virtue. Virtues, in turn, are the personal qualities that enable us to do the things that good people do. To use an analogy, a good watch is one that tells time well, looks stylish, and has other such virtues. Of course, the qualities of a good person are more complicated than those of a good watch and require agreement on the proper ends of humankind. Among the most prominent present-day proponents of virtue theory, Alasdair MacIntyre[5] has argued that an important feature of modern societies is their inability to reach agreement on such matters. But we can possibly agree that the human virtues probably include truthfulness, courage, and so on. These virtues come into play in different human *practices*, or spheres of endeavor, each of which has distinct goods and virtues. Thus, the main goods of playwriting may include witty wordplay, while the goods of news writing may prominently include being informative and concise, and the virtues of the practitioners of each of these fields vary accordingly.

David Stewart's work[6] on developing ethical habits in business is influenced by virtue theory. Stewart argues that virtue theory has much to teach modern businesspeople. He argues that businesses would perform better if they concentrated on developing virtues or excellences like quality, rather than focusing exclusively on the bottom line. And just as Aristotle emphasized the importance for the individual of cultivating friendships, Stewart emphasizes the importance to the firm of developing good long-term relations with partners such as suppliers and customers. Stewart argues that Japanese firms have long followed such "communitarian" business practices, which in part account for their remarkable successes.

In Catholicism's version of virtue theory, one is called to base one's life on that of Jesus and the Saints. In contrast to self-interest as the virtue of economic man, Christianity provides an alternative view. In a world where competition is the dominant mode of relating with others, Jesus models a different way; the way of *compassion* where we are called "to be the kind of people who are moved to absorb the terror of pain and suffering that threatens to isolate those in need and destroy their dignity."[7] As compassionate people we are called to reach beyond ourselves and into the community—to the poor, the homeless, immigrants, and all those marginalized by racism, sexism, and homophobia. Compassion enables us to walk side-by-side with them.

A recently published book entitled *Compassionomics*[8] summarizes many past studies, providing significant evidence that in health care, at least, compassion in the form of human connection matters in astonishing ways. They conclude that: compassion has vast benefits for patients across a wide variety of conditions; missed opportunities for compassion can have devastating health effects; compassion can help reverse the cost crisis in health care; compassion can be an antidote for burnout among health care providers; 40 seconds of compassion can save a life.

Although I have argued for the incorporation of the moral aspects of the individual into economic theory, I argue against seeing the moral aspects of the world as a limited and distinct area in which special rules apply. It is thus not enough merely to qualify economic rationality in a few areas where moral considerations are important. Morality interpenetrates all economic life; its implications are sweeping and do not apply to only certain areas. For example, in considering work life, the moral value of work, and not just preferences, must be considered. Moreover, moral behavior undergirds all the economy, which would quickly disintegrate if large numbers of people attempted to cheat one another or failed to honor their contracts. Thus, moral considerations require a radical rethinking of all of economics.

THEORIES OF JUSTICE

Having briefly discussed ethics at the individual level, I now turn to a discussion of ethics for society as a whole.[9] There are differences between ethics at the individual level and at the societal level, since societal ethics refer not only to the ethics of individuals comprising it, but also ethics regarding the rules and regulations that affect all individuals and govern how individuals interact with each other, how individuals affect each other and how they fare in relation to each other. For these reasons, it is difficult to have a discussion of justice or ethics at a societal level which completely parallels the discussion of ethics at the individual level in terms of virtue, actions, and consequences. However, there are elements of virtue, deontological and consequentialist ethics to be found in the different theories of justice discussed below.

I will discuss five theories of justice: (1) egalitarian theories that focus on equality; (2) theories that focus on consequences, as exemplified by utilitarianism; (3) theories that focus on individual rights and the notion that people should receive what they contribute or what they deserve; (4) theories which base principles of justice on freely made contracts between self-interested individuals; and (5) theories that focus on a communitarian ideal of the common good.

Egalitarian Theories of Justice

The first category covers approaches to justice which emphasize equality, the well-being of the least advantaged people in society, and focus on the satisfaction of basic needs of all people.

There are many modern egalitarian conceptions of justice, some of which argue that equality is good in itself, especially if inequality is involuntary, and if it concerns the distribution of some broad thing—such as health care, housing, education, or more generally, income—that people value.

A focus on equality leads to a number of questions concerning what it is that we seek equality of. One question is whether what is good is equality of opportunity among people, or the equality of outcomes. If it is the equality of outcomes, how do we measure outcomes? Should our goal be to equalize income across people, or to equalize some other goods that we think are important, for instance, equality of health conditions. If it is equality of opportunity, how do we ensure such equality by creating a level playing field? Should the rules that are in place treat all individuals in the same way, or address problems of certain types of differences, such as handicaps? If large inequalities in outcome persist, how can we be sure that opportunities actually are equal? See Chapter 9, "Pope Francis and Inequality," for further discussion of egalitarian views.

Utilitarianism and Related Theories

Utilitarianism is the exemplar of theories that involve the maximization of social good. It was developed by British philosophers in the 18th and 19th

centuries such as Jeremy Bentham (1748-1832), John Stuart Mill (1806-1873) and Henry Sidgwick (1838-1900) and has been described as the theory which seeks to achieve the "greatest good for the greatest number of people." More specifically this approach to justice involves the maximization of the sum of utility of all individuals in society. Individual utility reflects the balance between positive and negative feelings of individuals and is generally taken to be the amount of pleasure people obtain minus the amount of pain they experience. Social changes, such as those involving government policies, are considered to be good if they increase the sum total of individual utility, and the aim of society should be to maximize total utility for society as a whole.

Utilitarianism, as defined above, represents a form of consequentialist ethics, since good and bad are judged in terms of consequences or social outcomes. It also takes a hedonistic approach to the good since it evaluates consequences by summing up the net pleasure (that is, pleasure minus pain) obtained by individuals.

There are a number of problems with utilitarianism in addition to its neglect of freedom and rights. First, is the question about the definition and measurement of pleasure and pain. Utilitarianism based on pleasure and pain has to a large extent been replaced among economists by the implications of choice theory. People are assumed to be better off (and therefore obtain more utility) when they choose something over something else when they could have chosen the latter. However, this is true by definition. If you didn't get more utility, you wouldn't have chosen that bundle. While this overcomes the problem of measuring pleasure and pain, it has the problem that it assumes away the problem of buyer's remorse. Second, utilitarianism has the problem that it requires comparing the utility of different people and summing them up, that is, it involves interpersonal utility comparisons. That is, there is no way to equate two different people's utility gains or losses without a common measuring rod and none have been found.

Equity, Desert, and Rights-Based Theories

The theories of justice considered here are based on the concepts of proportionality and individual responsibility. Equity theorists trace the roots of their theory in the *Nichomachean Ethics*, in which Aristotle described a theory of justice based on proportionality between a person's contribution to an exchange or interaction, and the outcome in terms of consequences the person receives, positive or negative. In other words, if two people are involved in an exchange or interaction, the ratio of what a person receives to his or her input should be equal for the two people: the one who provides more inputs should get proportionally more output. Difficulties relate to quantification of inputs and outputs, and also what kinds of inputs are considered appropriate in this approach. Some equity theorists argue that the class of inputs relevant to the equity approach should only be those over which the agent exercises control.

The American philosopher Robert Nozick argues that a distribution of goods is just if it is brought about by free exchange among consenting adults from a just starting position, even if large inequalities subsequently emerge from the process. This approach is concerned with the entitlement, or rights of individuals to what they possess, or their "holdings," and at the core of this approach are two principles: (1) the principle of justice in acquisition, that is, how things came to be originally owned, and (2) the principle of justice in transfer, that is, how these holdings were transferred between people.[10] Nozick argues that these two principles are violated by theft, fraud, enslavement, and forcible exclusion from participating in exchange. This view draws on the English philosopher John Locke and Kant, but is opposed to utilitarianism because he takes individual choices to be paramount rather than attempts to promote the social good.

Theories of desert aim to provide people with their just desert, or what they deserve. These theories usually distinguish between different factors that affect the distribution of claims on income and wealth. The American economist and Nobel Laureate James M. Buchanan, like Nozick, envisions a limited role for state intervention and dominant role for individual choice and action. However, he specifies four factors which determine income and wealth distribution, that is, luck, choice, effort, and birth. He argues that of these, the relevance of effort in justifying inequality is least controversial, and the only one which conflicts with widely held views of justice are those caused by birth.[11] In this view, inequality caused by effort, choice and luck would not be considered unjust.

The approaches discussed in this section are usually associated with libertarianism, which gives a very small role to government, and with a fairly wide acceptance of inequality, at least when it results from these acceptable causes. It can, however, be rooted in both deontological and utilitarian ethical theories. Thus, the minimal role of government can be advocated because it seems to deny people some basic right. Government intervention is argued to have the bad consequence of reducing people's choices and, in addition, of lowering levels of production by reducing people's incentives. Similarly, inequality can be justified by an appeal to the natural right to private property, as advocated by the British philosopher John Locke, or in terms of the consequentialist argument that inequality induces people to excel and to increase economic growth.

Contract Theories of Justice

Contract theories derive principles of justice from what individuals in a group would choose voluntarily even when there are conflicts of interest but may still yield mutually beneficial results.[12] Contract theories try to derive ethical principles that individuals may choose, given their objectives which may involve solely the pursuit of self-interest. The idea that the principles of justice can be derived from (possibly implicit) contracts between individuals has early roots in the writings of Plato, Hobbes, Kant and Rousseau. Brian Barry distinguishes between two broad categories of contract theories as applied to justice: (1) those based on mutual advantage, in which self-interested individuals agree on a bargain that furthers each individual's advantage; and (2) those based on impartiality, which examines what individuals who are impartial (about their place in society) would pursue certain ends which may, but need not be, self-interested.[13] A variant of the latter is what the American philosopher John Rawls calls the reciprocity approach in which individuals pursue the common good provided that others reciprocate, while impartiality may imply an unconditional commitment to the common good.

Rawls is the central figure in modern contract theories of justice. Rawls's theory of justice[14] has been extremely influential in reinvigorating an interest in justice issues among philosophers, and in framing discussions of justice among social scientists, including economists. Rawls's theory is partly a critique of utilitarianism, and builds on the theory of social contract—in which self-interested individuals come together and voluntarily agree upon a social contract—developed by Locke, Rousseau and Kant, and equality plays a central role in it, including the duty to help people in need. Rawls's principle of justice, which provides a standard against which the distributional aspects of the basic structure of society can be assessed, is one "that free and rational persons concerned to further their own interests would accept in an initial position of equality."[15] He called this the "original position," a hypothetical situation in which people stand behind a "veil of ignorance" which prevents them from knowing their social status, wealth, abilities, etc. Rawls claims that two justice principles would be chosen by everyone in such a position. He states these principles as:

1. Each person has an equal right to a fully adequate scheme of equal basic liberties which is compatible with a similar scheme of liberties for all.
2. Social and economic inequalities are to satisfy two conditions. First, they must be attached to offices and positions open to all under conditions of fair equality of opportunity; and second, they must be of greatest benefit to the least advantaged members of society.

In Rawls's view the first principle takes priority over the second which implies that he is giving absolute priority to liberty compared to other considerations, including social equality. That is, personal liberties cannot be violated for whatever reason. The first part of the second principle ensures that public opportunities are open to all; no one can be excluded from such opportunities on grounds, say, of race or religion. The second part, which has come to be called the "difference principle" is taken to mean that a social state is an improvement if it increases the amount of "primary goods" going to the least well off. "Primary goods," for Rawls, refers to general-purpose means to meet people's ends such as "rights, liberties and opportunities, income and wealth." For example, high salaries for doctors may be justified by improved medical care for all other strata of society including the lowest. If such an argument cannot be made, then doctors' salaries should be no higher than those for other workers. Rawls's principles of justice are intended to indicate how major social institutions should distribute rights and liberties, or what Rawls calls the "basic structure of society" but does not apply to the formation of government or individual market transactions.

Rawls's approach is appealing for a number of reasons. It is fair and evenhanded in the sense that it prohibits parties in the original position from choosing a theory designed to unfairly favor particular parties. If there was some chance that you would either be a doctor or a nurse's aide, you would be unlikely to insist on policies that unfairly allowed doctors to feather their nests at the expense of less well paid health care workers. Moreover, it is related to individual self-interest. People choosing the structure of society behind the veil of ignorance would be risk-averse, and since everyone has a chance of being part of the poorest strata of society, the social contract is constructed to benefit the least well-off members.

However, Rawls's theory has also been subject to a great deal of criticism. Libertarian critics on the right, such as Robert Nozick, who defend a minimalist state, argue that Rawls's theory of justice requires an extensive state which would interfere continually in individual's free choice and infringe on people's natural rights to private property. Marxist critics on the left take the view that Rawls's approach does not address what they consider the root of the problem of injustice, that is, the capitalist system and the unequal ownership of productive assets, and by giving priority to the first principle over the difference principle it limits the extent to which income can be redistributed.

Virtue and Communitarian Approaches

Another approach to justice is what has been called communitarian justice which defends the communitarian ideal of the common good.[16] Writers in this tradition often regard their work as being rooted in Aristotelian virtue theory. Some proponents have defended their approach by criticizing the welfare liberal conceptions of justice of the utilitarians and Rawls. An example of this is the work of Michael Sandel[17] who claims that the western liberal view of justice is based on an inadequate conception of human nature; one that is composed of the particular wants, interests, or ends that we have does not constitute who we are essentially. Sandel argues that welfare liberals espouse this conception of the self because it is fundamental to their conception of justice, one that gives priority of individual rights over the common good. MacIntyre also characterizes liberalism as attempting to separate the rule defining right action from conceptions of the human good, and argues that these forms of liberalism fail and are bound to fail because the rules governing right action cannot be adequately grounded independent of a conception of the common good. As mentioned earlier, MacIntyre stresses the importance of internal goods generated in terms of practice within communities which generate good qualities in people within that community. MacIntyre's focus on internal goods like achieving high standards of excellence within the practice makes external goods like money and status unimportant to the pursuit of the common good. His focus on the community and good internal to it draw attention to the fact that virtue cannot be defined for individuals alone, but individual virtue depends on the virtues of communities—so that the whole of society is more than the sum of the parts, that is, its members—and that different communities may, in principle, emphasize different lists of goods which represent virtues. However, MacIntyre does not argue that any notions of excellence that are developed by a community are virtuous, and therefore does not take the view that all communities are intrinsically good.

Sen's approach, in terms of functionings and capabilities in achieving goods that are valued, usually includes goods such as good health, education, etc., but Sen argues that the precise content of these goods is to be determined by societies in the process of public deliberation.[18] Others in the virtue tradition, such as Nussbaum, argue for a universal list of goods which are common to all communities, although communities can add additional goods to this list.

St. Thomas Aquinas and a Faith-Based Approach

Despite being a virtue ethicist, in the mold of Aristotle, Aquinas's ethical writings[19] demonstrate how all three moral theories play a role in actual practice. In the classifications I have used above, Aquinas's thought reflects a theory of justice of the communitarian type. He focuses on people as Christians acting morally that yield morally good outcomes. Agreeing with Aristotle, Aquinas argued that private ownership of property is morally legitimate because it is both natural and serves utilitarian purposes; for example, people take better care of what they own than common property. But he goes on to argue that owners must use their property for the common good. That is, it is a stewardship theory of property. The earth and all in it belong to God and people are merely trustees of that property for the common good and cannot use it just to promote their personal gain.

Social responsibility is inherent to private property because God's gift of the earth is to all people in common. People can own property, but once their needs are met, the needs of others must be met out of their surplus. It is this common purpose in use which justifies, in cases of extreme necessity, the right of the poor to take for their needs the property of the rich. In other words, whatever one has in "superabundance"–that is, above and beyond what will reasonably satisfy the needs of them and their family—"is owed, of natural right, to the poor for their sustenance." In support of this view Aquinas quoted Ambrose, one of the four original Great Doctors or teachers of the church. He also cited the *Decretum Gratian*, a twelfth-century compilation of canon law, that contains the powerful statement: "The bread which you withhold belongs to the hungry: the clothing you shut away, to the naked: and the money you bury in the earth is the redemption and freedom of the penniless."

Note those words *owed* and *belongs*. For Christians sharing their surplus wealth with the poor is not a matter of charity, but of their duty and their rights. Aquinas even went so far as to say: "It is not theft, properly speaking, to take secretly and use another's property in a case of extreme need: because that which he takes for the support of his life becomes his own property by reason of that need."

Aquinas does not leave the enforcement of the social responsibilities of private ownership solely to the consciences of individuals. He is sure that social supervision (the level will depend on circumstances) is needed. He cites Aristotle, who reasoned that the regulation of possessions helps to preserve states or nations because, if a few gain control of property and income, the future of the community may be undermined. Everyone needs a sufficiency of material goods because this is necessary to lead a virtuous life, a life of human well-being of human dignity. Extreme disparity in the distribution of income and wealth frequently results in social discontent because it is an affront to the human sense of fairness and justice. It is the responsibility of the state to regulate the use of private property (and of the resulting markets) so that the common good is maintained. The state is responsible to make equitable property laws, impose taxes, and generally exercise jurisdiction over property and economic activity. Again, following Aristotle, Aquinas argues it is up to the good legislator to decide how this is to be done. The legislator has the duty to ensure that an adequate amount of the necessities of life are available to all who are ready and willing to work for them. In return the citizen is expected to contribute to the common good.

These social responsibilities, which are demands of justice, must be met if society is to be peaceful and well-ordered. But Aquinas argues they are not enough by themselves. Justice removes obstacles to peace and community, but more is needed. Justice alone will not produce the required social cohesion, the solidarity that only can come from the virtue of charity. Charity implants the desire to help one's neighbor which is needed for social cohesion. Good laws can help and are necessary but there is much they cannot achieve. Much must be done by private individuals motivated by the virtues, particularly that of charity. Self-seeking and greed will always be part of property ownership and justice will not always be able to be done. To Aquinas the proper moral and spiritual values are essential for the common good in any community.

Ever since the late Middle Ages, Aquinas's moral thought on social issues has shaped the growth and development of Catholic teaching. His social teachings make up a coherent whole because he taught that the same moral norms that govern an individual's actions and choices are the ones that should govern social, political, and economic activities. It is religious faith that provides a moral framework for choice and an ethical standard for action. We will see more in Chapter 6 when we take up CST.

CONCLUSION

This chapter has briefly discussed some major approaches to the theories of ethics and justice. It has first distinguished between virtue, deontological and consequentialist ethics from the perspective of individual actions, and then distinguished between societal ethics in terms of theories of justice which take egalitarian, utilitarian, and equity, desert and rights-based, contractual and communitarian perspectives. I will end with three comments.

First, the discussion has many deficiencies. The coverage of approaches to ethics and justice has by no means been exhaustive. Nor could it be expected to be, given the length of this chapter. I will discuss many of the issues discussed here in more detail in later chapters.

Second, despite its deficiencies, the discussion here (plus the earlier discussions in Chapters 2 and 3) suggests that the theory of ethics implicit in mainstream economics is a very limited and partial one which follows a consequentialism that is related to a particular form of utilitarianism based on the Pareto principle and the social welfare function, and which for the most part ignores virtue and deontological concerns and theories of justice based on egalitarian and communitarian concerns.

Third, with the exception of Aquinas, I have only discussed philosophical approaches to ethics and justice. The next chapter on Catholic Social Thought and the Common Good attempts to show how CST, as a religious based communitarian approach to justice can be useful to economic theory and economic policy.

NOTES

1. This section draws heavily on W. David Solomon, "Normative Ethical Theories," in *Economics, Ethics, and Public Policy*, ed. Charles K. Wilber (Lanham, MD: Rowman & Littlefield, 1998), 119-38.

2. Solomon, "Ethical Theories," 121.

3. Daniel M. Hausman and Michael S. McPherson, *Economic Analysis and Moral Philosophy,* 2nd edition (Cambridge: Cambridge University Press, 2006).

4. Amitai Etzioni, "Toward a Kantian Socio-Economics," *Review of Social Economy* 45, no. 1 (April 1987): 37-47.

5. See Alasdair MacIntyre, *After Virtue: A Study in Moral Theory,* 2nd ed. (Notre Dame, IN: University of Notre Dame Press, 1984), and Alasdair MacIntyre, *Dependent Rational Animals: Why Human Beings Need the Virtues* (Open Court Publishing Co., 2001).

6. See David Stewart, *Business Ethics* (New York: McGraw-Hill, 1995). Also see Richard P. Nielsen, "Arendt's Action Philosophy and the Manager as Eichman, Richard III, Faust, or Institution Citizen," *California Management Review* 26, no. 3 (Spring 1984): 191-201.

7. Richard M. Gula, PSS, "Moving Hearts," *Give Us This Day*, July 2019, 104-5.

8. Stephen Trzeciak and Anthony Mazzarelli, *Compassionomics: The Revolutionary Scientific Evidence That Caring Makes a Difference* (Pensacola, FL: Studer Group, 2019).

9. This section draws on Dutt and Wilber, *Economic Ethics*, chapter 3 "Approaches to Ethics and Justice."

10. Robert Nozick, *Anarchy, State and Utopia* (New York: Basic Books, 1974).

11. James M. Buchanan, *Liberty, Market and State: Political Economy in the 1980s* (New York: New York University Press, 1986), 129-130.

12. For a good, brief discussion on justice and contractualism, see Will Kymlicka, "The Social Contract Tradition," in *A Companion to Ethics*, ed. Peter Singer (Oxford: Blackwell, 1991), 186-96.

13. Brian M. Barry, *Treatise on Social Justice,* vol. 1, *Theories of Justice* (Berkeley, California: University of California Press, 1991).

14. John Rawls, *A Theory of Justice* (Cambridge, MA: Harvard University Press, 1971).

15. Rawls, *Theory*, 11.

16. For a critical discussion of communitarian and other approaches to social justice, see James Sterba, "Social Justice," in *Economics, Ethics and Public Policy*, ed. Charles K. Wilber (London: Rowman and Littlefield, 1999), 187-215.

17. Michael Sandel, *Liberalism and the Limits of Justice* (Cambridge: Cambridge University Press, 1982).

18. See Amartya K. Sen, *On Economic Inequality* (Oxford, UK: Oxford University Press, 1973, expanded edition, 1997).

19. See Charles K. Wilber, "Thomas Aquinas," in *The SAGE Encyclopedia of World Poverty*, Second Edition, ed. Mehmet Odekon (Los Angeles, CA: SAGE Reference, 2015): Vol. 1, 74-6.

Chapter Six

Catholic Social Thought and the Common Good

CST raises larger questions about the economic system itself and the values it expresses. These are questions that cannot be ignored in the Catholic vision of economic justice. For example:

> Does our economic system place more emphasis on maximizing profits than on meeting human needs and fostering human dignity? Does our economy distribute its benefits equitably or does it concentrate power and resources in the hands of a few? Does it promote excessive materialism and individualism? Does it adequately protect the environment and the nation's natural resources? Does it direct too many scarce resources to military purposes? *Economic Justice for All*, para. 132

I will focus on three issues in this chapter. First, drawing on the CST outlined in Chapter 1, I will more fully develop the conception of the common good first mentioned there and then as an economist try to flesh out its meaning to me. Second, I will explain some of the ways that economic theory can be useful to policy makers in attaining that common good. Third, I will suggest some practical changes to the way the actual economy operates.

THE CATHOLIC SOCIAL THOUGHT TRADITION AND THE COMMON GOOD

As we saw in Chapter 1, the tradition of CST is rooted in a commitment to certain fundamental values—the right to human dignity, the need for human freedom and participation, the importance of community, and the nature of the common good. These values are drawn from the belief that each person is called to be a co-creator with God, participating in the redemption of the world and the furthering of the Kingdom. This requires social and human development where the religious and temporal aspects of life are not separated and opposed to each other.

As a result of these fundamental values two principles permeate CST. The first is a special concern for the poor and powerless, which leads to a criticism of political and economic structures that oppress them. The second is a concern for certain human rights against the collectivist tendencies of the state and the neglect of the free market.

In the United States, both liberals and conservatives support markets. The economies of Sweden, Germany, Japan, South Korea, France, South Africa, and Brazil are all built upon markets. The issue that divides people is how much and what kinds of social regulation are appropriate, how much trade-off is there between efficiency and equity. There is little in CST to support the free market policies of the U.S. since the 1980s and much that would oppose the burdens placed upon the poor by those policies.

In 1986 the United States Catholic bishops issued a pastoral letter, *Economic Justice for All*, that summarized this tradition of CST and applied it to the U.S. economy.[1] In my opinion, the process of writing the letter was as important as the actual message. In 1980 the bishops approved a pastoral letter on *Communism and Christianity*, written by a Yale philosopher in consultation with the bishops. It was decided to do one on *Capitalism and Christianity*. A five-member committee of bishops was appointed to do so.

The five bishops met and appointed a group of theological and economic advisers, including myself. We quickly realized that such a pastoral would be next to impossible and be little read, the typical fate of past pastoral letters. The first questions were "which Christianity," "which capitalism"? Given the time—early 1980s—we decided to focus on Catholic Social Thought and the U.S. Economy. This was a period of recession and a time of attacks upon the poor and on poverty programs. Inflation was seen as public enemy number one and concern for unemployment was relegated to the back burner.

Hearings were held over several years with many different groups—government officials, business CEOs, labor leaders, welfare mothers, academic economists, social action people from the church, representatives of other churches, et al. Meetings of the committee were held about once a month, usually in Washington, D.C., but also in San Francisco, New York, and at Notre Dame in Indiana.

Many meetings of the committee were held where drafts of parts of the letter were debated, amended, and tentatively approved. In 1984 a first draft was submitted to the assembled bishops for discussion. In addition, they were asked to hold consultations in their dioceses and submit back to the committee any comments and recommendations they wanted. Many dioceses held widespread meetings of the laity right down to the parish level. Also, bishops consulted with their key advisers. The bishops submitted more than 10,000 pages of material to the committee, including 500 pages written by the bishops themselves. Over the next year this material was utilized, along with additional hearings, to write a second draft of the pastoral.

This second draft was submitted to the bishops for discussion at their annual meeting in 1985. From this meeting further amendments were made to the text. The Vatican reviewed the draft and suggested a meeting with a group of Latin American bishops to discuss the section on the international economy. A third draft was submitted to the bishops in 1986 and approved by a vote of 220 to 9. This is the document released to the public.

There are two points that need to be made clear when discussing the message of the pastoral letter. First, the bishops decided to address the pastoral to two audiences—the policy making community and to Catholics and other people of good will generally. Second, the intent of the bishops was to initiate a debate, not conclude it. That is, they wanted to show that public policy making needs to be informed by moral concerns. They hoped the letter would stimulate public discussion toward more humane policy. Also, they wanted to create church structures that would generate greater understanding of CST among the faithful. They set up an implementation office with the responsibility of getting courses on CST taught in every Catholic high school and every seminary.[2]

The bishops' pastoral letter *Economic Justice for All* is fundamentally a moral document, concerned with the effects of the economy on the lives of millions of human beings. It argues that concern for human dignity in social solidarity is at the core of Christian faith. Because economic institutions and policies have a major impact on human dignity, they are not only technical but moral concerns as well. Therefore, the bishops argue, every perspective on economic life that is human, moral, and Christian must be shaped by three questions: What does the economy do for people? What does it do to people? And how do people participate in it? In addition, the bishops argue that in pursuing the common good, special concern must be given to the economy's impact on the poor and powerless because they are particularly vulnerable and needy.

Basically, the bishops have set out a moral vision to guide both policy makers and individual Christians. To quote them at some length:

> We have outlined this moral vision as a guide to all who seek to be faithful to the Gospel in their daily economic decisions and as a challenge to transform the economic arrangements that shape our lives and our world. These arrangements

embody and communicate social values, and therefore have moral significance both in themselves and in their effects. Christians, like all people, must be concerned about how the concrete outcomes of their economic activity serve human dignity; they must assess the extent to which the structures and practices of the economy support or undermine their moral vision.

Such an assessment of economic practices, structures, and outcomes leads to a variety of conclusions. Some people argue that an unfettered free-market economy, where owners, workers, and consumers pursue their enlightened self-interest, provides the greatest possible liberty, material welfare, and equity. The policy implication of this view is to intervene in the economy as little as possible because it is such a delicate mechanism that any attempt to improve it is likely to have the opposite effect. Others argue that the capitalist system is inherently inequitable and therefore contradictory to the demands of Christian morality, for it is based on acquisitiveness, competition, and self-centered individualism. They assert that capitalism is fatally flawed and must be replaced by a radically different system that abolishes private property, the profit motive, and the free market.

Catholic social teaching has traditionally rejected these ideological extremes because they are likely to produce results contrary to human dignity and economic justice.(1) Starting with the assumption that the economy has been created by human beings and can be changed by them, the Church works for improvement in a variety of economic and political contexts; but it is not the Church's role to create or promote a specific new economic system. Rather, the Church must encourage all reforms that hold out hope of transforming our economic arrangements into a fuller systemic realization of the Christian moral vision. The Church must also stand ready to challenge practices and institutions that impede or carry us farther away from realizing this vision.

In short, the Church is not bound to any particular economic, political, or social system; it has lived with many forms of economic and social organization and will continue to do so, evaluating each according to moral and ethical principles: What is the impact of the system on people? Does it support or threaten human dignity?[3]

The bishops go on to say that: "The fundamental moral criterion for all economic decisions, policies, and institutions is this: They must be at the service of *all people, especially the poor*."[4]

To understand the common good in practical terms and the economic problems that keep us from attaining it, we need to realize that, as the bishops point out, the economic system is a human creation. As such it solves certain problems for us while creating others. Two facts stand out from an examination of the history of market economies. They have been successful in producing amounts of goods and services unprecedented in history; *and* they have done so in an extremely uneven manner.

As I noted in earlier chapters, the new consumers' goods, the new methods of production or transportation, the new markets, the new forms of industrial organization also incessantly revolutionized the economic structure *from within*, incessantly destroying the old one, incessantly creating a new one. This process of Creative Destruction is the essential fact about capitalism.[5] It is scant solace to the skilled worker thrown out of a job or the town which progress left behind. So, the strengths of the economic system are also its weaknesses.

The great economic debate in the U.S. has been and still is: Can the destructive side of markets be mitigated while doing minimal damage to the creative side? Free-market advocates say that there is no alternative to allowing the "natural" laws of the economy to work themselves out. Attempts to reform the market system, or even worse to replace it, will only cause greater harm. The counterargument is that, in fact, markets can be reformed, though for the reforms to be effective, they must consider the dynamics of the system. This is the stance of most economists today.

Many steps to affect the economy can be taken by a variety of actors: individuals, unions, corporations, churches, neighborhood associations, and other mediating institutions. Government as a social institution must also play an important role. Clearly not all government actions are positive, but government can be an important instrument wielded by men and women to attenuate the effects of the destructive side of market operations.

The Catholic common good concept is rooted in a communitarian vision of society.[6] Because of this it emphasizes both the dignity of the human person and the essentially social nature of that dignity. As we saw in Chapter 1, both civil and political liberties on the one hand and social and economic needs on the other are essential components of the common good. It is not the aggregate of individual welfare as in traditional economics. It is a set of social conditions, such as full employment and universal healthcare, necessary for the realization of human dignity, which transcend the arena of private exchange and contract. Such conditions or goods are essentially relational. To exist they must exist as shared.

To sum up, and repeat, every person is made in the image of God, putting concern for human dignity at the core of Christian faith. Because economic institutions and policies have a major impact on human dignity, they are not only technical but moral concerns as well. The following seven principles highlight the major themes from *Economic Justice for All* (and CST documents generally) and flesh out the call to evaluate every economic policy by what it does for people, to people and how it allows people to participate:

1. *Dignity of the Human Person*: All people are sacred, made in the image and likeness of God. People do not lose dignity because of disability, poverty, age, lack of success, or race. Ethiopians are as important to God as Americans. This emphasizes people over things, being over having.

2. *Community and the Common Good*: The human person is both sacred and social. We realize our dignity and rights in relationship with others, in community. "We are one body; when one suffers, we all suffer." We are called to respect all of God's gifts of creation, to be good stewards of the earth and each other.
3. *Rights and Responsibilities*: People have a fundamental right to life, food, shelter, health care, education, and employment. If this means they must immigrate to secure these rights they are entitled to do so. All people have a right to participate in decisions that affect their lives. Corresponding to these rights are duties and responsibilities to respect the rights of others in the wider society and to work for the common good.
4. *Option for the Poor*: The moral test of a society is how it treats its most vulnerable members. The poor have the most urgent moral claim on the conscience of the nation. We are called to look at public policy decisions in terms of how they affect the poor.
5. *Dignity of Work*: People have a right to decent and productive work, fair wages, private property, and economic initiative. The economy exists to serve people, not the other way around.
6. *Solidarity*: We are one human family. Our responsibilities to each other cross national, racial, economic, and ideological differences. We are called to work globally for justice. In the economic arena, as in other areas of life, competition must be complemented with cooperation.
7. *Subsidiarity*: Catholic thought sees society as made up of a dense network of relations among individuals, families, churches, neighborhood associations, business firms, labor unions, and different levels of government. Thus, every level of society has a role to play in ensuring basic human rights and the common good. In Catholic Social Thought this is expressed as the "principle of subsidiarity."

HOW CAN ECONOMICS SERVE THE COMMON GOOD?

Mainstream economic theory is rooted in an individualist conception of society. Society is seen as a collection of individuals who have chosen to associate because it is mutually beneficial. The common good is simply the aggregation of the welfare of each individual. Individual liberty is the highest good, and traditional economic theory attempts to provide a rigorous demonstration that rational individuals, left free to engage in voluntary exchange, will construct competitive market institutions that yield optimal levels of individual freedom and material welfare. In the absence of market failures this economic theory of individual rationality indicates that intervention by public authorities or the forming of collective groups such as trade unions lower efficiency and thus the level of output and welfare.

Economists, however, do not rest here. They also explore how what are called market failures can prevent market outcomes from being efficient. Market failures include such things as:

1. Monopolies and other departures from perfect competition. Monopoly producers may produce less than what is efficient for the economy because they want to create an artificial scarcity and keep the price of their product high in order to make high profits.
2. Externalities, in which people and firms affect others adversely or positively without either paying or being paid. Firms may emit too much pollution which makes other firms and people worse off because the latter, rather than they, bear the costs of pollution.
3. Public goods which no private firms will want to produce because they cannot make people pay for them. Public goods are those which can be enjoyed by all at the same time (like listening to radio programs off the air) and which the producer cannot prevent people who don't pay from consuming it (for instance, national defense—a producer of this service cannot selectively protect some people from foreign invasion without protecting others who do not pay).
4. Imperfect information, in the sense that buyers and sellers do not possess all the relevant information to produce efficient outcomes. Imperfect information implies that at least some individuals in the economy do not have complete information that allows them to make appropriate decisions: for instance, if consumers do not have complete information about the properties of medicines, they may buy those which do not work, or not buy those which actually work but which they think do not (in the latter case both the consumers will be better off by using the medicines and the firms would make more profits if they did).

If market failures do occur, economists analyze how they can be made to operate more efficiently, for instance, with government breaking up monopolies, imposing fines for pollution, supplying public goods, and by certifying whether medicines work. Some economists tend to think these market failures are rare and that government as the solution would frequently make matters worse. Other economists tend to believe these market failures are common and that, within limits, government can correct for these problems.

Moreover, markets may, and often do, result in outcomes that are thought inequitable. Markets may be efficient, but the free-market outcome does not prevent someone from getting all the goods and some people getting very little or even nothing. Thus, the market may be unable to provide people with things they need even for basic biological subsistence, while others may get more goods than they can ever use. The rapid increase in inequality in advanced industrial economies, including the United States, since 1980 has generated new research that questions the ability of free markets to produce fair results.[7]

Economists usually respond by arguing that trying to correct for fairness by changing market prices, as for example through rent controls, will be counterproductive. The preferred way to deal with these justice issues is to redistribute resources (wealth) which will not result in distorting prices. However, when doing so, care must be taken that incentives are not adversely impacted. New research[8] shows that moderate redistribution, through increased progressive taxation on the rich, may increase a country's growth rate by increasing opportunities for the poor and middle classes.[9]

Furthermore, economic theory can provide several tools to help policy makers working toward the common good. Concepts of scarcity, choice, and incentives drawn from microeconomics are important as are concepts such as effective demand[10] drawn from macroeconomics.

For example, one important role economic theory can play in helping achieve the common good is a negative one. Economics is at its best when showing that a policy has unintended consequences that contradict the desired outcome. Scarcity requires choices and choices result in opportunity costs, and choices are affected by incentives. For example, if the desired goal is to provide cheaper housing for the poor, rent controls that put a ceiling on price generate a disincentive for landlords to provide rental housing. Instead they will have an incentive to get around the price ceiling by cutting up the unit into multiple rentals, charging for key deposits, and reducing maintenance. Another example is the "no free lunch" one. A dollar spent on cancer research cannot be spent on unemployment benefits. Economics challenges policy makers to explain why doing X is better than alternatives, Y and Z. There are many such examples.

Developments in microeconomic theory and game theory go further and demonstrate that in a world of interdependence and imperfect information, individual self-interest can result in socially irrational outcomes. As a result, cooperative behavior is needed to complement self-interested behavior to yield efficient economic outcomes. If interdependencies are the rule, not the exception, market failures due to ubiquitous "externalities"[11] make it impossible to attain the common good without some form of collective intervention.

There are two lines of argument I will pursue. The first focuses on how the existence of externalities requires market outcomes to be over-ridden. The second is that scholarly work in economics recognizes the criticisms and flaws in free markets and that under conditions of interdependence and imperfect information, rational self-interest frequently will lead to socially irrational results unless that self-interest is constrained by government intervention, group self-regulation, or an embodied moral code.

Externalities and the Common Good

Using the concept of externalities, economic theory can, in fact, provide a legitimate basis for public intervention into the market process. Specifically, I argue that individual rationality can provide an economic basis for the type of public employment and social programs derived from the common good philosophy embodied in CST generally and specifically in the U.S. bishops' pastoral letter on the economy.[12]

Many privately produced goods generate externalities, both positive (social benefits) and negative (social costs), which affect people who are not involved in the transaction. Pollution is a social cost inflicted on others by those who produce and those who use automobiles. Since the pollution cost is not borne by the producer or individual consumer, too much pollution is produced (and more automobiles than if their price included the cost of cleaning up the pollution caused by their manufacture). When one neighbor maintains his or her house, it raises the value of all the houses in the neighborhood. This is an example of a positive externality yielding a social benefit to all the neighbors. Since not all the benefits are captured by the one maintaining his or her house there is less incentive to do so and thus less "maintenance" than is optimal is produced.

The existence of externalities results in market failure. That is, the market system under-produces private goods with social benefits and over-produces private goods with social costs. When, because of externalities, social costs and benefits diverge from private costs and benefits, what is best for each individual is not what is best for society. Government, having the power to compel payment or compliance, has been seen traditionally by economists as the institutional mechanism to correct these market failures.

Now I want to apply the concept of externalities to several situations that demonstrate how economic theory can be useful for a communitarian conception of the common good.

Free-market economists such as the late Nobel Laureate Milton Friedman have long recognized that education is a special commodity that requires government intervention.[13] It has positive externalities since education has a greater value to society as a whole than to the individual alone. For example, an educated person, it is argued, makes a better voter and more generally is necessary to keep our modern, complex society operating.

However, many commodities besides education possess positive externalities. Health is certainly one example. Preventing or curing a worker's illness or accident not only benefits him or her but also those who suffer from his or her lost output. Also preventing communicable diseases and illnesses has benefits to all who are exposed. The measles outbreak of 2019 in the United States is an example. The small number of misinformed parents that prevented their children from getting vaccinated caused an epidemic. Thus, controls and subsidization of health care carries the same logic as the subsidization of education. The coronavirus pandemic of 2020 is a particularly serious example. Wearing face masks in public protects other people from getting the virus from you. Many people hate wearing masks and claim their freedom is being restricted. Here again, what I want hurts all of us as a community.

The argument can be extended. Many production processes generate negative externalities in the form of environmental pollution. Economic theory would suggest that the pollution should be taxed as a way to get producers to clean up the production process. Using incentives for people and companies to act in their self-interest is more efficient than trying to regulate pollution via administrative control. A carbon tax is often suggested by economists to reduce pollution of the environment.

I have focused on the issue of externalities because it holds out the greatest hope for understanding between adherents of economic theory and advocates of the common good philosophy. As the pervasiveness of externalities, and thus interdependence, is recognized, the practical policy conclusions derived from individualist economic theory converge to those obtained from a more communitarian conception of the common good. Of course, there may be argument over the best way to subsidize commodities that generate positive externalities and to tax those that generate negative externalities.

Imperfect Information, Strategic Behavior, and the Need for an Embodied Moral Code

As noted above, traditional economic theory assumes independence of economic actors and perfect information. However, work in Behavioral Economics[14] demonstrates that the more realistic assumptions that one person's behavior affects another's behavior and that each has less than perfect knowledge of the other's likely behavior can give rise to strategic behavior.

A classic example is the situation where both the employer and worker suspect that the other one cannot be trusted to honor their explicit or implicit contract. For example, the employer thinks the worker will take too many coffee breaks, spend too much time talking with other workers, and generally work less than the employer thinks is owed. The worker, on the other hand, thinks the employer will try to speed up the pace of work, fire him or her unjustly if given the chance, and generally behave arbitrarily. When this is the case, the worker may tend to shirk, and the employer will increase supervision to stop the expected shirking. If the worker would self-supervise, production costs would be lower. Thus, this distrust between employer and worker reduces efficiency.

In this case the pursuit of individual self-interest results in the worker and the employer as individuals and as a group becoming worse off than if they had been able to cooperate, i.e., not shirk and not supervise. The problem is simple and common. The employer and worker are interdependent and do not have perfect knowledge of what the other will do, and the resulting lack of trust leads to behavior that is self-defeating. This outcome is made worse if distrust is accompanied with feelings of injustice. For example, if the worker feels that the contract is unfair (low wages, poor grievance machinery, etc.), the tendency to shirk will be increased.

This case and others like it have two things in common. They have a group (workers and their employers) with a common interest in the outcome of a particular situation. And, second, while each attempts to choose the best available course of action, the result is not what any member of the group desires. For example, employers must pay for additional supervision costs, and workers receive lower wages because of lowered productivity. In these cases, the individual motives lead to undesired social and individual results.

Why is it so difficult for the individuals involved to cooperate and make an agreement? The reason is that exit is cheap, but voice is expensive.[15] Exit means to withdraw from a situation, person, or organization and depends on the availability of choice, competition, and well-functioning markets. It is usually inexpensive and easy to buy or not, sell or not, hire or fire, and quit or shirk on your own. Voice means to communicate explicitly your concern to another individual or organization. The cost to an individual in time and effort to persuade, argue, and negotiate will often exceed any prospective individual benefit.

In addition, the potential success of voice depends on the possibility of all members joining for collective action. But then there arises the free rider problem. If a person driven only by self-interest cannot be excluded from the benefits of collective action, he or she has no incentive to join the group agreement. Self-interest will tempt him or her to take the benefits without paying the costs, i.e., watching educational television without becoming a subscriber. This free riding explains why union organizing is next to impossible in states that prohibit union shops (where a majority of the workers voting for a union means all workers must pay the equivalent of union dues).

Allan Schmid refers to these problems as social traps.[16] These are situations where there is some act under the individual's unilateral control that promises to produce a short-run welfare improvement for that individual, but at the same time is not consistent with what individuals who share a common preference want to obtain as a long-run result.

How can we spring these social traps generated by interdependence and imperfect information? The resolution of the problem is not easy, for they are persistent and frequently intractable. There are three possibilities: government intervention, group self-regulation, and institutional reinforcement of those moral values that constrain self-interested behavior.

Government Intervention

Market failures such as pollution or monopoly have generally been seen as warrants for government intervention. However, there are ubiquitous market failures of the imperfect information variety in everyday economic life. In these cases, private economic actors can also benefit from government measures for their protection, because interdependence and imperfect information generate distrust that can lead the parties to self-defeating behavior. Certain kinds of government regulation—from truth-in-advertising to food-and-drug laws—can reduce distrust and thus economic inefficiency, providing gains for all concerned. However, government regulation has its limits. Where the regulated have concentrated power (e.g., electric companies) the regulators may end up serving the industry more than the public. Well-financed lobbies can sway legislators to pass laws that benefit special interests rather than the common good. In addition, there are clearly situations in which government operates to serve the self-interest of the members of its bureaucratic apparatus. Another major limitation on the ability of government to regulate is the willingness of people to accept enlarged government activity necessary to carry out the new policies. Government can serve the common good, but it has clear limits.

Self-regulation

The second way to spring these social traps is self-regulation. Sellers could voluntarily discipline themselves not to exploit their superior information. This is the basis of professional ethics. Surgeons, for example, take on the obligation, as a condition for the exercise of their profession, to avoid performing unnecessary operations, placing the interest of the patient first. The danger is that their professional association will end up protecting its members at the expense of others. There is substantial evidence that more surgeries are performed than necessary.[17]

Institutional Reinforcement of Moral Values

This leads to the final possibility—developing institutions to heighten group consciousness and reinforce moral values that constrain self-interested behavior so that the pursuit of short-run rewards and free riding can be controlled. Is it possible to rebuild institutional mechanisms so that long-run interests and moral values become more important in directing economic behavior? Yes, but the view of people as simply self-interested maximizers needs to be re-thought.

CST claims that all policies and institutions of society must honor the dignity of the human beings involved. Thus, economic and ethical issues become intertwined in such a way that they cannot be separated. In *Laborem Exercens*,[18] John Paul II argues that the workplace is key to human development and dignity of the worker is as important as productivity. In his encyclical, *Caritas in Veritate*,[19] Pope Benedict XVI builds on this modern CST while honoring the 40th anniversary of Paul VI's *Populorum Progressio*. His central argument is an extension of the analysis of love and charity from *Deus Caritas Est*[20] to address the economic, cultural, and political concerns of our world today. What Benedict XVI argues is that economic relations themselves can and should be an occasion for solidarity, guided by the philosophy of gift. I will develop this in the next chapter on CST and labor issues.

Economists need to study whether habits of benevolence and civic spirit can be furthered by bringing groups together to solve common problems. Growth of worker participation in management, consultation between local communities and business firms to negotiate plant closings and relocations, establishment of advisory boards on employment policy that represent labor, business, and the public, are some policies that need to be examined to establish whether indeed self-interest alone is insufficient and that mutual responsibilities are necessary in a world where interdependence and imperfect information tempt individuals into strategic behavior that, in turn, generates distrust and self-defeating results. The bishops made a start in their 1986 pastoral letter on the economy.[21]

ALTERNATIVE MEASURES OF THE ECONOMY

This chapter has been occupied primarily with how economic theory might aid the attainment of the CST concept of the common good with some attention to policy issues. I want to add a concrete proposal that has some possibility of being accepted in the real world of economic policy making and that also would be a step forward in closing the gap between our present individualist society and the common good.

The assumption that the economic order is the most important one and that progress is to be viewed primarily as economic progress is the assumption that renders economic theory so important. The emphasis on quantification in economics adds another element to its notion of the good. Measurements of the common good focus on means and ends that can be quantified. One practical outcome of this is a heavy emphasis on "things" over interpersonal relationships, education, cultural affairs, family, workplace organization, etc.

Many working within the Roman Catholic tradition would argue that we must broaden our view of human welfare from that of a simple consumer of goods and services with consumer sovereignty as the goal. Instead, drawing upon Scripture, Tradition, and cross-cultural studies which have attempted to find absolute needs or needs that are expressed in a variety of societies, three components of human welfare can be specified for an economy.[22]

The first is what Denis Goulet calls "life-sustenance," which corresponds generally to physiological needs or basic material goods. People need the basic goods that are necessary for life—adequate food, water, housing, clothing, education, and health care—and an economy is successful if it can provide them.

A second component of human welfare is esteem and fellowship. An economy should provide a sense of worth, of dignity to its citizens. One's goods can be a measure of societal esteem, but surely there are other important elements. For Christians, Jesus's life and ministry were an apparent failure. Those who confess the Lordship of one executed as a political criminal can never simplistically identify virtue with success.

The institutions in which citizens work should support them physically and give them a sense of belonging and of contributing to an important undertaking. Society should have clubs, churches, and other entities which support the individual. If the family is the basic social and economic unit, as is the case in the United States, the economy should provide support and encourage in families a sense of self-esteem that can help sustain them. See Chapter 12 for further discussion of this important issue. A general term for this need is fellowship; the economy should promote right relations among its participants, and to the extent it can, should keep life from being "nasty and brutish," while providing basic material goods to lengthen it.

The third component of human welfare is freedom. However, freedom is a difficult goal to specify clearly. It obviously does not mean that all individuals may do whatever they wish, for that would be anarchy and the death of community. At its weakest, an increase in freedom means that the range of options open to the individual or the group has increased, that there are more choices available. This has its physical side in choice of goods, but it can also operate in other spheres such as the political or religious.

There are three component parts to the goal of freedom. The first, and the one which is usually at the center of much economic theorizing in the United States, is the provision of consumer sovereignty. Individuals should be able to choose the goods that they wish to consume.

The second part is worker sovereignty. People must have a choice of jobs, jobs they find meaningful and that enhance their human capacities.[23] Somehow workers must be given a voice in their workplace. See Chapter 8 for a fuller discussion of this point.

Third, a society must provide citizen sovereignty, a mechanism to aggregate peoples' preferences for community. What kind of community do people want? What kind of environment do they want? The concept of citizen sovereignty implies that a way to express preferences and to control communities is provided to the citizen. Several mechanisms may be found which satisfy this requirement, in addition to the democratic voting procedures used in the United States. One way of enhancing citizen sovereignty could be through strengthening local groups for citizen participation in decision making, e.g., parent-teacher organizations, zoning boards, and citizen review boards of police departments and other public agencies. Or perhaps local residents might participate in the operation of local industries in their areas, by electing representatives to firms' boards of directors to minimize the negative aspects of industrial production such as noise and pollution.

If the economy were viewed as CST does, as one among several important parts of society, that all contributed to human welfare, we would need to modify our national accounting system. The use of Gross Domestic Product as the measure of progress and per capita change as the measure of well-being is questioned by many and certainly is not a measure of the common good as seen in CST. [24]

Toward a New National Accounting System

A number of ways of modifying our national accounting system have been proposed, such as the Measure of Economic Welfare proposed over 40 years ago by economists William Nordhaus and James Tobin in 1972.[25] These measures add components involving leisure, nonmarket work, especially women's household work, and the services of government and consumer capital (such as government infrastructure and consumer durables), and subtracts things such as commuting costs, regrettable necessities such as military expenditures, and an estimate of dis-amenities due to urban overcrowding and pollution. Many recent efforts in this direction involve subtractions for environmental damage. While some of the issues addressed, such as household work and environmental damage, are straightforward and noncontroversial, their proper valuation raises all kinds of difficulties, which poses the question of whether one should aggregate all these into one indicator of well-being, or whether they should be tracked separately.

The best developed attempt to find a better measurement is the Social Progress Index.[26] It defines social progress as the capacity of a society to meet the basic human needs of its citizens, establish the building blocks that allow citizens and communities to enhance and sustain the quality of their lives, and create the conditions for all individuals to reach their full potential. To do this it measures 50 social and environmental indicators to create a clearer picture of what life is really like for everyday people. The index does not measure people's happiness or life satisfaction, focusing instead on actual life outcomes in areas from shelter and nutrition to rights and education. To do this the index divides these indicators across three broad dimensions of social progress: Basic Human Needs, Foundations of Wellbeing, and Opportunity.

There are several other attempts to construct alternatives to GDP but none of them is completely satisfactory since all still are focused on economic variables. Catholic Social Thought does not equate economic well-being with well-being in general. Except at very low levels of living there is very little correlation between economic well-being and personal happiness. Much of what is most important to real people, as opposed to "economic man"—such as the quality of their relations to others, contentment, sense of meaning, etc.—is missed by GDP and its alternative measures. However, the Social Progress Index is clearly better than GDP at measuring well-being no matter how defined. The 2020 Index,[27] released on September 10, 2020, shows a depressing picture for the United States. We rank #1 in the world in quality of higher education, but only #91 in access to quality basic education. We lead the world in medical technology, yet we are only #97 in access to quality health care. "The United States, despite its immense wealth, military power and cultural influence, ranks 28th—having slipped from 19th in 2011. The index now puts the United States behind significantly poorer countries, including Estonia, Czech Republic, Cyprus and Greece."[28]

The decline of the United States as measured by the Social Progress Index is a reminder that the country faces structural problems in the economy and the society at large that have festered and grown over the past 40 years under leaders of both parties.

CONCLUSION

To conclude I will attempt to pull together the various pieces of this chapter to indicate what I think are possible policies for a common good that promotes human flourishing; policies that follow from economic theory; policies attainable in the present political environment. This is an imperfect world populated by imperfect people, so the least imperfect way to think about the common good is as a process not an end state. That is, what policies hold out hope of moving us in the right direction?

Doing so requires the cooperation of both the public and private sectors. The private sector produces goods and services efficiently but distributes them in ways often unfair. The public sector can deliver payments such as Social Security and Medicare quite efficiently but is less capable and more bureaucratic in producing goods or services. Thus, greater taxation to reduce inequalities and the subsidization of education and medical care are important roles of the public sector in achieving the common good. A strengthening of anti-trust policies is needed to reduce the power of large corporations. But more is needed.

In a market economy, most people earn a living by working and it is an important way that a person participates in society. Therefore, any concept of the common good that includes the importance of human dignity has to include policies that provide work for everyone capable and willing to do so. This may require more than monetary and fiscal stimulus. Public works programs may be required. Allowing people to earn their living provides greater dignity than receiving handouts through welfare programs.

Present and future business managers need to be taught how greater worker participation and morale can lead to greater productivity. Here is a real challenge to business schools and M.B.A. programs in Catholic colleges and universities. Business managers cannot introduce policies that reduce profits if they are to remain competitive with firms that do not introduce such policies.

Finally, the common good transcends purely economic values, and a public accounting system needs to recognize what is important and what is not. Thus, the creation of a replacement for GDP is essential in developing and popularizing the idea of a common good and human flourishing.

These are policies that I believe will help move us along the road to the common good. The precise form they should take needs to be settled by the trial and error of what works. The balance between government and private sector action will need to be determined through the rough and tumble of the public policy process. It is here that CST needs to make its voice heard.

In these first six chapters I have used CST to chart out the direction we should move in constructing a more realistic and useful economic theory. The social economics I outlined is an important first step in re-envisioning economics, but there is still a long way to go.

I believe these six chapters show we must:

1. Accept the fundamental role of a world view in economics and make explicit the values embodied in our own world view
2. Propose and develop alternatives to the neo-classical definition of economic welfare
3. Broaden our conception of economic behavior beyond the motive of self-interest
4. Examine the actual nature of human preferences, including the processes by which they are formed and change over time
5. Recognize the reality of economic interdependence and imperfect information, including the fundamental uncertainty of the future
6. Shed light on the nature, existence, and resolution of social traps
7. Counter the notion of altruism or other moral values as scarce resources with an alternative perspective emphasizing that they respond positively to practice
8. Counter the notion that creation of a market necessarily increases the area of individual choice
9. Study not only the efficiency effects of public policies but also their effects on values and income and wealth distribution
10. Be able to distinguish between cases where self-interested behavior and internalized moral behavior are substitutes and where they are complements. Clearly, there is much work to be done. The remaining chapters utilize these characteristics of a more useful economics to analyze important issues such as poverty, development, inequality, and financial crises.

NOTES

1. U.S. Catholic Bishops. *Economic Justice for All: Pastoral Letter on Catholic Social Teaching and the U.S. Economy*. U.S. National Catholic Conference of Bishops: Washington, D.C., November 18, 1986. http://usccb.org/upload/economic_justice_for_all.pdf

2. This office was funded for five years and its success was spotty at best.

3. USCCB, *Economic Justice*, para. 127-30.

4. USCCB, *Economic Justice*, para. 24.

5. Joseph A. Schumpeter, *Capitalism, Socialism, and Democracy*, 3d ed. (New York: Harper & Brothers, 1950), 83.

6. For this section on the common good, I have drawn heavily on David Hollenbach, *Claims in Conflict: Retrieving and Renewing the Catholic Human Rights Tradition* (New York: Paulist Press, 1979). Also see Herman E. Daly and John B. Cobb, Jr., *For the Common Good: Redirecting the Economy toward Community, the Environment, and a Sustainable Future*, 2nd ed. (Boston: Beacon Press, 1994).

7. Thomas Piketty, *Capital in the Twenty-First Century* (Cambridge: Belknap Press, 2014).

8. Jonathan D. Ostry and Andrew Berg, "Treating Inequality with Redistribution: Is the Cure Worse Than the Disease?" *IMFdirect: The International Monetary Fund's Global Economy Forum*, posted February 26, 2014. http://blog-imfdirect.imf.org/2014/02/26/treating-inequality-with-redistribution-is-the-cure-worse-than-the-disease/

9. For a popular explanation see Paul Krugman, "Inequality Is a Drag," *New York Times*, August 7, 2014. http://www.nytimes.com/2014/08/08/opinion/paul-krugman-inequality-is-a-drag.html?emc=edit_th_20140808&nl=todaysheadlines&nlid=41712839

10. There is little space here to treat macroeconomic issues, but it needs to be said that government fiscal and monetary policies to combat unemployment and inflation are crucial tools to achieve the common good.

11. Externalities occur when producing or consuming causes an impact on third parties not directly related to the transaction. They can be positive or negative.

12. USCCB, *Economic Justice*, chapter 3.

13. Milton Friedman, *Capitalism and Freedom* (Chicago: University of Chicago Press, 1962), 85-107.

14. See Matthew Rabin, "Behavioral Economics," in *New Frontiers in Economics*, ed. Michael Szenberg and Lall Ramrattan (Cambridge, UK: Cambridge University Press, 2004).

15. See Albert O. Hirschman, *Exit, Voice, and Loyalty* (Cambridge, MA: Harvard University Press, 1970), and Albert O. Hirschman, *Rival Views of Market Society* (New York: Viking, 1986), 77-101.

16. See A. Allan Schmid, *Property, Power, and Public Choice* (New York: Praeger, 1978).

17. According to a *USA Today* review of government records and medical databases, tens of thousands of patients undergo unnecessary surgery each and every year. Among the most commonly performed unnecessary surgeries are cardiac angioplasties, pacemakers, back surgery, knee and hip surgeries, hysterectomy, and Cesarean sections. See https://www.usatoday.com/story/news/nation/2013/06/18/unnecessary-surgery-usa-today-investigation/2435009/.

18. John Paul II, *Laborem Exercens*.

19. Benedict XVI, *Caritas in Veritate*.

20. Benedict XVI, *Deus Caritas Est*, encyclical letter, Vatican website, 205. http://www.vatican.va/content/benedict-xvi/en/encyclicals/documents/hf_ben-xvi_enc_20051225_deus-caritas-est.html

21. USCCB, *Economic Justice*, chapter 4.

22. See the various documents of CST, particularly *Economic Justice for All*, plus Denis Goulet, *The Cruel Choice: A New Concept in the Theory of Development* (New York: Atheneum 1971); Kenneth P. Jameson, James H. Weaver, and Charles K. Wilber, "Strategies of Development: A Survey," in *Development Economics: Theory, Practice, and Prospects*, ed. Thomas R. DeGregori (Kluwer Academic Publishers, 1989), 137-177; Charles K. Wilber, "Sustainable Development, Consumerism, & Catholic Social Thought," in *Looking beyond the Individualism & Homo Economicus*

of Neoclassical Economics, ed. Edward J. O'Boyle (Milwaukee, WI: Marquette University Press, 2011) 129-43.

23. See John Paul II, *Laborem Exercens.*

24. Our corporate-dominated markets have a fatal character flaw. They must grow and continue to grow. They must grow or the system itself will collapse. Let me quote a fascinating article:

> There is no sufficiency principle, no ability to say "enough." Every last scrap of material, every last inch of earth, every last iota of human attention and experience, must become a commodity in order to feed the market maw. There is no other option. A system that supposedly embodies "choice" in the end doesn't give us any. The mechanism grinds on, out of synch with both the natural systems that sustain it and the needs of the humans who comprise it. "Prosperity" becomes another word for ecological and social dysfunction, and a staggering increase in illth.
>
> This dysfunction is a daily experience for most of us. Yet for most economists it does not exist. In their view an increase of expenditure is by definition an increase in well-being, so there is no need to inquire further. To the contrary, problems make the GDP go up. Cancer begets costly cancer treatments; stress leads to the consumption of prescription drugs, and on and on. (See Jonathan Rowe and David Bollier, "The Missing Sector: Enlarging Our Sense of the Economy," http://jonathanrowe.org/the-missing-sector.)

25. William Nordhaus and James Tobin, *Is Growth Obsolete?* (Washington, D. C.: National Bureau of Economic Research, 1972).

26. See https://www.socialprogress.org/index/global/methodology for a detailed map of its components.

27. See the 2020 Index at https://www.socialprogress.org/index/global.

28. Nicholas Kristof, "'We're No. 28! And Dropping!,'" *New York Times*, September 9, 2020. https://www.nytimes.com/2020/09/09/opinion/united-states-social-progress.html

Part II

APPLICATIONS

Chapter Seven

Economics of Labor Markets and Theory of the Gift

In this chapter I will do a quick review of the philosophical foundations of economic theory and CST that we already have covered in earlier chapters. Then I will compare their views on two labor market issues—minimum wage laws and labor unions. Then, I will look at the concept of gift in Pope Benedict XVI's encyclical, *Caritas in Veritate*, and show how it can be used to analyze wage behavior within firms. I will conclude by looking at worker shared ownership.

Possibly the most important difference between traditional microeconomic theory and CST is that the former is based on an individualist conception of society and the latter on a communitarian vision. Flowing from that difference is the economic belief that labor is onerous and that leisure is preferred. In contrast, CST claims, in the words of Pope John Paul II, that "work is a good thing for man."[1] Work is how most people participate in society. As we saw in Chapter 6, the United States bishops in their pastoral letter *Economic Justice for All* argue that how people are able to participate is one of the key ways to judge an economy. Workers are people, human beings created by God with infinite human dignity. From the beginning of modern CST in the 1891 encyclical *Rerum Novarum*, workers' rights were a central focus. In *Laborem Exercens*, Pope John Paul II said:

> In fact there is no doubt that human work has an ethical value of its own, which clearly and directly remain linked to the fact that the one who carries it out is a person, a conscious and free subject, that is to say a subject that decides about himself. . . . In the light of the above, the many proposals put forward by experts in Catholic social teaching and by the highest Magisterium of the Church take on special significance: proposals for joint ownership of the means of work,

> sharing by the workers in the management and/or profits of businesses, so-called shareholding by labour, etc. (para. 6, 14)

Let me now look at some of the ways that CST can challenge the standard economic theory of labor markets.

ETHICS, LABOR, AND EMPLOYMENT

Ethical issues are particularly important in the field of labor economics because of the fact that it deals with not just a factor of production, but with human beings. There are numerous ways in which ethical issues enter labor economics. The fact that workers, as human beings, have ethical beliefs has implications for labor market outcomes, wage rigidity, and unemployment. Furthermore, labor markets have a crucial role to play in determining the overall personal distribution of income through its effects on the labor share of output, and thus have an important bearing on the question of distributive justice. In the following, I briefly discuss two issues concerning labor economics.

The Minimum Wage

The microeconomics section of standard introductory textbooks usually stresses the fact that a minimum wage set above the market clearing wage reduces employment by raising the cost of hiring workers for firms, causing unemployment among the very low wage workers it was designed to help. Thus, the standard story—which makes some people critical of minimum wage legislation—argues that the minimum wage results in inefficiency. There may be additional problems which result from this. Firms who face higher wage costs may increase the prices of their products, which can make consumers worse off. Moreover, if profits are squeezed, business firms may have less internal funds which they could have used for investment purposes, making their businesses grow.[2]

So why do the U.S. bishops call for increases in the minimum wage, citing CST as their reasoning. The conclusion that the minimum wage or its increase reduces employment and causes or increases unemployment is usually demonstrated using a simple perfectly competitive framework in which both firms and workers are wage-takers, that is, they are such small parts of the market that when they decide how much to work or how many to employ, they do not think they will have any effect on the wage. If, however, firms are large in relation to the labor market, they may realize that if they increase the number of workers they hire, they will drive up the wage and cut into their profits. This will induce them to reduce their level of employment in an effort to keep the wage down and increase their profits. In the case of a monopsony, where there is only one firm hiring labor, the imposition of a minimum wage above the profit maximizing wage in effect makes the firm a wage taker, removing its incentive to reduce employment and reduce the wage. Hence, employment will actually increase, and unemployment will fall. Although the practical relevance of the one-firm monopsony idea may be limited, large employers in small towns and the costs of job search can result in monopsonistic features which drive wages down.

Beyond monopsony issues, if the wage rate is in fact increased by the minimum wage, and this translates into increases in the real wage, the redistribution from profits to wages may increase consumption spending, both at local and macro levels, which may increase employment and output, and even increase profits and investment. Thus, even the growth effect may not necessarily be negative. Empirical evidence on the effects of the imposition or increases in the minimum wage on employment and unemployment do not clinch the issue, although it suggests that the textbook view about a necessary increase in unemployment seems to be incorrect. Card and Krueger[3] examined the effect of an increase in the minimum wage on low-wage jobs in U.S. states and find that unemployment did not rise, but very likely fell. Two new, as yet unpublished studies, support the Card and Krueger findings.[4] One study, focused on nursing homes, shows that the raised minimum wage led to increased productivity that resulted in improved mortality rates of the patients and no fall in nursing home profits. This was possible because they could raise prices due to no substitutes for their services. Also, the improved mortality rates made the price increases more acceptable. The second study, focused on department store clerks in a chain of 2,000, found that a higher minimum wage increased employee performance with no significant impact on store profits. Other studies, however, find mixed results.[5]

With the efficiency and employment effects still up for debate, CST evaluations of the minimum wage have turned to ethical considerations. It has been defended on the ground that it increases the wage of the lowest-paid workers and increases, overall, the wage share because it sets a floor to the wage and pushes up wages for other jobs as well. However, there is concern that the distributional consequences might be negative if one is interested in improving the position of the worst-off members of a society and the labor market.[6] Many poor people are in fact not minimum wage workers and sometimes outside the labor force, and employers sometimes blunt the effects of the minimum wage by making minimum wage jobs more onerous. The minimum wage is sometimes criticized from an individual rights perspective because it is thought to adversely affect freedom of contract. It is claimed that minimum wage laws are a denial of the human right to sell one's labor to a willing buyer and to make one's decisions about whether or not to take paid work at the going rate. In contrast, CST claims that minimum wage laws can be defended with the argument that no one should be forced to sell their labor for less than a living wage. A worker is not freely choosing, but circumstances are coercing him or her. A fundamental human right, at least in a prosperous society, is the right to earn a minimum livelihood. If markets do not yield minimum wages that provide for a living income, then society has not just a moral right but an obligation to intervene and enact minimum wage laws. Without these laws human life is corrupted in the sense that life itself is threatened. It is a similar argument to the one against allowing people to sell themselves into indentured servitude.

The key question—is there a better way to increase the income of low wage workers than using minimum wage laws? Family allowance programs are widespread in Europe and wage subsidy plans have potential. Neither of these has many supporters in the United States.

The Role of Labor Unions

CST has long believed that solidarity via labor unions is required to right the imbalance of bargaining power between large businesses and their employees. Pope Leo XIII wrote that joining unions is a natural right.[7] Pope John Paul II argued that history has shown that unions are "an indispensable *element of social life*."[8] Both Pope Benedict and Pope Francis have urged strong support for labor unions.[9]

Globalization has caused significant unemployment and downward pressure on wages due to "increased power to move jobs and investments around the globe; supply chains that allow firms to deny responsibility for poor labor conditions; a much larger pool of unemployed and underemployed workers; and substantial restructuring in the public sector."[10] Market forces unleashed by globalization have weakened unions, *and* workers' rights to unionize have been under attack since the early 1980s.[11]

Therefore, many workers do not have a mechanism by which they can protect themselves against employers that exploit them by paying paltry wages and forcing them to work in inhumane conditions.[12] It is astonishing but sweatshops exist in the world's richest country in the twentieth century. A recent report indicates that workers in many low-wage industries in U.S. cities are subject to wage theft, denial of breaks, retaliation for trying to form unions or complaining about working conditions and other forms of abuse.[13]

There is, however, a fairly widespread view among economists that labor unions are bad for the economy. The issues are in some respects similar to the arguments against the minimum wage, and thus our discussion can be brief. The labor union is viewed as introducing a monopoly element in the labor market: when workers form unions they become in effect a single seller of labor, restricting their supply of labor to obtain a higher wage, so that, compared to the perfectly competitive situation, the wage is higher and the level of employment lower. By raising wages, unions squeeze profits and slow down growth, at least to the extent that profits drive investment, technological change, and growth. Paralleling the discussion of the minimum wage, the counterarguments are that unions do not create inefficiency, but merely correct it, since labor markets typically have monopsonistic elements which make the wage low compared to the perfectly competitive one, and unions bring the wage closer to it.

Moreover, at the macroeconomic level, it is possible that the increase in the wage share expands markets (under the plausible assumption that workers have a higher propensity to consume than profit recipients), increases sales, and in fact increases profits, which in turn may increase investment, technological change, and growth, rather than reducing it. A higher wage share may also be considered good from a CST view, if labor unions actually increase the wage and do not increase unemployment.

Labor unions, moreover, introduce additional elements that are not present in the discussion of the minimum wage. First, since not every sector of the economy is unionized, if unionization raises the wage and reduces employment in the unionized sectors, these unemployed workers will increase the labor supply in non-unionized sectors, exerting downward pressure on the wage in those sectors. Since wages are likely to be relatively low in those sectors, wage inequality will increase in this case. The position of the worst-off in society, in fact, may be worsened, as in the case of the minimum wage. It is argued, in fact, that unions represent insiders, and do not represent the interests of outsiders who are unemployed, in the wage bargaining process. Second, unions not only bargain over wages but also change power relations in the workplace and give workers a voice. The effects of this on efficiency are not obvious. On the one hand, they may make workers more aggressive, less productive because of work norms and opposition to technological change, and create industrial strife. On the other hand, they may increase cooperation between workers and supervisors, who meet on relatively more equal terms and therefore trust each other more. This can increase labor productivity and productive efficiency, and also help to improve technology as workers, with their direct knowledge of production shop-floor practices, can contribute to improving technological and organizational methods. By providing voice as an option, and not just exit, as discussed by Hirschman,[14] unions can improve overall efficiency, since decisions will reflect the views of all workers, and not just the marginal worker who is most likely to leave. Participation in unions can build community among workers which may increase worker cooperation and efficiency, in addition to being good for developing fellow-feeling and fraternity. Third, unions can provide a check of unethical business practices, such as arbitrary dismissal and noncompliance with regulations about working conditions and safety. Labor unions can have a countervailing influence on the power of big business, not only at the firm level, improving efficiency, but also at the broader political level thereby making the political playing field more even and fair.[15]

Though the economic impact of unionization remains mixed, it or some form of worker participation is necessary to give workers a voice in making the workplace enhance human dignity rather than detracting from it.

GIFT EXCHANGE AND EFFICIENCY WAGES

In *Caritas in Veritate,* issued in honor of the 40th anniversary of Paul VI's *Populorum Progressio*, Pope Benedict XVI builds on modern CST. His central argument is an extension of the analysis of love and charity from *Deus Caritas Est* to address the economic, cultural, and political concerns of our world today. Since Leo XIII's *Rerum Novarum*, the church has insisted on the fundamental principle of human dignity and urged various means of solidarity complemented by the principle of subsidiarity. Benedict does not revise or revoke these principles. He repeats and summarizes them. But "Charity in Truth" goes beyond this. The paragraphs cited below introduce a theme important to the encyclical and its application.[16]

> The Church's social doctrine holds that authentically human social relationships of friendship, solidarity and reciprocity can also be conducted within economic activity, and not only outside it or "after" it. The economic sphere is neither ethically neutral, nor inherently inhuman and opposed to society. It is part and parcel of human activity and precisely because it is human, it must be structured and governed in an ethical manner.
>
> The great challenge before us, accentuated by the problems of development in this global era and made even more urgent by the economic and financial crisis, is to demonstrate, in thinking and behaviour, not only that traditional principles of social ethics like transparency, honesty and responsibility cannot be ignored or attenuated, but also that *in commercial relationships the principle of gratuitousness and the logic of gift as an expression of fraternity can and must find their place within normal economic activity* (italics added by author). This is a

> human demand at the present time, but it is also demanded by economic logic. It is a demand both of charity and of truth.

This is new and exciting to an economist like me. I have always thought of solidarity as a series of measures to complement or to correct what "normal economic activity"—that is, the market—could not achieve. What Benedict XVI argues, however, is that economic relations themselves can and should be an occasion for solidarity, guided by the philosophy of gift.

What does this mean in real life? Let me explore that question by relating Benedict's position to Adam Smith's economics and then focusing on the real-life issue of worker-employer relations. Let me start with another quote from the pope:

> The social doctrine of the Church has unceasingly highlighted the importance of distributive justice and social justice for the market economy, not only because it belongs within a broader social and political context, but also because of the wider network of relations within which it operates. In fact, if the market is governed solely by the principle of the equivalence in value of exchanged goods it cannot provide the social cohesion that it requires in order to function well. Without internal forms of solidarity and mutual trust, the market cannot fulfill its proper economic function.[17]

As we saw in an earlier chapter, the Smith that is known to most modern economists is a caricature of the real Adam Smith. The popular image of Smith represents him as arguing that the so-called invisible hand of the free market and the pursuit of self-interest by individuals drives the economy to achieve the social good.

However, a more careful reading of Smith's writings, especially his *Theory of Moral Sentiments,* shows that he had a pluralist view of human nature, in which sympathy—the ability to perceive things from another person's perspective—has an important role. He also emphasized that "rules of conduct" influence people's behavior in a positive manner: "Those general rules of conduct, when they have been fixed in our mind by habitual reflection, are of great use in correcting misrepresentations of self-love concerning what is fit and proper to be done in our particular situation."[18]

He thought that "humanity, justice, generosity, and public spirit, are the qualities most useful to others,"[19] and believed while self-interest is useful in certain situations, these other virtues are useful in others. For Smith, the way that the connecting principles of the economy, through the invisible hand, give rise to order reflects the planning and handiwork of the Deity as designer.[20] So Adam Smith, economist and philosopher, would be quite comfortable reading *Caritas in Veritate.*

Let's apply Benedict's idea of gift to a specific issue within worker-employer relations. In the light of economists' claims about the importance of incentives for the operation of markets, is the treatment of work in CST, and more particularly, the concept of gift in *Caritas in Veritate*, viable? An economist might argue that "humanization" of work may be impossible because of: (a) the way markets create a bifurcation of people as consumers/workers, coupled with the competitive pressures that force business firms to become ever more efficient; and (b) the consumerism which is rooted in human greed *and* the workings of the business system.

Because of competition one firm cannot improve working conditions, raise wages, or democratize the workplace if the result is an increase in production costs. Competition from other firms will keep the costs from being passed on in higher prices and, thus, profits will decline. The bifurcation of people into consumers/workers means that what they prefer as consumers—lower prices—makes what they prefer as workers—better working conditions and wages—less obtainable. Reliance on the market as the primary decision-making mechanism bifurcates the decision into separate areas. What people want as workers will not be ratified by those same people as consumers. Since competition is now worldwide, even a whole country faces difficulty in mandating workplace improvements that raise costs.

The problem is reinforced both by human greed and the constant effort of business to promote consumption as the ultimate end of life. This creates constant pressure to reduce labor costs, undercutting attempts to improve the quality of work life. Thus, the only hope may be to change work organization in ways that are both humanizing *and* efficient.

Let me present an example. Consider a business firm which employs workers and produces for the market. This relationship is not just a simple market relation. Unlike many markets in which the two parties enter into a transaction and that is the end of their relationship, the relationship here is very likely to be a relatively long-term one—sometimes for a month or a year, or more usually an indefinite period—and one in which the firm is not hiring a certain amount of labor services, but a certain number of explicit or implicit hours of labor. When the labor contract is made the employee knows his or her wage but has not yet provided the labor services. The employer may not be able to monitor exactly how hard the employee works, especially in more complex jobs, even with supervisors, and the employee has a great deal of leeway about how much effort he or she will put into the job. The degree of effort, in turn, will depend on how the employee believes he or she is being treated by the firm. A symbol of this treatment is the wage paid, although other conditions of work also count. This can be likened to a gift exchange: if employees believe that they are being well treated and well paid, they will in return be loyal to the employer and buy into the employer's goals. The main point is that if they believe they are unfairly treated, they will not be loyal and feel no sense of duty to get the job done; they will shirk and only work the least amount that they can get away with, and may even sabotage the production process. If, however, they feel that they are treated more than fairly, they will feel satisfied with their job and proud of working for the employer, and therefore put in a great deal of effort. The result will be that if employers believe that this is the way their employees will respond; they will pay a fair wage and will try to provide a good working environment. Productivity and wages will be higher than if they did not pay a fair wage and provide for good working conditions. Moreover, there are likely to be fewer labor–firm disputes, which will have a positive effect on efficiency. And there probably will be less need for supervisory personnel.

This story of a gift relation has some similarities with the standard efficiency wage theory in economics. According to this theory employers pay workers a wage higher than the lowest needed to obtain workers. They do so in order to reduce shirking. At this higher wage workers would not like to get caught shirking and lose their jobs (something that they would not mind so much if they were paid the lower wage, since they could obtain another job at that same wage). In the efficiency wage model, there is unemployment in equilibrium because the wage is at a level higher than the labor market-clearing level, and because firms have no incentive to reduce the wage since their profits will be adversely affected by lower productivity due to increased shirking. Unemployment and the higher real wage provide a carrot and a stick to workers which make them provide greater effort because of the fear of getting fired and becoming unemployed.

However, the gift exchange story is different because it explicitly brings in the issue of fairness. People react well when treated fairly, and not well when they feel unfairly treated. The story involving fairness is not only more realistic than the one that only involves shirking and the fear of losing one's job but is also better able to withstand criticism as an explanation of high wages. Shirking can be avoided by giving workers the incentive of seniority rights without paying higher wages to all workers, and workers may fear being fired and losing their reputation as good workers and thus exert a high level of effort without being paid high wages.[21] Moreover, in work which requires group effort and where the individual's contribution is hard to measure, workers may free ride on the efforts of their colleagues while getting paid higher wages. The fairness argument is able to withstand all these objections.

Another argument can be made for the importance of the gift relation in commercial affairs. Reliance on financial incentives can have the unfortunate result of driving out the moral dimension of decision making, as was briefly noted in Chapter 6 when discussing virtue-based ethical problems with markets. The general idea that economic incentives may sometimes backfire has received some empirical support in recent years. Building on work in social psychology, Frey and Oberholzer[22] argued that the introduction of monetary payments may reduce the intrinsic motivation to behave altruistically or perform one's civic duty. They illustrated this with the case of monetary compensation for the location of a nuclear waste repository facility.

As noted in Chapter 6, a growing experimental literature testing monetary incentives also suggests that financial incentives can be counterproductive.[23] In a field experiment on day-care centers in Israel, Gneezy and Rustichini[24] furthermore found that introducing a fine increased the number of late-coming parents. Consistent with this finding, several recent laboratory experiments suggest that the introduction of fines or minimum performance requirements can reduce performance.[25]

Barry Schwartz, Professor of Psychology at Swarthmore College, argues that 35 years of research demonstrates that "incentives don't just fail; they often backfire."[26] He goes on to say that these studies show that financial incentives remove the moral dimension from decisions by, among others, corporate executives. Attempts to use an index to measure performance results in the index being manipulated to boost the index that the incentive bonus is based on even to the detriment of company welfare. This is clearly the case in the banking industry that took on excessive amounts of risk and became over-leveraged in the pursuit of bonuses. Concern for the welfare of their clients took a back seat.

Economists have made a major mistake in treating love, benevolence, and particularly public spirit as scarce resources that must be economized lest they be depleted.[27] This is a faulty analogy because, unlike material factors of production, the supply of love, benevolence, and public spirit is not fixed or limited. These are resources whose supply may increase rather than decrease through use. Also, they do not remain intact if they stay unused.[28] These moral resources respond positively to practice, in a learning-by-doing manner, and negatively to non-practice. Obviously, they can also be overused.

People learn their values from their families, their religious faith, and from their society. In fact, a principal objective of publicly proclaimed laws and regulations is to stigmatize certain types of behavior and to reward others, thereby influencing individual values and behavior codes. Aristotle understood this: "Lawgivers make the citizen good by inculcating habits in them, and this is the aim of every lawgiver; if he does not succeed in doing that, his legislation is a failure. It is in this that a good constitution differs from a bad one."[29]

Habits of benevolence and civic spirit, in addition to heightened group consciousness, can be furthered by bringing people together to solve common problems. Growth of worker participation in management, consultation between local communities and business firms to negotiate plant closings and relocations, establishment of advisory boards on employment policy that represent labor, business, and the public, all are steps toward a recognition that individual self-interest alone is insufficient, that mutual responsibilities are necessary in a world where interdependence and imperfect information generate distrust and tempt individuals into strategic behavior that, in turn, results in sub-optimal outcomes.

The way that I have juxtaposed ethically based behavior and self-interest might give the impression that they are always mutually exclusive. But proximity to self-interest alone does not defile morality. Moral values are often necessary counterparts in a system based on self-interest. Not only is there a "vast amount of irregular and informal help given in times of need"[30]; there is also a consistent dependence on moral values upon which market mechanisms rely. Without a basic trust and socialized morality, the system would be much less efficient.

Thus, Pope Benedict XVI's argument in *Caritas in Veritate* that gift relations must exist inside normal economic activity has some support in economics as a real-world possibility.

Economists, influenced by CST, have much to offer by studying the impact of cooperative institutions on strategic behavior and free riding. Chapter 4, "A New American Experiment: Partnership for the Public Good," from the bishops' pastoral letter *Economic Justice for All* on the U.S. economy can be a fruitful beginning point for theologians and economists to further the development of Catholic social thought for the twenty-first century.

WORKER-SHARED OWNERSHIP

CST has long taught that workers should be able to participate in the management and profits of the firms they work for. As long ago as 1919, the United States bishops' *Program for Social Reconstruction* called for co-partnerships and even worker cooperatives. Pope Pius XI urged that the employment contract be replaced by a partnership contract allowing workers to "become sharers in ownership and management or participate in some fashion in the profits received."[31] Pope John Paul II called for "associating labor with the ownership of capital."[32] Chapter 4 of the bishops' 1986 pastoral letter *Economic Justice for All* also urges more formal cooperation among labor, business and government.

In actual practice in the United States, there is a growing practice of sharing the fruits of ownership with a company's workers, as documented by research at the National Bureau of Economic Research, which holds out hope of realizing work that supports them physically and gives them a sense of esteem and of contributing to an important undertaking.[33] In the United States, 44 percent of employees have part of their pay linked to company performance, either through ownership, stock options, profit-sharing or gain-sharing.

There are several ways in which firms share the rewards (and risks) of business with workers in what is called shared capitalism: *Profit-sharing* rewards workers based on the profit of the company by paying workers cash through bonuses or by placing the workers' share of profits in a retirement plan. Sometimes profit sharing is paid to workers in company stock, so what is received as a profit share becomes employee ownership. *Gain sharing* offers workers payments based on the performance of their work units rather than of the whole enterprise. *Employee ownership* offers employees ownership of part or all of a firm through shares of listed firms or through comparable legal arrangements of non-listed firms. *Employee Stock Purchase Plans* allow workers to buy stock with deductions from their paychecks with a discount from the market price. Finally, *stock options* are a hybrid between profit sharing and employee ownership. A stock option gives the worker the right to buy the stock at a set price anytime during a specified period following the option grants. The employee can get the upside gain of a rise in the share price without the downside risk of losing part of their investment.

The Bureau of Economic Research's "Shared Capitalism" Project[34] is the major research on the extent to which workers' earnings depend on the performance of their firm or work group in the United States and Europe and on the impact of sharing arrangements on economic behavior. Their evidence shows that: (1) a large and growing proportion of workers are covered by shared capitalism through worker profit-sharing, bonuses, or worker ownership of shares; (2) outcomes for workers and firms are higher under shared capitalism than under other work and pay arrangements; and (3) that worker co-monitoring helps overcome the free rider problem that arises when part of pay depends on the productivity and effort of all workers.

In a report[35] published by the Center for American Progress in March 2011, the principal researchers from the National Bureau project point out a strange anomaly in current United States tax policy: Companies are allowed to write off costly stock options that represent incentive pay for top executives, despite little to no evidence that they work to improve company performance. Professor Nancy Folbre[36] has suggested a policy of restricting these tax benefits to companies that provide the same type of incentive pay for all full-time employees, stipulating that the value expended on the bottom 80 percent of employees by salary must equal at least that expended on the top 5 percent. She points out that similar restrictions have long been in effect for employee retirement and health plans. The costs of these health programs are not tax-deductible unless they are offered in a nondiscriminatory way to all workers.

If we want to reshape our individualist economy into a more communitarian form called for by CST, we need to support modest changes in tax incentives that could expand worker share of the economy.

NOTES

1. John Paul II, *Laborem Exercens*, para. 9.
2. However, the 2017 income tax reduction led to firms buying back their stocks, not increased investment or higher wages.
3. David Card and Alan Krueger, *Myth and Measurement* (Princeton, NJ: Princeton University Press, 1995).
4. Seema Jayachandran, "A Raise for Workers Can Be a Win for All," *New York Times*; June 21, 2020.
5. See Stephen Bazen, "Minimum Wages and Low-wage Employment," in Mary Gregory, Wiemer Salvedra, and Stephen Bazen, eds., *Labour Market Inequalities* (Oxford: Oxford University Press, 2000), pp. 124-30. Also see Gary S. Becker and Guity Nashat Becker, *The Economics of Life: From Baseball to Affirmative Action to Immigration, How Real-world Issues Affect Our Everyday Life* (New York: McGraw-Hill, 1996), pp. 37-8.
6. T. M. Wilkinson, "The Ethics and Economics of the Minimum Wage," *Economics and Philosophy*, 20 (2004), pp. 351-74.
7. Leo XIII, *Rerum Novarum*, para. 49, 51.
8. John Paul II, *Laborem Exercens*, para. 20.
9. Benedict XVI, *Caritas in Veritate,* para. 64; Francis, *Address to World Meeting of Popular Movements*, October 28, 2014.
10. Stephanie Luce, *Labor Movements: Global Perspectives* (Chichester, Great Britian: Polity, 2011), 121.
11. See James A. Gross, *A Shameful Business: The Case for Human Rights in the American Workplace* (Ithaca: ILR Press/Cornell University Press, 2010), 79-80.
12. Gerald J. Beyer. "The Principle of Mercy in the World of Work Today," in *Ekonomia a chrześcijaństwo: świat biznesu przez pryzmat encyklik św. Jana Pawła II Centesimus annus i Laborem Exercens*, ed. Agnieszka Lekka-Kowalik (Warszawa: Instytut Papieża Jana Pawła II, 2017), 141-68.
13. Annette Bernhardt et al., "Broken Laws, Unprotected Workers: Violations of Employment and Labor Laws in America," *A Report of the National Employment Law Project*, available at http://www.nelp.org/content/uploads/2015/03/BrokenLawsReport2009.pdf?nocdn=1, 2-6.
14. Hirschman, *Exit, Voice and Loyalty.*

15. John Kenneth Galbraith. *American Capitalism. The Concept of Countervailing Power* (New York: Houghton Mifflin Company, 1952).
16. Benedict XVI, *Caritas in Veritate*, para. 36.3 and 36.4.
17. Benedict XVI, *Caritas in Veritate*, para. 35.
18. Adam Smith, *Theory of Moral Sentiments*, 160.
19. Adam Smith, *Theory of Moral Sentiments*, 190.
20. Jerry Evensky, "Ethics and the Invisible Hand" *Journal of Economic Perspectives* 7, no. 2 (1993): 197-205, reprinted in Charles K. Wilber, ed. *Economics, Ethics and Public Policy* (London: Rowman and Littlefield, 1998).
21. George A. Akerlof and Robert J. Shiller, *Animal Spirits* (Princeton, NJ: Princeton University Press, 2009).
22. Frey and Oberholzer–Gee, "The Cost of Price Incentives."
23. See Gneezy and Rustichini, "Pay Enough or Don't Pay at All," 791-810.
24. Gneezy and Rustichini. "A Fine Is a Price," 1-17.
25. See Chapter 4, endnote 17 for references.
26. Barry Schwartz, "The Dark Side of Incentives," *Business Week*, November 23, 2009.
27. Albert O. Hirschman, *Rival Views of Market Society* (New York: Viking, 1986), 155.
28. Hirschman, *Rival Views of Market Society*, 155.
29. Aristotle, *Nicomachean Ethics*, 1103b
30. Arrow, "The Gift Relationship," 345.
31. Pius XI, *Quadragesimo Anno*, encyclical letter, Vatican website, para. 65 (1931). http://www.vatican.va/content/pius-xi/en/encyclicals/documents/hf_p-xi_enc_19310515_quadragesimo-anno.html
32. John Paul II, *Laborem Exercens*, para 14.
33. Douglas L. Kruse, Richard B. Freeman, and Joseph R. Blasi, eds., *Shared Capitalism at Work: Employee Ownership, Profit and Gain Sharing, and Broad-based Stock Options* (Chicago: University of Chicago Press, 2010).
34. See their website at http://www.nber.org/papers/w14830#navDiv=2.
35. Richard B. Freeman, Joseph R. Blasi, and Douglas L. Kruse, "Inclusive Capitalism for the American Workforce: Reaping the Rewards of Economic Growth through Broad-based Employee Ownership and Profit Sharing," *Center for American Progress*, March 2011. http://www.americanprogress.org/issues/2011/03/pdf/worker_productivity.pdf
36. Nancy Folbre, "Shared Capitalism," *Economix: New York Times Blog*, May 30, 2011. http://economix.blogs.nytimes.com/2011/05/30/shared-capitalism/.

Chapter Eight

The Causes of Poverty

One day in a conversation with a close friend, I said Christian liberals (typically Democrats) and Christian conservatives (typically Republicans) have completely opposite views on the causes of poverty and, therefore, the solutions to the problem. The liberals blame institutional factors such as differential parental income, racism, neighborhood schools that result in segregation by income, etc. Conservatives focus on personal factors such as lack of ambition, short-sightedness, and genetic differences. These personal factors are compounded by poor government policies that give improper incentives. For example, unemployment benefits reduce the incentive to work, high taxes reduce the incentive to invest, etc.

A January 2014 poll found that 51% of Republicans agreed that "lack of effort on his or her part" was the primary reason that a poor person would find him- or herself in poverty, while only 32% put the blame on "circumstances beyond his or her control." Conversely, Democrats were more likely to blame circumstances rather than a lack of effort, 63% to 29%. Independent voters tracked more closely to Democrats on this issue as well, with 51% blaming circumstances and 33% blaming laziness for poverty.[1]

In short, liberals blame the institutions of capitalism and the failure of government to correct for those failures. Conservatives blame personal behavior failures and government policies to offset those failures. Who is right? My friend responded, "They both are." In this chapter I look at the arguments and the available evidence to see if we can come up with a clearer answer.

As Christians, whether we are liberals or conservatives, we know we are called to be our "brothers' and sisters' keeper." Central to the biblical view is that justice in a community is most directly tested by its treatment of the powerless in society, most often described as the widow, the orphan, the poor and the stranger (non-Israelite) in the land. Jesus followed in the prophetic tradition, taking the side of those who are powerless or on the margin of his society. Jesus's description of the final judgment in Matthew 25 (31-46) still haunts me with its powerful message of what it means to be a Christian. But how are we to serve the poor as if they were Jesus? CST provides an answer that both conservatives and liberals can endorse:

> The principle of participation leads us to the conviction that the most appropriate and fundamental solutions to poverty will be those that enable people to take control of their own lives. For poverty is not merely the lack of adequate financial resources. It entails a more profound kind of deprivation, a denial of full participation in the economic, social, and political life of society and an inability to influence decisions that affect one's life. It means being powerless in a way that assaults not only one's pocketbook but also one's fundamental human dignity. Therefore, we should seek solutions that enable the poor to help themselves through such means as employment. Paternalistic programs which do too much for and too little with the poor are to be avoided. (*Economic Justice for All*, para. 188)

Some personal experiences have shaped my own beliefs about the causes of poverty. I was born during the depression and my father, who was a carpenter by trade, was unemployed, so he, my mother, my brother, and I followed the migrant picking trail throughout Oregon and part of Washington. I do not remember much but the family stories remain vivid about the hard work and the outright cruelty of some of the overseers. Years later in the late 1950s, while investigating working conditions among the strawberry workers in Oregon, I saw how hard they worked and how little they earned. In the 1960s in a Maryland suburb of Washington, D.C., a friend—African American, chemist at Fort Meade, and farm property owner in the south—was turned down for a small home improvement loan from a local bank. I went to that same bank and borrowed the same amount on my signature alone. I was still in graduate school and teaching at a small college earning quite a bit less than my friend. I then loaned him that same amount. In 1985, Mary Ellen and I, along with three other couples, founded the Holy Family Catholic Worker House in South Bend, Indiana to shelter homeless families. From 1985 to 2000, we volunteered there and from 2000-2006 at the South Bend Homeless Center. I saw over and over how an illness could lead to homelessness; how a car breaking down making you late for work meant losing the job; how lack of childcare made it impossible to have a regular job; and the list could go on. Clearly, I bring a bias toward the liberal position from my experiences. However, experience is often a useful complement to theory and statistics.

Let me begin a more dispassionate analysis by laying out some overall statistics to situate the issue. The official poverty rate[2] in 2018 was 11.8%

resulting in 38.1 million people in poverty. Breaking that down by racial category: White, not Hispanic 15.7 million, 8.1%; Hispanic, any race 10.5 million, 17.6%; Black 8.9 million, 20.8%; Asian 2 million, 10.1%. Even as the economy continued its steady growth from the beginning of the Great Recession in 2008 until early 2020, with unemployment falling to a 50-year low of 3.5%, there was a large number of workers earning wages low enough to leave them and their families extremely vulnerable. A recent study from the Brookings Institution "found that 53 million Americans between the ages of 18 to 64—accounting for 44% of all workers—qualify as 'low-wage earners.' Their median hourly wages are $10.22, and median annual earnings are about $18,000."[3] The onset of the coronavirus and the consequent lockdown has changed everything. Unemployment now ranges between 13-20 percent, depending on how it is counted. Government spending on relief is approaching $3 trillion. The outcome will not be known for years. What we do know is that the existing issues of poverty and inequality have been magnified by the crisis.

THE RATE OF POVERTY AND SYSTEMIC CAUSES

Before taking up the dispute between liberals and conservatives I need to deal with a crucial issue. The causes for the level of poverty being some rate or another, say 12% or 15%, is my concern here. If the rate is determined by economy-wide systemic issues such as inadequate aggregate demand to achieve full employment and/or by too many jobs that pay less than a living wage, then the poverty rate is determined by these systemic forces, and it is only the distribution of poverty among individual members of the population that is the result of the factors that liberals and conservatives argue over.

> Imagine for a moment that income is distributed according to the results of a footrace. All of the income in the United States for each year is put into a giant pool and we hold a race to determine who gets what. The fastest fifth of the population gets 48 percent of the income to divide up, the next fastest fifth splits 23 percent, the next fastest fifth gets 15 percent, the next fifth 10 percent, and the slowest fifth divides 4 percent. The result would be an unequal distribution of income, with each person in the fastest fifth getting nine times as much money as each person in the slowest fifth, which is what the actual distribution of income in the United States looks like.[4]

To see why some fifth of the population must be poor no matter how fast people run, all we have to do is look at the system itself. It uses unbridled competition to determine not only who gets fancy cars and nice houses, but who gets to eat or has a place to live or access to health care. There has to be a bottom fifth so long as the system is organized as it is. Learning to run faster may keep you or me out of poverty, but it will not get rid of poverty itself. To do that, we have to change the system along with how people participate in it.

To show the importance of this issue, here is a more realistic example. Suppose we can significantly lower racial barriers to good education and jobs. Will this reduce the poverty rate? If there are no more good jobs than before, you simply will have fewer minority families in poverty and more white families taking their place. That is, poverty will only be redistributed. To reduce the poverty rate, you must improve the quantity and quality of jobs. Or you must transfer income from the rich to the poor by taxing the former and distributing it to the poor in the form of subsidized medical care, housing, etc.

Here is one more example. Education increases the competitive advantage of individuals but only as long as others do not do likewise. If everyone got a college degree, we would still have millions working at poverty level jobs—retail clerks, maids, flipping hamburgers, etc. The only change is they would now have college degrees.

Let me provide some data to illustrate the importance of this issue. The able-bodied poor between 18 and 64, who were in the labor force full-time or less than full-time, were 9.5 million and those who did not work at least one week 15 million. And many of the job openings were in the low-paying retail sector. When you count dependents plus seniors and disabled persons not in the work force you get to the 43.1 million people officially poor. Thus, unemployment and employment at below poverty level wages is a crucial factor in explaining the poverty rate.

What is the evidence for systemic forces explaining the overall poverty rate in the country? The Poverty Center at Syracuse University argues there is some supportive evidence: "For example, there is the failure of poverty to fall during periods of large training programs, and the failure of poverty to fall with rise in general educational levels of the population."[5]

Between 1970 and May 2019, employment in manufacturing declined from 23% of the civilian workforce to 8%. Since overall unemployment is low, the lost manufacturing jobs must have been replaced by people leaving the work force or by getting new jobs. Lost manufacturing jobs were primarily replaced by lower-wage, lower-hours service jobs.

Chad Shearer and Isha Shah, in another study from the Brookings Institution, identified good jobs for workers without bachelor's degrees by defining "good jobs" as those paying median earnings or more for a given metropolitan area and providing health insurance. They found that such jobs are relatively scarce, held by only 20% of workers without bachelor's degrees in large metro areas. Another 13% are in "promising" jobs, in which incumbent workers are likely to progress to a good job within 10 years.[6] An analysis by Kyle Fee, Keith Wardrip, and Lisa Nelson came to similar findings.[7] They defined good jobs for workers without a bachelor's degree as those paying at least the national median wage adjusted for local cost of living. The analysis found that for every good job there are 3.4 working-age adults with less than a bachelor's degree.

What do these new service jobs, replacing manufacturing ones, look like? The Leisure & Hospitality sector is our largest with about 15 million non-management employees. In this sector workers, on average, are paid $16.58 per hour and work 25.8 hours per week. This results in a weekly income of $428 or just over $20,000 per year, well below the poverty line for a family.

The high percentage of "bad jobs" in the economy helps explain another new reality in the current economy—the low participation rate of middle-aged males in the work force. Workers are reluctant to re-enter the workforce if the only jobs available are these low-paid, dead-end ones.

The policies necessary to overcome these systemic problems—true full employment policies that guarantee work at living wage levels—will be both financially expensive and politically intractable. It is worth pointing out that the United States Catholic Bishops in their 1986 pastoral letter *Economic Justice for All*, recognizing that jobs are the main source of income and of participating in society, call for a full employment policy and a total revamping of welfare programs.[8]

THE DISTRIBUTION OF POVERTY

Let us now turn to the *distribution* of poverty and why it is these particular people who are poor and not someone else.

The Conservative Argument

"Anyone unwilling to work should not eat. For we hear that some of you are living in idleness, mere busybodies, not doing any work. Now such persons we command and exhort in the Lord Jesus Christ to do their work quietly and to earn their own living." (2 Thess 3:10b-12) Conservative theorists and policy types argue that individual poverty is primarily the result of dysfunctional behavior in the face of what is required to succeed in the economy and society more generally. Moreover, due to long running poverty in certain geographic areas and among certain races and classes, it is further argued that this dysfunctional behavior is magnified by the so-called "culture of poverty" thesis.[9] This thesis argues that the dysfunctional behavior of individuals becomes over time a culture that is passed on to each succeeding generation. That is, dysfunctional parents raise dysfunctional children. Conservatives argue further that government welfare policies have made the problem worse by adding dependency to this culture of poverty. The result has been rising rates of divorce, female-headed single-parent families, teen pregnancy, drug/alcohol abuse, and general criminal activity. The final result is a vicious cycle of poverty that few manage to escape.

Charles Murray's *Losing Ground* [10] argued that the post-war boom in the economy had been reducing poverty rapidly but that President Johnson's War on Poverty, which emphasized cash assistance, created welfare dependence and family disintegration.

Because of these arguments, conservatives oppose long-term welfare. Rather they see the need to provide opportunities for poor and low-income workers to become self-reliant. They believe that it is more compassionate and effective, rather than keeping them dependent on government funding.

In July 2018, the White House Council of Economic Advisers issued a report enthusiastically endorsing work requirements for the nation's largest welfare programs. The council favored "negative incentives," tying aid to labor-market effort, and dismissed "positive incentives," like tax benefits for low-income workers, because the former is cheaper. The council also claimed that America's welfare policies have brought about a "decline in self-sufficiency." Is that true?

Actually, the able-bodied, poor, and idle adult is a rare creature. According to the Brookings Institution, in 2016 one-third of those living in poverty were children, 11 percent were elderly, and 24 percent were working-age adults (18 to 64) in the labor force, working or seeking work. The majority of working-age poor people connected to the labor market were part-time workers. Most could not take on many more hours either because of caregiver responsibilities, as with many single mothers, or because their employer did not offer this option, rendering them involuntary part-time workers. Among the remaining working-age adults, 12 percent were out of the labor force owing to a disability (including some enrolled in federal programs that limit work), 15 percent were either students or caregivers and 3 percent were early retirees. That leaves 2 percent of poor people who did not fit into one of these categories. That is, among the poor, two in 100 are working-age adults disconnected from the labor market for unknown reasons. The nonworking poor person getting something for nothing is a lot like the cheat committing voter fraud: pariahs who loom far larger in the American imagination than in real life.[11]

Ted Bradshaw has provided several examples of policies that flow from the conservative position.[12] A county directed its schools to identify children missing school more than ten days per school-year without medical excuses, and then if the family received Temporary Assistance for Needy Families (TANF) benefits, the child's portion of the family welfare payments were withheld to enforce school attendance and ensure that welfare kids not get left behind for another generation. This policy flowed from the belief that poverty is perpetuated by individual or family irresponsibility which must be countered with stiff penalties. In another case pre-school programs were developed and used to help poor kids gain skills and internalize the value of learning that would help them succeed in school, and after-school programs were designed to keep children away from negative influences of unsupervised street cultures. This example also flowed from the belief that subcultures of poverty must be battled by acculturating poor children in mainstream values. It should be noted that these differ little from many liberal policies. The difference being that liberals see discrimination, unemployment, and poverty itself as the causes of perpetuated poverty that need to be combated directly and by measures such as these.

Explicitly or implicitly, individual deficiencies have been an easy policy target. The key initiatives today are to push the poor into work as a primary goal. Indeed, this move is accompanied by an increasing emphasis on "self-help" strategies for the poor to pull themselves from poverty, strategies encouraged by the elimination of other forms of welfare. The earned income tax credit is one aspect of the strategy to ensure that the poor work even at below living-wage jobs. Many contemporary anti-poverty programs are designed to use punishment and the threat of punishment in order to change behavior and get people off public assistance. The best example of this response to poverty is to limit the number of years people can be on family assistance and to require participation in work activities after some period, for example, the two years on welfare in the 1996 welfare reform. This punitive approach justifies policies that restrict public assistance to services and goods instead of cash because there is a lack of trust in the discretion of poor people. Providing food at school for children or offering homeless people shelters rather than cash to pay for housing are examples. Bradshaw reported on a study he did of a program (MERCAP) that reduces assistance payments to families if their children fail to attend school, hoping that children will eventually graduate from high school and not become another generation of welfare recipients. He found, however, that the punishment did little to change behavior.

With a focus on culture as well as individual behavior, policy proposals such as Head Start and after school programs are popular among both conservatives and liberals and have shown some signs of success in providing an alternative socialization for the coming generation.

The election of President Trump in 2016 has allowed the conservative view to dominate poverty policy in Washington. His first released budget was built on the belief, discussed above, that the government should help only those who can't work or if they can be willing to do so. Those who are not willing should be removed from all the benefit programs. To carry out this philosophy the budget proposed cuts to the Supplemental Nutrition Assistance Program (food stamps) of $192 billion over the next 10 years. Medicaid was to be cut $800 billion and TANF (Clinton's welfare reform of 1996) by $21 billion. Put together this would result in a sharp reduction in the safety net for the poor and disadvantaged. There is much more—the elimination of funding for Pell Grants for higher education, of support for Americorps and Vista Volunteers—that can be explained more by an anti-government philosophy than poverty policy per se.

The intent is clear. Mick Mulvaney, the White House budget director, who believes that too much help for the poor by government creates dependency and discourages work effort, said: "We are going to measure compassion and success by the number of people we help get off of those programs and get back in charge of their own lives." To emphasize this philosophy the budget adds a work requirement for the receipt of food stamps.

What does the evidence say? Much of the research has focused on the behavior of the poor. For example, it is claimed that poor people do not value education because the evidence is that they do not show up for parent teacher conferences and similar on-site, publicly visible, school programs. However, this is misleading given that poor parents face difficult childcare costs, transportation problems, and little chance to take time off from their low-paid work. Other studies that try to get at attitudes find poor parents as interested in their children's education as non-poor parents. The claim that poor people are lazy is belied by what evidence we have. For example, one study found that poor working adults worked an average of 2,500 hours a year, roughly the equivalent of one and a quarter to a half full-time job. And these jobs were often hard manual labor where the worker needed to patch together a number of low-paying part-time jobs. Of course, there are also people who become addicted to alcohol and/or drugs and cannot function in the economy. For example, a survey of recreational manufacturing firms in Elkhart, Indiana showed that 40 percent of job applicants over 2016-2017 failed the required drug tests. However, many studies show that addiction rates are just as high among higher-income groups, but their income allows them to cope better. Also, the "war on drugs" over the past 40 years with its stiff minimum sentencing has left significant numbers of people with felony records that keep them from being hired by most employers.

The Liberal Argument

The liberal argument focuses not on individual behavior or the detrimental effects of culture but on the economic, political, and social system which causes people to have limited opportunities and resources with which to achieve income and well-being. Pope Francis expresses this view:

> The need to resolve the structural causes of poverty cannot be delayed, not only for the pragmatic reason of its urgency for the good order of society, but because society needs to be cured of a sickness which is weakening and frustrating it, and which can only lead to new crises. Welfare projects, which meet certain urgent needs, should be considered merely temporary responses.[13]

First, we need to recognize there is a history to the present poverty and inequality. And it is not simply a tale of expanding free markets where some worked hard and got ahead, and others did not or had bad luck. No, there is substantial truth to Karl Marx's argument that "primitive capital accumulation" is the source of much of the system's wealth. In the United States we have to accept that stealing the land of Native Americans and locking them up in reservations located on barely arable land, was a major source of wealth for white people and a continuing curse for Native Americans.

The slave trade and the dependence of southern agriculture on slave labor was a major source of wealth creation for white people and its denial to African Americans. Even after the Civil War and Reconstruction, the enactment of "Jim Crow" laws that lasted up to the civil rights movement in the 1960s, denied African Americans access to quality education, the right to vote, and made it possible for them to be deprived of what wealth they had in the form of land. An important cause of African American poverty today is the estimated "11 million acres black people had lost, in many cases through fraud, deception and outright theft, much of it taken in the last 50 years."[14] White control of property laws and tax rolls allowed manipulation of markets so that African Americans were displaced from their lands for all kinds of "lawful" reasons and sold at auction to whites.

If the problem of poverty is in the system and in its manipulation rather than in the poor themselves, an adequate response must be to change the system and curb its misuse. This is easy to say but hard to do, which may explain why so many liberal policy programs, as noted above, revert to trying to change individual behavior. How can one get more jobs, improve schooling for the poor, equalize income distributions, remove discrimination bias from housing, banking, education, and employment, and ensure equal political participation by poor persons? None of these tasks are easy and all require interventions into the systems that create the barriers that block poor persons from gaining the benefits of society.

Even more difficult is the question of how, if at all, Native American and African Americans should be compensated for the damages inflicted upon their people and that leave them woefully behind today. How do you get a level playing field without special programs, whether called reparations or not.

The Nobel Prize–winning economist James Heckman concludes in a 2013 book, *Giving Kids a Fair Chance*, that "the accident of birth is the greatest source of inequality in America today. Children born into disadvantage are, by the time they start kindergarten, already at risk of dropping out of school, teen pregnancy, crime, and a lifetime of low-wage work. This is bad for all those born into disadvantage and bad for American society."[15]

Warren Buffett said as much recently: "The American Dream has been very real for millions and millions of people over the years but there has been an American Nightmare that accompanied that, where people who equally tried to get educated and worked hard and had good habits and found themselves living a life that's been on the edge throughout their entire lives and the same for their children; and America can do better than that."[16]

Two facts stand out from an examination of the history of the American economy. As has been noted several times already in previous chapters, the economy has been successful in producing amounts of goods and services unprecedented in history; *and* it has done so in a temporally and spatially uneven manner, i.e., it has proceeded very unevenly among regions within the country. Certain regions became dynamic centers of development while others stagnated on the periphery. Then the process shifted, and once-growing areas stagnated and stagnant ones developed. And, of course, development has proceeded cyclically through booms and busts in each region and in the country as a whole. This process extends to individual industries and even households. For example, the textile industry started in New England, then migrated to the southern states and finally moved overseas leaving abandoned plants and unemployed workers behind at each stage.

This dynamic process of Creative Destruction is the fundamental impulse that sets and keeps the capitalist engine in motion. It creates new consumers' goods, new methods of production or transportation, new markets, and new forms of industrial organization. The price of this creation of new products, new jobs, new technologies, and new industries is the destruction of the old products, jobs, technologies, and industries. And the closing or relocation of plants with their loss of jobs hurts families and communities—here and now. The new plants and jobs frequently are located elsewhere and use a new generation of workers. The gains are in new and lower-cost products for people as consumers.

In addition, this creative-destructive process has gone global creating socio-political tensions both because of its uneven nature and because of its challenge to traditional values and ways of life. Today this is true particularly in countries such as the United States where the result has been a sharp increase in income and wealth inequality.

Robert Putnam, in his masterful study *Our Kids: The American Dream in Crisis*,[17] charts the decline of Port Clinton between 1959 and 2013. The decline of good blue-collar jobs with the resultant sharp increase in income inequality, breakup of the family, and collapse of social mobility mirror what has happened in the country as a whole. In the county-wide area of Port Clinton, the average worker real wage had not increased in over 50 years. The average worker was now earning 16 percent less than their grandparents were in the early 1970s.[18] During this period optimism turned into a collapse of hope.

Thus, both the total rate of poverty and the distribution of poverty among the population is partly, at least, determined by systemic forces. The market economy creates an inadequate number and quality of jobs because of the creative/destructive nature of the economy and the failure of the public sector to create demand for labor to rebuild our crumbling infrastructure and other essential public services. In addition, the distribution of poverty can be thought of as a foot race where some must jump hurdles while others have an open field. Poverty itself is a high hurdle to overcome with its attendant poor housing and schools. Discrimination, racial, ethnic, age, etc. provide additional hurdles to overcome. A poor African American child in a big city faces hurdles that an upper-middle-class suburban white child does not. A 50+-year-old white man with blue collar skills in a small town whose chief employer has just closed the plant faces hurdles of equal, if different, challenge.

CONCLUSION

What to suggest? First, we need a full employment policy that includes providing public jobs that pay above poverty level for able bodied adults that can't find work in the private economy. This will require also providing low-cost childcare. All policies need to be analyzed for their incentive effects as well. For example, if moving from public assistance to a job in the private sector causes a loss of the family's Medicaid, the incentive will be to stay on public assistance. Public employment should replace unemployment insurance. Maybe it is here that Christian conservatives and liberals can agree, good jobs are the solution. And maybe they will be willing to listen to Pope Francis and Pope Benedict XVI:

> We were created with a vocation to work. The goal should not be that technological progress increasingly replaces human work, for this would be detrimental to humanity. Work is a necessity, part of the meaning of life on this earth, a path to growth, human development and personal fulfillment. Helping the poor financially must always be a provisional solution in the face of pressing needs. The broader objective should always be to allow them a dignified life through work. Yet the orientation of the economy has favored a kind of technological progress in which the costs of production are reduced by laying off workers and replacing them with machines. This is yet another way in which we can end up working against ourselves. The loss of jobs also has a negative impact on the economy "through the progressive erosion of social capital: the network of relationships of trust, dependability, and respect for rules, all of which are indispensable for any form of civil coexistence." In other words, "human costs always include economic costs, and economic dysfunctions always involve human costs." To stop investing in people, in order to gain greater short-term financial gain, is bad business for society.[19]

NOTES

1. Morgan Whitaker, "Most Republicans Think Poverty Caused by Laziness, New Poll Finds," January 23, 2014. http://www.msnbc.com/politicsnation/gop-blames-poverty-laziness#49786
2. United States Census Bureau, "Income and Poverty in the United States: 2018," September 10, 2019, https://www.census.gov/library/publications/2019/demo/p60-266.html
3. Martha Ross and Nicole Bateman, "Low-Wage Work Is More Pervasive Than You Think, and There Aren't Enough 'Good Jobs' to Go Around," Brookings, Thursday, November 21, 2019. https://www.brookings.edu/blog/the-avenue/2019/11/21/low-wage-work-is-more-pervasive-than-you-think-and-there-arent-enough-good-jobs-to-go-around/
4. Allan G. Johnson, "Why Is There Poverty?", excerpt from Allan G. Johnson. *The Forest and the Trees: Sociology as Life*, Practice, and Promise. Temple University Press; 3rd edition (September 12, 2014), https://www.agjohnson.us/essays/poverty/
5. Maxwell School, Syracuse University
6. Chad Shearer and Isha Shah, "Exploring the Industries That Concentrate Good and Promising Jobs in Metropolitan America," Brookings, December 18, 2018. https://www.brookings.edu/research/opportunity-industries/
7. https://www.philadelphiafed.org/-/media/community-development/publications/special-reports/identifying_opportunity_occupations/opportunity_occupations_revisited.pdf

8. USCCB, *Economic Justice for All.*

9. H. R. Rodgers, *American Poverty in a New Era of Reform* (New York: M. E. Sharpe, 2000).

10. Charles Murray, *Losing Ground: American Social Policy 1950-1980* (New York, NY: Basic Books, 1984).

11. Matthew Desmond, "Americans Want to Believe Jobs Are the Solution to Poverty, They're Not," *New York Times*, September 11, 2018. https://www.nytimes.com/2018/09/11/magazine/americans-jobs-poverty-homeless.html

12. Ted K. Bradshaw, "Theories of Poverty and Anti-Poverty Programs in Community Development," Oregon State University, Rural Poverty Research Center, Working Paper No. 06-05 (February 2006), p. 22.

13. Francis, *Evangelii Gaudium*, encyclical letter, Vatican website, 2013, para. 202. http://w2.vatican.va/content/francesco/en/apost_exhortations/documents/papa-francesco_esortazione-ap_20131124_evangelii-gaudium.html

14. Andrew W. Kahrl, "Black People's Land Was Stolen," *New York Times*, June 21, 2019.

15. James J. Heckman, *Giving Kids a Fair Chance* (Boston: The MIT Press, 2013).

16. Dustin Wicksell, "Warren Buffett: Poverty Is the 'American Nightmare'," Inquisitr, May 9, 2015. https://www.inquisitr.com/2077281/warren-buffett-poverty-is-the-american-nightmare/

17. Robert D. Putnam, *Our Kids: The American Dream in Crisis* (New York: Simon & Schuster, 2015).

18. Putnam, *Our Kids*, 19-23.

19. Internal quotes from Benedict XVI, *Caritas in Veritate*; Francis, *Laudato Si*, para. 128.

Chapter Nine

Pope Francis and Inequality

The following quote from Pope Francis expresses what has been the heart of CST ever since Pope Leo XIII's 1891 encyclical, *Rerum Novarum*.

> Every economic and political theory or action must set about providing each inhabitant of the planet with the minimum wherewithal to live in dignity and freedom, with the possibility of supporting a family, educating children, praising God and developing one's own human potential. This is the main thing; in the absence of such a vision, all economic activity is meaningless.[1]

Poverty has been the key issue. However, Pope Francis has gone further and as noted in the quote below, condemned economic inequality itself. Why does he make this claim and is he justified in doing so?

> Today we also have to say 'Thou shalt not' to an economy of exclusion and inequality. Such an economy kills . . . . Today everything comes under the laws of competition and the survival of the fittest, where the powerful feed upon the powerless. As a consequence, masses of people find themselves excluded and marginalized: without work, without possibilities, without any means of escape. Human beings are themselves considered consumer goods to be used and then discarded. . . . The socioeconomic system is unjust at its root.[2]

In this chapter, as an economist and a believer, I try to understand and support this claim in non-theological terms. One way to do so is to show that economic inequality (1) makes it more difficult to overcome absolute poverty and (2) leads to cultural deterioration. In doing so I draw upon economic theory and economic ethics.

VERTICAL EQUALITY: FAIRNESS IN DISTRIBUTION

Questions of fairness, distribution and equality play an important role in economics and policy analysis. Broadly speaking, economists hold one of three views about these questions. One view is that efficiency and fairness are the two main goals for appraising how well an economy is doing and for devising, implementing, and evaluating economic policy. More specifically, every economic policy change—which usually impacts people differently—needs to be scrutinized for its distributional implications. This is the view held by social economists and CST. A second view is that fairness necessarily involves value judgments, and economists, as scientists, should concentrate only on efficiency, leaving judgments about fairness to society as a whole. A third view is that questions of equality and distribution are unimportant and divert attention from the important goals of efficiency and growth. The second view is untenable as we saw in Chapter 2, both because the notion of efficiency itself involves a value judgment, and because, more generally, one cannot avoid making value judgments in economics. The third view is rejected by CST and by most Americans. However, economists need to explain what they mean by equality, how it relates to fairness, and why distributional equality and inequality are worthy of attention.

Many ethical questions arise when we discuss equality and inequality: (1) Why should equality be considered a desirable goal? While, for some people, there is something intrinsically good about equality, others question whether it has any ethical value. For some others, while equality has no intrinsic worth, it may be related to other things that we value, either positively or negatively. (2) Another question concerns what it is that we are discussing the equality of, that is, if we equalize, what it is that we should equalize or at least make less unequal? For instance, should we make less unequal people's incomes, or their happiness, their health conditions, or their opportunities in life? (3) Yet another set of questions addresses among whom should we be equalizing, among people, groups, or countries, and if it is between people and groups, should we equalize between individuals who have more or are better off and those who have less or are worse off, or between people of different types distinguished by other characteristics, such as ethnicity, gender, and where they live? See Chapter 5 for a fuller discussion of alternative views of equality.

These questions, of course, are interdependent, because the validity of arguments about why equality is good may well depend on the equality of some things and not other things, and among some entities and not others. Despite their interdependence, I will introduce these three types of questions in turn.

First, I will discuss the reasons for or against equality; second, I will address the issue of equality of what, and finally, equality among whom. I will end with some concluding comments.[3]

It is useful to start with the idea of fairness. Although it can be described in a number of ways, a central feature of it is the demand for impartiality and recognizing the interests and concerns of others. This raises a number of issues. First, some sense or another of fairness appears to be universal among people everywhere. Even young children are often heard to emphatically declare, "That's not fair!" Second, although it can tell us that certain things are unfair, it is not clear whether it can tell us what specifically it is to be fair, to act fairly, or to have a fair outcome. To the Christian, of course, it is the Golden Rule, "Do unto others as you would have them do unto you," though honored more in words than actions. Third, and related to the second point, it is not clear what is the relation between equality and fairness.

Why Equality?

It is standard practice in the discussion of ethics to distinguish between intrinsic and instrumental reasons for taking the view that something is good. Intrinsic reasons are those that assert that something is good or bad in itself, while instrumental reasons are those that assert that something is good or bad not in itself, but because it affects something else which is intrinsically good or bad. This distinction does not imply that something cannot be both intrinsically and instrumentally good or bad, or good in one sense or bad in another, but just clarifies two different senses in which things may be good or bad. When we say something is intrinsically good, we cannot just say that our intuition tells us that it is good in itself (because one person's intuition may be different from someone else's), but we have to defend its intrinsic goodness in some way.

In terms of this distinction, equality may be good in itself or it may be good if it affects something else that we value, for instance, how happy people are, whether it leads to higher levels of output, or whether it increases freedom. Let us consider each type of reason in turn.

Intrinsic Arguments

It may be argued that inequality in the distribution of something is bad in itself. It is not clear, however, why this is so. There may be nothing intrinsically good about equality, because different people do not have to be the same, and that differences may be good because it promotes diversity. While diversity may be good for a number of reasons, and homogeneity may be considered bad, especially if it is enforced, we can still defend equality in terms of equality of things that are considered to be good intrinsically or instrumentally.

First, inequality in income may imply inequality in political voice or in access to health and education, which may exacerbate inequality in each other. For example, the Supreme Court's decision in the Citizens United case, which allows unlimited spending on elections, allows those with high incomes to potentially control who gets elected and, thus, what policies get enacted. As another example, in Ferguson, Missouri, the city government relied on fines to finance their activities. The fines were on things like speeding, overtime parking, littering, etc., with those fines doubling if not paid on time. The result is that it was the poorer citizens who found the fines difficult to pay. When a white policeman shot and killed a black man the city exploded with the anger over the fines adding fuel to the rioting.

High levels of inequality, also, may result in a loss of self-respect as well as the failure to obtain the respect of others, and these may be valuable intrinsically and instrumentally (for instance, for having the capability of contributing to society). Third, inequality can create obstacles to the achievement of social solidarity and create obstacles to friendship and relationships. Finally, high levels of inequality may allow some people to subjugate and dominate others, which most would consider intrinsically bad. This is the common case in many of the poor countries of the world and is what Pope Francis is referring to when he says "the structural causes of inequality" must be combatted.

Instrumental Arguments

Turning from intrinsic to instrumental arguments, many variants have been made. The instrumental argument may not convince some people because they believe that there is no justification for taking people out of poverty and early mortality if they choose not to work hard and attend to their health. However, it seems that some who take the view that inequality is acceptable, especially if it reflects people's choices and efforts, may agree that everyone is entitled to some minimum absolute level of well-being, so that those who are worse off may have some priority over those who are better off, in terms of getting more of that in which there is inequality. This, of course, is the position of CST. The U.S. Catholic bishops say that "decisions must be judged in light of what they do *for* the poor, what they do *to* the poor and what they enable the poor to do *for themselves*. The fundamental moral criterion for all economic decisions, policies, and institutions is this: They must be at the service of *all people, especially the poor*."[4]

It is not clear that the argument in favor of priority of the poor and for people obtaining some absolute minimum level of well-being is independent of the argument for a certain measure of equality. First, it is not clear what an absolute minimum level of well-being in a particular society is. In evaluating how someone is doing we invariably make comparisons, for instance, we examine how someone is doing compared to how he or she was doing in the past, or with how that person can potentially do. Since potentials are difficult to measure precisely, one way of doing so is by examining how others are doing, so that inequality becomes an issue. Second, relative positions in some spheres may imply absolute positions in other spheres. For instance, if there is inequality in income and the availability of resources, and if people who are worse off feel absolutely worse off, they may not be able to maintain their dignity or self-respect. Adam Smith wrote in *The Wealth of Nations*:

> By necessaries I understand not only the commodities which are indispensably necessary for the support of life, but what ever the custom of the country renders it indecent for creditable people, even the lowest order to be without. . . . Custom . . . has rendered leather shoes a necessary of life in England. The poorest creditable person of either sex would be ashamed to appear in public without them.[5]

The need being fulfilled here is the need of not being ashamed; Smith is clearly arguing that the number of commodities capable of satisfying this need depends on custom, and is therefore changeable as customs change, which in turn changes with average levels of income. This argument may be interpreted as being subjective, dependent on the feelings of people. However, a number of objective factors also play a role. For instance, the worth of a high school education in terms of getting "good" jobs depends on whether most people have secondary school education, high-school education, college education, or post-graduate education, and the need for having a car to travel depends on whether most people have cars and their willingness to support public transportation.

A final set of instrumental arguments regarding equality arise from connections between inequality of income and other things in the economy as a whole that we may consider valuable. Economists have been greatly concerned with the relationship between the distribution of income on the one hand and the level of output of the economy or its growth rate on the other. An argument that has a long history in economics is that equality may have an adverse effect on the growth rate of the economy because the rich save a higher proportion of their income than the poor, so that inequality leads to higher saving, investment, and economic growth. Another argument relates to the efficiency-equity tradeoff discussed by Arthur Okun[6] using the leaky bucket metaphor: if I try to distribute water between people, carrying it in leaky buckets, the total amount of water will be diminished due to the leaks. In other words, attempts at redistributing income may result in lower levels of total output due to the creation of disincentives (a tax on incomes may reduce the amount of work people want to do), or allocation inefficiencies (taxes on some kinds of activity may make people engage less in these activities and more in others which are not taxed). However, theoretical and empirical evidence suggests that although these tradeoffs may exist sometimes, but not always, there are a number of reasons why more equal distributions of income may lead to higher levels of output and growth. More equality can lead to higher levels of consumption demand (because the poor consume a higher proportion of their income than the rich), aggregate demand, output, investment, capital accumulation and growth.[7] Improvements in health and education may also occur with a more equal distribution of income giving greater access to these resources; which can increase output in the economy by allowing the deprived to become more economically productive members of society. The existence of high levels of inequality may lead to crime, conflict, and violence,[8] which could reduce output and income. Poor health conditions of the poor could result in epidemics which could affect the health of the entire population or require higher levels of spending on health which may reduce the production of other types of goods. Inequality may also lead to an improper functioning of the democratic process with votes being bought and sold and obtained by domination and subjugation, rather than a fair process of discussion and debate which leads to good outcomes. These arguments do not automatically clinch the instrumental case for greater equality, since there is a fair amount of empirical controversy about the direction of effects, and because some arguments are about absolute levels of well-being and not necessarily inequality. However, the point remains that there are many possible ways in which greater equality may promote better aggregate outcomes for society.

Equality of Outcome or Equality of Opportunity

A problem with any form of outcome equalization is that it does not distinguish between people who put in more effort, or who make different choices, than others. In other words, equalizing outcomes may take away the incentives people have for doing better. One can decide then to bypass both means and outcome variables, but instead make the "rules of the game" fair, so that everyone has an equal chance of doing well as defined generally or by the individual. The supposed benefit of this is that it will preserve incentives and allow people to earn what they deserve from what they choose. There are difficulties with this approach as well. First, how do we know that the playing field is really level and that the disadvantages some people have in terms of birth, luck, and societal constraints and other factors have in fact been eliminated? One can look at whether there is enough social mobility, but even then, perhaps the true test of equal opportunity is that incomes are at least made less unequal. Second, one can ask why one needs to promote incentives of certain kinds which do not really result in social improvements or even personal improvements. Hard work and saving, for instance, may not improve matters for society as a whole and for individuals. Many people are overworked because they are trying to consume more compared to others with the result, they are not better off by their own reckoning because others do the same and because they work more than they would like to.

How Unequal Are We?

We need to understand that every economy, including that of the United States, has regulations and norms. The notion of "free markets" is a myth. Lobbyists are always helping businesses gain special advantages. For example, our tariffs block cheap sugar imports to help sugar plantation owners. If we have excessive inequality, it's because our economic regulations and norms allow or encourage it. According to the U.S. Census Bureau inequality increased 24 percent from 1968 to 2012. We now have more inequality than any other affluent democracy in the developed world. Income disparities have become so pronounced that America's top 10 percent now average more than nine times as much income as the bottom 90 percent. Americans in the top 1 percent tower stunningly higher. They average over 40 times more income than the bottom 90 percent. But that gap pales in comparison to the divide between the nation's top 0.1 percent and everyone else. Americans at this lofty level are taking in over 198 times the income of the bottom 90 percent. The top 1 percent of America's income earners have more than doubled their share of the nation's income since the middle of the 20th century. American top 1 percent incomes peaked in the late 1920s, right before the onset of the Great Depression.

Wages in the United States, after taking inflation into account, have been stagnating for more than three decades. Typical American workers and the nation's lowest-wage workers have seen little or no growth in their real weekly wages. Unions have a much smaller economic presence than they did decades ago. With unions playing a smaller economic role, the gap between worker and CEO pay was eight times larger in 2016 than in 1980.

The result of this erosion in the condition of the less well-off has been devastating in the United States. Sir Angus Deaton, a Nobel Economist, says:

> Capitalism is not delivering to large fractions of the population; in the US, where the inequalities are clearest, real wages for men without a four-year college

> degree have fallen for half a century, even at a time when per capita GDP has robustly risen. Mortality rates are rising for the less-educated group at ages 25 through 64, and by enough that life expectancy for the entire population has fallen for three years in a row, the first time such a reversal has happened since the end of the first world war and the great influenza epidemic. Less educated Americans are dying by their own hands, from suicide, from alcoholic liver disease, and from overdoses of drugs. Morbidity is rising too, and they are also suffering from an epidemic of chronic pain that, for many, makes a misery of daily life. . . .
>
> Less-educated white men and women in America have had their lives progressively undermined, starting in the 1970s, and showing up, since 1990, in rising numbers of deaths from suicide, alcoholic liver disease, and drug overdoses. African Americans experienced a similar disaster thirty years earlier and the improvements in their lives since then have protected them to an extent. In the face of globalization and innovation, many of us would argue that American policy, instead of cushioning working people, has instead contributed to making their lives worse, by allowing more rent-seeking, reducing the share of labor, undermining pay and working conditions, and changing the legal framework in ways that favor business over workers. Inequality has risen not only due to wealth generation from innovation or creation, but also through upward transfers from workers. It is not inequality itself that is hurting people, but the mechanisms of enrichment.[9]

In the United States, wealth inequality is even more pronounced than income inequality. Wealth is total assets minus liabilities. Assets are everything owned from a personal residence and cash in savings accounts to investments in stocks and bonds, real estate, and retirement accounts. Liabilities are what a household owes: a car loan, credit card balance, student loan, mortgage, or any other bill yet to be paid. The most visible indicator of wealth inequality in America may be the *Forbes* magazine list of the nation's 400 richest. In 2018, the three men at the top of that list—Amazon founder Jeff Bezos, Microsoft founder Bill Gates, and investor Warren Buffett—held combined fortunes worth more than the total wealth of the poorest half of Americans. In 2018, Jeff Bezos accumulated roughly $150,000 per minute, as his net worth grew by $78.5 billion that year.[10]

In 1982, the "poorest" American listed on the first annual *Forbes* magazine list of Americas' richest 400 had a net worth of $210 million in today's dollars. The average member of that first list had a net worth of $590 million. In 2018, rich Americans needed net worth of $2.1 *billion* to enter the *Forbes* 400, and the average member held a net $7.2 billion, over 10 times the 1982 average after adjusting for inflation.[11]

If we want to shift the balance of winners and losers, then the regulations and norms must change. Some regulations are preventative, and others are corrective. Progressive tax schedules are corrective and redistribute excessive economic gains. Safety nets and social welfare programs are also corrective: they support those who suffer financially. Every nation has preventative regulations that govern economic fairness. During and after the Great Depression of the 1930s a wide variety of regulations were established around the world to prevent excessive inequality. Yet many of these rules were later weakened or removed, especially in the 1980s and 1990s. The result was an avalanche of deregulation and excess, culminating in the Great Recession of 2008. Under the Trump administration deregulation and tax cuts favoring the higher income brackets and corporations have increased inequality even further.

We cannot fix inequality without changing the rules that govern labor markets, tax levels, land use, etc. Decades of regressive legislation has built the current mountain of inequality. The sales tax itself is regressive, hitting lower income earners with a higher tax rate on their income. Some of the most popular proposals include: Raise the minimum wage; increase taxes on super-high incomes; a tax on wealth above a minimum level; close tax loopholes; cap CEO pay; and strengthen laws on nondiscriminatory hiring, compensation, and promotion practices for women and minorities.

HORIZONTAL EQUALITY: AMONG DIFFERENT GROUPS

Inequality is most commonly measured in terms of income by income groups, that is, vertical inequality. Such measures could also apply to expenditures, wealth, land holdings and other indicators which can be added across people.

A different measure of inequality, called horizontal inequality, refers to inequality of income or some other valued thing among different identifiable groups in an economy, such as ethnic or religious groups, gender, class or region. Thus, one may be interested in whether there is a difference between average incomes of whites, African-Americans and people of Hispanic origin in the United States, or between the average incomes of Hindus and Muslims in India, or between men and women who work for a wage, or between different provinces in China. The reason why we may be interested in this kind of inequality is that it can be explained by causes which are different from those of vertical inequality, it may raise different kinds of issues about why we should care about inequality, and it may require different kinds of public policies to reduce the inequality.

An important cause of inequality of the horizontal kind is discrimination along ethnic, religious, regional and gender lines. Let us begin with some data on wealth and income inequalities among racial groups. In 2016 the median

Black family, with just over $3,500, owned just 2 percent of the wealth of the nearly $147,000 the median White family owned. The median Latino family, with just over $6,500, owned just 4 percent of the wealth of the median White family. Put differently, the median White family had 41 times more wealth than the median Black family and 22 times more wealth than the median Latino family.

Families that have zero or even "negative" wealth (meaning the value of their debts exceeds the value of their assets) live on the edge, just one minor economic setback away from tragedy. Black and Latino families are much more likely to be in this precarious situation. The proportion of Black families with zero or negative wealth rose by 8.5 percent to 37 percent between 1983 and 2016 compared to 15.5 percent for white families. The proportion of Latino families with zero or negative net worth declined by 19 percent over the past 30 years but was still more than twice as high as the rate for Whites.

Income gaps across racial and ethnic groups persist and, in some cases, are wider than in 1970. Large gaps between the incomes of blacks and whites have narrowed only modestly in recent decades. In 2016, blacks at the 90th percentile of their distribution earned 68% as much as whites at their 90th percentile, the same as in 1970. At the median, blacks earned 65% as much as whites in 2016, up from 59% in 1970. Similarly, lower-income blacks narrowed the gap slightly from 47% in 1970 to 54% in 2016. While the income gap between blacks and whites closed somewhat from 1970 to 2016, Hispanics fell even further behind at all income levels. For example, at the high end of the income distribution, Hispanics earned 65% as much as whites in 2016 compared with 74% in 1970.

The gender wage gap in weekly earnings for full-time workers in the United States in 2017 was 18.1 percent, given that the ratio of women to men's median weekly full-time earnings was 81.8 percent. If part-time workers were included, the ratios of women to men's earnings would be even lower, as women are more likely than men to work reduced schedules, often in order to manage childrearing and other caregiving work.

This discrimination may be the result of the beliefs and behavior of individuals and groups in societies—for instance, white employers may discriminate against blacks in their hiring or salary decisions—or there may be discriminatory policies by a group which controls the state apparatus against other groups, by excluding these groups from positions of power and influence, and through the allocation of resources. If there is discrimination by private people, one could examine why such discrimination exists: is it purely due to prejudice or are there other underlying reasons such as competition for jobs?

We may be concerned about inequality because it may imply that people are being denied certain resources and rights purely based on prejudice which is difficult to defend as fair. But is discrimination based on inborn characteristics—such as race—always bad? Clearly, if a firm does not hire someone, or pays a lower wage to someone, only because of reasons of race, the answer should be obvious. However, in some cases it gets more complicated. For example, suppose an employer does not hire a person of a certain race because there is statistical evidence to show that *on average* people who belong to that race perform less well than others at this job. Further assume it is too costly or impossible to obtain detailed information on how these *particular people* will perform compared to the average? Although the employer is not necessarily prejudiced, this form of discrimination is problematic, partly because it is possible that if there is no discrimination, the statistical evidence of inferiority or what is called statistical discrimination may disappear in the longer run; because, given more chances, people from these categories could show that they are not inferior. The result is people of that type would not be hired or be hired much less frequently than people of other types. Is that unethical? While it may not be unethical for individuals, it may well be argued to be unethical from a social perspective. The fact that people of that type have less education may be because of past discrimination and that they do not have the incentives, since they are less likely to obtain the jobs. This is an example of the cumulative causation mechanism that makes racial and other inequalities persist, without there being any fundamental difference between people of different types. This is uneconomic and unethical, because different people who are not really different in ability are being treated differently by being treated as a class and because society would be more efficient if these people were hired because they would become more educated and more productive. In 2020, in the aftermath of the police murder of George Floyd, this reality has been recognized by many in the dominant white population (what African Americans have always known) for what it is—*systemic racism*.

Moreover, such inequality may have effects which are different from vertical inequality. For instance, it has been found that although vertical inequality is not a major explanation for violent civil conflicts, horizontal inequality may well be, because solidarity based on common ethnic or religious background may make it easier for different groups to coalesce against other groups. See Chapter 12 for details. Finally, some measures such as income redistribution through progressive income taxes may not be able to address inequality of this type; other methods, such as affirmative action in hiring and distribution of resources, proportional representation in government or seat reservations in legislative bodies may be called for.

Another dimension of horizontal inequality is the unit or domain in which it is measured. So far, we have focused mainly on a country. But other units are relevant too. For instance, one may be interested in inequality at a larger level, such as at the world level, or inequality at smaller levels, say within a family or within an urban area. Inequality within a family between men and women may be extremely important to understand the position of women in a society. In 2017 women earned 81.8 percent of men. Women's lower earnings are due to a number of factors, including lower earnings in occupations done mainly by women; lack of paid family leave and subsidized childcare; and discrimination in compensation, recruitment, and hiring. Measures to improve the quality of jobs held mainly by women, tackle occupational segregation, enforce equal pay and employment opportunities, and improve work family benefits for all workers will help the incomes of women and their families grow and strengthen the economy.

Inequality at the world level is important for a variety of reasons, especially in an increasingly interconnected world. Inequality has been on the rise across the globe for several decades. Some countries have reduced the numbers of people living in extreme poverty. But economic gaps have continued to grow as the very richest amass unprecedented levels of wealth. Credit Suisse defines "wealth" as the value of a household's financial assets plus real assets (principally housing), minus their debts. Among industrial nations, the United States is by far the top-heaviest, with much greater shares of national wealth and income going to the richest one percent than any other country. The world's richest one percent, those with more than $1 million, own 45 percent of the world's wealth. Adults with less than $10,000 in wealth make up 64 percent of the world's population but hold less than 2 percent of global wealth. The world's wealthiest individuals, those owning over $100,000 in assets, total less than 10 percent of the global population but own 84 percent of global wealth.

Since 1980, the share of national income going to the richest 1 percent has increased rapidly in the United States, Canada, China, India, and Russia and more moderately in Europe. World Inequality Lab researchers note that this period coincides with the rollback in these countries and regions of various post–World War II policies aimed at narrowing economic divides. By contrast, they point out, countries and regions that did not experience a post-war egalitarian regime, such as the Middle East, sub-Saharan Africa, and Brazil, have had relatively stable, but extremely high levels of inequality.

Rapid economic growth in Asia (particularly China and India) has lifted many people out of extreme poverty. But the global richest one percent has reaped a much greater share of the economic gains. Although their share of global income has declined somewhat since the 2008 financial crisis, at more than 20 percent it is still much higher than their 16 percent share in 1980.

CONCLUSION

The question of equality is a complex matter which raises many important ethical issues. Reasonable people can argue about whether or not equalization is a good idea, what should be equalized, and among whom equalization should take place. All these questions raise a number of issues which are not very easy to resolve, but surely worth considering carefully. I conclude with four comments.

First, there is no particular reason to expect the answers to these questions to be the same in all spheres of life. The principles governing different aspects of social, political, and economic life may be different, so that the issues concerning equality may have to be different to reflect these different principles.

Second, as noted earlier, inequality in some spheres may be causally related to inequality in other spheres, and these connections should be carefully borne in mind. For instance, inequality in education can lead to inequality in income, and inequality in income can lead to inequality in political voice and social connections, which in turn feed back into each other. Also, for instance, inequality between men and women inside the home may well interact with inequality in the workplace, because if women are not well paid at work their position at home may be adversely affected, and if women have an inferior position at home and have to bear the brunt of housework and childrearing, their opportunity to be equal participants in the labor market are adversely affected. This observation implies that there is a case for stressing equality in some spheres which have stronger effects on equality in other spheres, and that one should not confine attention to examining inequality in each sphere separately, because of the possible spillover effects.

Third, sometimes debates about equality are couched in favor or against perfect equality. In fact, most relevant analytical and policy discussions in economics are not about removing inequality altogether (whatever that means), but about *reducing* inequalities. There may be more agreement about this incremental view of equality rather than about complete equalization.

Thus, even if one believes that some inequality is justified because of the incentives and desert arguments, one may believe that the existing amount of inequality is too high in comparison to what is justified. It is clearly the case that inequality itself distorts incentives and restricts opportunities. How does this apply in the United States?

Compare two groups of children: one group is born into wealthy families, with parents willing and able to provide books, museum visits, high-quality schooling including private universities. A second group has parents who struggle to put food on the table, who live in areas where the schools are run-down and under-staffed, and where expectations are low and hope for the future not re-enforced in home or school. The impact of the coronavirus pandemic on schooling in the United States in 2020 highlighted the importance of inequality. When schools closed to live classes and sent students home for on-line learning it became clear that millions of low-income families did not have access to high speed internet services. We should expect children from the first group almost invariably to do better economically and they do. While some children from very disadvantaged backgrounds achieve success, most do not. The reality is that our vaunted social mobility is mostly a myth.

In fact, the United States has less social mobility than most other developed countries. Ron Haskins and Isabel Sawhill of the Brookings Institution show in their book *Creating an Opportunity Society*[12] how poorly the United States does. For example, 42 percent of those born in the bottom fifth of the income distribution remain there as adults. On the other hand, only 6 percent of those born into a family from the bottom fifth climb to the top fifth as adults. The United States at 42 percent mired in the bottom fifth has the least mobility when compared to Denmark at 25 percent, Sweden at 26, Finland at 28, Norway at 28; and Britain at 30.

Extreme income inequality shifts ever more political power from lower- and middle-class households to the richest. The Supreme Court decision in *Citizens United*, enabling the growth in Super PAC spending, is making this problem worse by increasing the importance of money in politics. The disparity in the distribution of wealth is even greater than that of income, so great, in fact, that the richest 400 people in the United States control more wealth than the entire bottom 50 percent of households. A number of these 400 are pouring in millions of dollars to influence elections which allows them to change the rules in their favor—for example, banning collective bargaining by public employees in Wisconsin and enacting so-called right-to-work laws in Indiana.

Fourth and finally, I have mostly discussed arguments about equality and inequality, and paid very little attention to the question of how to equalize incomes or whatever one is seeking to equalize. There are a number of possible policies that could help reduce inequality and substantial disagreement among economists and policy makers on which ones are the best. I will list a few that are typically endorsed by CST.

As far back as Pope Leo XIII's 1891 encyclical *Rerum Novarum*, CST has argued that it is a natural right for workers to form unions to bargain over wages and hours, conditions of work, and other issues that arise between workers and their employers. The growth in union membership in the late 1930s and early 1940s coincided with a falling share of income going to the top 10 percent. A strong labor movement means workers have more power to negotiate with their employers for a proportionate share of income growth. That power is precisely what corporations and policymakers doing their bidding have increasingly been eroding. Attacking unions makes sense from a bottom-line perspective: for corporations, an easy path to profits is in suppressing wages. As union membership has declined over the past 40-plus years, the top 10 percent have captured a greater and greater share of income. Breaking the momentum of rising inequality will require a much-strengthened labor movement. This in turn will require ambitious reforms to the laws governing union organizing and collective bargaining to level the playing field and return bargaining power to workers.

Most recently, anti-union interests have focused their attack on public-sector workers—the workforce with the highest rate of union representation. In 2018, a small group of foundations with ties to the largest and most powerful corporate lobbies celebrated their newest success: the Supreme Court decision in *Janus v. AFSCME Council 31*. The court ruling effectively stripped state and local government public-sector unions of their ability to collect fair share fees to cover the costs of representing workers who choose not to join their workplace's union. By eliminating fair share fees, the ruling goes a long way toward stripping workers of their ability to organize and bargain collectively.

A policy that helps reduce inequality *and poverty* is raises in the federal minimum wage law. It reduces inequality among wage earners because the minimum wage affects wages of low-wage workers and workers further up the wage scale by setting a wage floor. The minimum wage is also an important anti-poverty tool. The inflation-adjusted value of the federal minimum wage is about 25 percent less today than it was at its peak in 1968. Had policymakers enacted adjustments to keep the 1968 minimum wage rising with inflation, the black and Hispanic poverty rate would be 14 percent lower today, meaning 2.5 million fewer blacks and Hispanics would be in poverty.

Subsidiarity is a key part of CST. It calls for action first at the lowest levels possible for effective results. As an example, individual state policies are important in dealing with inequality and poverty. As an example, in 2010, the neighboring states of Wisconsin and Minnesota embarked on divergent political paths. Because these states were neighbors who had suffered similarly from the Great Recession that began in 2008, their post-recession economic performance provides useful evidence on the effect of divergent policy paths. The Wisconsin state legislature pursued an agenda centered on cutting taxes, shrinking government, and weakening unions. In contrast, Minnesota lawmakers enacted a slate of priorities: raising the minimum wage, strengthening safety net programs and labor standards, and boosting public investments in infrastructure and education, financed through higher taxes (largely on the wealthy). The evidence shows clearly superior performance—faster income (7.2 to 5.1 percent) and employment growth (11.0 to 7.9 percent)—in Minnesota.

In Chapter 12, I will elaborate on the importance of subsidiarity by focusing on the economic role of families and mediating institutions. But first, I will grapple with the global financial crisis in Chapter 10 and the development of poor countries in Chapter 11.

NOTES

1. Letter from Pope Francis to Prime Minister David Cameron for the G8 Meeting, June 17-18, 2013. http://w2.vatican.va/content/francesco/en/letters/2013/documents/papa-francesco_20130615_lettera-cameron-g8.html

2. Francis, *Evangelii Gaudium*, para. 53, 59.

3. This section draws upon joint work with Amitava Krishna Dutt from our book, *Economics and Ethics: An Introduction* (New York: Palgrave Press, 2010; revised paperback edition, 2013).

4. USCCB, *Economic Justice for All*, para. 24.

5. Adam Smith, *The Wealth of Nations*, 351-2.

6. Arthur Okun, *Equality and Efficiency: The Big Tradeoff* (Washington, D.C.: Brookings Institute, 1975).

7. One may wonder how it is possible for an increase in inequality to both increase growth through the savings argument mentioned earlier and reduce it by reducing aggregate demand, as just mentioned. Both effects are possible, but which one will prevail in a particular situation will depend on whether there is some degree of slack in the use of resources (like capital and labor) and whether technological change responds positively to the pressure of higher aggregate demand.

8. An impeccably mainstream neoclassical analysis suggests that there is a perfectly "rational" alternative to going hungry or doing without the basic goods needed for survival. After weighing all of the probabilities, costs, and risks, a person can choose to allocate part of his or her labor to such anti-social activities as selling drugs, burglary, shop lifting, and mugging. This is not to argue that when wages fall below some minimum level every such person threatens the peace by becoming a criminal. Rather the argument is that to some extent the amount of crime committed by an optimizing agent is a function of its opportunity cost. If there is no legal work available or only at less than subsistence wages, then the opportunity cost is low. Whether you believe desperate people are driven to crime by poverty or that weak people are enticed into crime because the risks are not high enough, the fact remains that crime creates enormous costs for the community in the form of negative externalities—loss of life and property, costs of law enforcement, and the psychic costs of fear and in-

security. See Andrew Schotter, *Free Market Economics: A Critical Appraisal* (New York: Palgrave Macmillan, 1984).

9. Sir Angus Stewart Deaton, "Nobel Economist Says Inequality Is Destroying Democratic Capitalism." http://evonomics.com/nobel-economist-angus-deaton-capitalism-democratic/

10. Thomas Piketty, *Capital and Ideology* (Belknap Press: An Imprint of Harvard University Press, 2020).

11. These and the above facts on income and wealth inequality are from https://inequality.org/facts.

12. Ron Haskins and Isabel V. Sawhill, *Creating an Opportunity Society* (Washington, D.C.: Brookings Institution Press, 2009).

Chapter Ten

The Economy as a Casino

Ethics and the Global Financial Crisis

In this chapter I want to focus on the financial crisis that erupted in the United States in 2007-2008 and then spread to global financial markets and the global economy.[1] The causes, nature and consequences of the crisis have been extensively examined and debated in the academic literature, policy discussions and the popular press, and the story is well known. I want to analyze it in this chapter both as an economist and in terms of CST and general ethical norms. Let me start with a quote from Pope Francis:

> The financial crisis of 2007-08 provided an opportunity to develop a new economy, more attentive to ethical principles, and new ways of regulating speculative financial practices and virtual wealth. But the response to the crisis did not include rethinking the outdated criteria which continue to rule the world. (*Laudato Si*, para. 189)

Starting in 2007-08 the U.S. financial system imploded followed by the collapse of the economy into a continuing recession with unemployment hovering around the 10 percent level. To many economists, this appeared to be an example of John Maynard Keynes's dictum of 70 years earlier: "Speculators may do no harm as bubbles on a steady stream of enterprise. But the position is serious when enterprise becomes the bubble on a whirlpool of speculation. When the capital development of a country becomes a by-product of the activities of a casino, the job is likely to be ill-done."[2]

The Obama administration inherited this collapsing economy and stock market and responded with a large program of government spending. With the Republican capture of the senate in 2010, constant restraints were put on expansive policies under the banner of fiscal responsibility. Despite this, recovery moved along with a revival in consumer spending and the stock market booming, finally getting unemployment down after 8 years to 4.7%. The Trump administration enacted a massive tax cut in 2017 that helped drive the unemployment rate to a 50-year low of 3.5 percent. Republicans did not raise issues of fiscal responsibility despite there being a trillion-dollar deficit. Unfortunately, the newest crisis, the coronavirus pandemic of 2020, has required massive cutbacks in work and production so that the unemployment rate has gone up to 15 percent. Hopefully, with the discovery of a vaccine, the economy will return to more normal operations.

Following the financial collapse that led to the Great Depression of the 1930s, the U.S. government passed the Glass-Steagall Act, which among other things separated commercial banking activities from riskier investment bank operations. However, since 1980 one of the main thrusts of public policy has been to free up markets by deregulation (including repeal of the Glass-Steagall Act), cutting taxes, and eliminating or reducing social programs such as welfare. These policies have been pursued by both Republican and Democratic administrations. The result has been constant federal deficits, a dramatic increase in income and wealth inequality, periodic financial scandals, decay of public services and infrastructure, the growth of large banks to ever greater importance, and finally the collapse of the financial services sector and the slow-to-overcome economic recession.

A widely-held view is that the stuff of crises—arrogance, greed, unacknowledged conflicts of interest, unethical behavior, lack of transparency, failed leadership, and insufficient accountability—fueled "an industry out of control." Banks and other financial institutions got themselves, and the whole economy, into trouble by overleveraging, that is, they borrowed heavily, used relatively little of their own capital, and bought extremely risky assets. In doing so, they used confusingly complex instruments. The prospect of high returns and thus high compensation led account managers to accept excessive risk, rather than seek more prudential investments. Banks made all these mistakes unknown to the public, because so much of what they were doing was "off the books"[3] financing. And the regulators appeared to be asleep, failing to use what little power the waves of deregulation had left them.

Beyond the discussion of these mistakes, which have received the greatest popular focus, attention has also been given to several other issues: the nature of the financial sector; the role of the economic profession and economic analysis in failing to predict the crisis and creating conditions increasing the likelihood of its occurrence; the implication of macroeconomic imbalances involving increases in debt and income inequality; and the political economy of changes in government policy resulting from the increasing influence of powerful interest groups.

Despite the plethora of issues that have been discussed, very little has been said specifically about ethical issues in economics and their relation to the global crisis, apart from some references to the role of "greed" in popular discussions.[4] To me, this provides another illustration of how economists and others think that economic and financial issues are separate from ethical considerations. I would argue, on the contrary, that ethical issues are very relevant for understanding the causes and effects of the crisis and subsequent recession and for reducing the possibility of their recurrence in the future. While it is beyond my scope to provide a comprehensive discussion of the issues involved, this chapter will comment on some ways that an analysis of economic ethics is relevant for understanding the crisis.

First, I will provide a brief review of some relevant features of the crisis by way of background. In the following two sections I will focus on how ethical issues affect the behavior of individuals and groups in the context of the crisis; examining first the notion of greed, which has been emphasized in the popular discussion, and relating it to social norms and then examining more broadly the role of changes in social norms in creating conditions which made the crisis more likely. In the final two sections I will discuss how the neglect of ethical issues in economics is at least partly responsible for bringing about the crisis; focusing first specifically on finance, and then I will comment on more general economic issues.

THE ECONOMIC CRISIS OF 2008

The financial crisis of 2008 illustrated vividly how markets often fail, yet economics textbooks went unchanged, failing to convey the fundamental flaws and systematic weaknesses of the free-market system. While most economists view financial markets as being self-adjusting and efficient, as shown, for instance, in efficient market theory, there are others who point to their inherent instability. A long view of financial history[5] and analytical approaches,[6] which take the future to be fundamentally uncertain (in the sense that there is no objective basis to determine the probabilities of future events and returns on assets), suggest that financial markets alternate between bouts of exuberant optimism, when asset prices and credit increase, and forlorn pessimism in which asset prices tumble and credit freezes. According to this view there is nothing special about the 2007-2008 crisis.

However, its severity and broad reach has been explained by the deregulation of United States financial markets; the appearance of new financial instruments, including derivatives such as mortgage-backed securities, collateralized debt obligations and credit default swaps; bank and leveraged buyouts of unregulated private equity funds; and remuneration policies in financial institutions that encouraged lending irrespective of future returns. All of these led to a huge increase in lending because banks were making loans and passing them on to other financial institutions which sold them by splitting them up in the form of derivatives. It also led to an increase in house prices which fuelled further borrowing and lending, linking the fortunes of large numbers of financial institutions. When the loans could not be repaid, there was a ripple effect throughout the financial system, which then froze lending. Since there are large movements of financial capital internationally, due to the removal of restrictions on international financial transactions, to compete for funds the financial crisis moved across national borders. Moreover, several other countries had their own financial bubbles based on real estate loans.

Greed and the Crisis

Blame for the crisis has often been placed on the greed of bankers and financiers. Following a 2009 speech on Wall Street supporting financial regulation, it was reported widely in the press that United States President Barack Obama's message was that the "[d]ays of reckless greed are over."[7] He is reported to have said that "We will not go back to the days of reckless behavior and unchecked excess that was at the heart of this crisis, where too many were motivated only by the appetite for quick kills and bloated bonuses." Other politicians, including the former presidential candidate Senator John McCain, also used the word greed in describing the behavior of Wall Street and corporate executives.

Greed is a vice which can affect how economies operate and which can result from, and be increased by, engaging in some types of social activities. Given its importance in discussions of the crisis, it is worthwhile trying to make the concept more analytically precise. Despite the attention that the concept has received, especially in religion, a clear definition is not easy to find.[8]

One approach is to use the neoclassical concept of *homo economicus*, according to which individuals are seen as maximizing utility given the constraints that they face, and where individual utility depends on what (a) affects people directly (rather than on what affects others); (b) is affected only (or at least primarily) by material goods and money (rather than, say, leisure time spent with others); and (c) is insatiable (that is, more is always better). While this kind of individual behavior can be called greedy, it can lead to the view that greed has positive consequences if the conditions of the first welfare theorem of neoclassical economics (perfect competition and absence of distortions) are satisfied. In this case, "greed . . . is good," as the character Gordon Gekko famously stated in Oliver Stone's film *Wall Street*.[9] If all that went wrong is that during the financial crisis the conditions of that theorem were not satisfied, then greed led to bad outcomes and that is why it is bad, in a consequentialist sense. However, in CST, greed is more appropriately conceptualized in virtue ethics terms as a character trait or behavior which is ethically problematic independent of its consequences.

A more reasonable approach is to interpret greedy behavior as that which violates some socially accepted norms regarding what is permissible and what is not. Although this conceptualization may appear to be vague, it does not have the problems of being consequentialist or requiring an objective interpretation of what it means to break a law. Using this approach, greed can be interpreted as characteristics of people that lead them to not internalize and adhere to norms that are socially acceptable, and greedy behavior is behavior in which individuals break these norms for personal gain. Examples range from providing information that one considers to be untrue or withholding true and relevant information, to doing things which increase one's income without adequately considering how those actions affect others or society as a whole.

Interpreted in this way, how is greed responsible, even if only in part, for the financial crisis? I confine myself to a few illustrative comments. First, greed led financiers to conceal information in order to increase loans and sell assets, which contributed to the increases in indebtedness and the instability in financial markets. Although greedy behavior is not logically necessary for such instability—indeed, fundamental uncertainty can feed asset bubbles and debt expansion and subsequent busts—it can clearly exacerbate it. Second, greed led financiers to devise compensation systems—bonuses for short-term profits—that allowed them to gain from activities which created incentives to engage in these kinds of destabilizing behavior, so that greed fed greed. Third, greed arguably led financial elites to pressure the government into relaxing and preventing financial regulations with the purpose of increasing their incomes, which made the financial system more vulnerable. Greed is not the only factor, since the power of academic ideas, as we will argue later, also had a role to play in financial liberalization, and greed did not necessarily result in making all financial elites better off although some certainly benefited. Fourth, more generally, greed on the part of the rich arguably had an important role in bringing about increases in overall income inequality in countries like the United States, for instance, by engaging in business practices that depressed wages, and by supporting tax breaks for themselves. The result was a stagnation of the real incomes of others, which, in addition to other factors that increased vulnerability, led to large increases in consumer debt. While this arguably maintained consumption and aggregate demand in the short run, it proved to be unsustainable in the longer run as debt burdens grew and asset bubbles burst.

There is no doubt that greed—in the sense of breaking social norms in the pursuit of personal aggrandizement—is always present to some degree and places, but its role is likely to increase in some circumstances. Two major aspects of the 2008 crisis was its financial source and its international scope. Changes in the structure of economies have increased the size of the financial sector compared to that of the non-financial or "real" sector in many countries, and changes in communication technology and changes in policies regarding international capital flows have increased the importance of international financial transactions. It can be argued that both changes have given greed a more important role. The financial sector is arguably more likely to be a fertile ground for the conduct of greedy behavior. The financial sector deals in assets which are intangibles—rather than goods and services whose properties are more easily perceived by buyers and sellers—the characteristics of which are not well understood by market participants, thus, there is greater scope for obfuscation and prevarication by those who are able to do so and gain from.[10] Second, the fact that many market participants are working in isolation using computers instead of dealing face-to-face with people, makes social restraints on greedy behavior less effective. Third, the fact that financial actors often work in organizations or are competing with other such actors, makes it more likely for greedy behavior to become infectious, due to its acceptance in the organization's culture or in the culture of the financial community at large. Finally, the fact that the amounts that are traded in a very small period of time in these markets can be very large, because they do not require the physical movement of goods and people, makes the effects of greedy behavior more pernicious. Regarding international transactions, it is possible that interactions between people from different countries can lead to their being less constrained by the social norms that are sometimes shared within a country.[11]

All these factors can explain why greedy behavior in the form of violations of social norms for private gain increased during the run up to the crisis. Such behavior, over time, is likely to change norms as well. A cumulative dynamic was arguably created which made the crisis more likely.

Social Norms and the Crisis

In addition to the specific characteristics of financial markets and international financial transactions which, I have argued, increased the role of greed, there were general socio-economic changes which altered social norms.

In 1980 the elections of Ronald Reagan in the United States and Margaret Thatcher in Great Britain represented an alternative social consensus to the prevailing Keynesian welfare state—a return to less government and freer markets. The result of these political changes has been the growth of an economic philosophy dominated by an ideology fixated on competition and success as the measure of a person's worth. Although many will deny that this describes the essence of U.S. economic philosophy,[12] daily events are reminders of its sway, as reflected in: the exaltation of sports and movie stars, and Wall Street and corporate executives; the negative attitude of Congress and the business community toward welfare legislation; and the whole philosophy of success which measures the value of people by their income.

The promotion of financial success and self-interest first became epitomized in the 1980s by Wall Street stockbrokers and merger specialists and the goal of newly minted Harvard MBAs to make $1 million a year before their thirtieth birthday. By 2000 it was hedge fund managers and derivates traders. Writing in 2019, billionaires, particularly those from the high-tech world, are the most admired and celebrated public figures. In 2016 a definitely low-tech billionaire was elected president of the United States.

It is easy to understand, if not condone, the greed-driven behavior within the financial sector that crossed the line to unethical insider trading, excessive risk taking, and the ignoring of their prudential obligations as custodians of other people's money. Since the movers and shakers of the financial world were the Masters of the Universe, it is clear how government regulators were easy to convince that all was well. And given everyone's acceptance of the economics profession's teaching that markets know best, there was little reason to question what appeared to be unending success. Thus, this social consensus led to an atrophy of the normal legal, institutional, and social mechanisms which, in earlier times, might have countered those ethical lapses and their consequences.

THE ETHICS OF FINANCE AND THE FINANCIAL SECTOR

From a discussion of greed and changes in social norms and their effects on individual and group behavior in bringing about the crisis, I turn to the problems that arose out of economists' neglect of the ethical aspects of the finance sector and the economy as a whole.

Although there has been some discussion of the effects of a rise in the financial sector, in general the ethics of finance have escaped attention.[13] Financial activity, like any other kind of activity, if done voluntarily, is not something on which it is believed "scientists" can or should pass value judgments. But if we reject this claim and delve into the ethics of finance, a central question we need to ask is whether the financial sector—especially as large as it has become—is good for society and whether the high level of returns to finance are justified.

There has been a tendency in the past to denigrate financial activities such as money lending. Religious traditions, including Jewish, Christian, and Islamic, all looked down upon usury, and some denounced and even forbade charging interest. Aristotle opined that money is barren and that usury, among all the businesses, "is most contrary to nature."[14] Many other classical Greek and Roman writers agreed with Aristotle as did most medieval authors including St. Thomas Aquinas.

However, Aristotle's argument was ridiculed by later writers, including Jeremy Bentham,[15] by drawing attention to the positive consequences of financial activity. They have a point. Indeed, there is no question that the availability of finance can make possible many kinds of activities, including production and consumption of expensive products such as housing, automobiles, and appliances. The provision of finance to low-income farmers can allow increases in production made possible using purchased inputs, which can increase the income of the farmers and help to increase food production and increase food security for others. The extension of finance to large firms can increase production and investment, increasing the rate of growth of the economy and increasing employment growth.[16]

But these possible *consequentialist* benefits do not address the *deontological or virtue* perspectives[17] to which Aristotle, Aquinas, and others drew attention, that is, whether the activity of financing, which does not involve the creative activity that innovation and production does, deserves the rewards it gets in terms of interest or other returns.[18] The financial services industry has frequently combined the nakedly honest pursuit of power and wealth for the few with a legal license for objectively criminal, immoral behavior that harms the many. The scope is wide and outright scandalous of the banking systems' deprivations:

> Examples of how banks . . . have ripped off ordinary clients include selling subprime mortgages to vulnerable customers, rigging inter-bank lending rates, fiddling foreign exchange transactions, levying usurious interest rates on payday loans and credit cards and imposing extortionate charges for overdrafts. Meanwhile, banks and other financial institutions have engaged in money laundering, tax avoidance, the promotion of toxic products, reckless risk-taking, the abuse of mortgage bearers (not least foreclosures and repossession) as well as clearly usurious extortion and gambling with people's savings.[19]

Moreover, the idea that financial activity invariably has good consequences is questionable, especially when the financial sector becomes very large in relation to the rest of the economy. Many writers in the history of economic thought have been concerned with the problems that can arise from financial markets. Sen discusses the views of the Indian politician and philosopher Kautilya (who flourished 300 BC), Aristotle and even Adam Smith, among others. As the quote in the opening paragraph of this chapter notes, John Maynard Keynes worried that the economy was being turned into a casino. Mainstream neoclassical economics, when it allows for asymmetric information, also implies that market failures can arise from informational problems, leading to inefficient outcomes.[20] In addition to inefficiency, the large size of the sector which is subject to financial fragility makes the entire economy more crisis prone and people more vulnerable. When asset prices tumble and credit freezes, the real sector is adversely affected as investment, output and employment drop and unemployment rises, leading to reductions in income and consumption. These effects were felt during the 2007-2008 crisis and subsequent recession, when many people lost their jobs due to the recession and their homes due to foreclosures. Also, large increases in income and asset inequality have occurred with the rise in the importance of the financial sector that are difficult to justify in terms of any theory of justice, including that of CST, and therefore are difficult to be seen as a good consequence. This rise in inequality also increases the power of financial interests to affect legislators and push for policy changes which are intended to bring about further increases in their income.

The neglect of these issues has led to the failure to ask what the financial sector does for society and whether and why the high rewards to financial activity are justified. This, in turn, has led to an uncritical acceptance of the growing size of the financial sector, an acceptance which arguably had consequences which made economists in general fail to recognize the crisis and what it could do, and to support policies which made the crisis more likely.

THE NEGLECT OF ETHICS, ECONOMIC ANALYSIS, AND THE CRISIS

The failure to examine the ethics of the financial sector is of course a reflection of the general tendency of many economists to neglect ethical issues. This neglect does not imply that ethics are left out of economic theory and policy analysis, which I argued in Chapter 3 to be impossible, but that particular goals of a good society have been emphasized by default, that is, the goals of promoting individual freedom and economic growth and efficiency.

In the analysis of the financial sector, this bias is reflected in the use of terms like the *efficient* market hypothesis, capital market *liberalization*, and financial *liberalization* as opposed to financial *repression*. This choice of words, discussed in Chapter 3, suggests hidden values in the apparently value-free terms.

The removal of regulations on banks, of the type embodied in the U.S. Glass-Steagall Act of 1933 that limited commercial banks' ability to engage in transactions involving financial securities and their association with securities firms, and the decision to not regulate markets for new securities, including derivatives, can be traced to this problem. The efficient-market hypothesis basically suggests that financial markets operate efficiently, in the sense that it fully uses all the information available at the time financial investment decisions are made, so that it is not possible for someone to make consistently higher returns on investments than the average returns in the market when risk is adjusted for. This hypothesis has been widely taken to provide a justification of deregulation: if the market operates efficiently by itself, why regulate it? Without going into the problems regarding the assumptions on which the hypothesis is based—such as utility maximization, objectively calculable risk rather than uncertainty, and the rational expectations which state that individuals consider all information available, and the empirical tests of that approach, I wish to stress here the implied focus on efficiency for supporting market freedom. The lack of regulation, of course, was caused by a variety of reasons, including the strong political pressures imposed by financial interests and by the role some economists played as their "hired guns."[21] However, the acceptance of these pressures arguably had something to do with the views of the economics profession in favor of relatively unregulated markets, especially financial markets, and to a large part this can be seen to be the result of the failure to take ethical issues seriously.

The focus on efficiency and growth also arguably had the effect of policymakers being more concerned with the problems of government debt; thereby reducing the ability of governments to pursue expansionary fiscal policies sufficient to reach full employment. It also meant not giving sufficient attention to the plight of the unemployed and the income of low-income groups. All of this is not just the consequence of not taking ethical issues seriously, it also is undoubtedly related to the nature of rewards in the economic profession, and also—as mentioned in the discussion on financial market policies—to the power and influence of those who believe that they benefit from such policies.

In contradiction to our argument, it has sometimes been claimed that the crisis in the United States is largely a consequence of government attempts to increase lending on housing for low-income households, to provide a salve to address their economic plight; so that it was government concern for equality that led to the crisis. The empirical evidence does not show how much of the housing bubble was caused by lending to low-income households, and to what extent this lending was the result of government policy rather than loan pushing by deregulated lenders. Regardless, this criticism does not negate the basic problems of irresponsible behavior in the financial sector, slack regulation by the public sector, and an overall policy stance which tolerated increasing inequality in the name of efficiency and market freedom.

WILL IT HAPPEN AGAIN?

A key question needs to be answered: has financial sector reform been enough to significantly reduce the risk of future implosions? In turn a key issue in answering that question is the very large size of the major banks and the fact that they are "too big to fail." This has an unfortunate incentive effect on bank executives if they know they will always be bailed out even if they are reckless in their risk taking. This gives rise to what in the insurance industry is called a "moral hazard." When a person buys auto theft insurance, for example, they have less incentive to be careful, say, by locking the car doors. If their car gets stolen, they will be compensated by the insurance company. Likewise, bank executives will be tempted to take on more risk than is prudent when they know they will be bailed out by government as happened in the 2008 financial crisis.

Hoping to prevent another financial crisis in the United States, Congress passed and President Obama accepted the Dodd-Frank Act; that, among many provisions, put in place controls to keep big banks from failing. A key requirement forces too-big-to-fail banks to make themselves less dangerous by adding lots of capital to safeguard against losses, undergo stress tests and come up with a road map for how to safely unwind them.

The Dodd-Frank law has not kept the banks from getting bigger than ever. At the beginning of 2018, for example, JPMorgan had amassed an incredible $2.56 trillion in assets.[22] That's nearly twice as much as at the end of 2006 when the subprime mortgage bubble was beginning to burst. A chunk of JPMorgan's growth is due to its government-backed rescues of failing Bear Stearns and Washington Mutual. Bank of America and Deutsche Bank are ranked one level below JPMorgan on the "systemically important" list published by the Financial Stability Board. Bank of America's asset holdings have risen by 56% since the end of 2006 to $2.28 trillion. Deutsche Bank's asset size has increased by 21% over that span, according to FactSet. Wells Fargo, which acquired failing Wachovia during the financial crisis, holds assets of $1.93 trillion. That is up nearly 300% since the end of 2006. "If and when another crisis hits, the biggest players will be far larger than they were in the last crash," S&P Global Market Intelligence wrote in a report.[23]

Despite their growing size, big banks are considered much healthier than a decade ago. They have raised more than $1.5 trillion in capital since the crisis, giving them vast resources to cushion losses in a future crisis. U.S. banks are considered particularly sturdy given the 2010 Dodd-Frank Wall Street reform law.[24]

However, "too big to fail" is a threat that should not be ignored. The financial system is the life blood of the economy. Firms need to raise funds for investment purposes from banks, other financial institutions, and from the bond and stock markets. Consumers borrow from banks and credit unions to finance lumpy purchases such as automobiles, houses, appliances, and the like. Thus, the financial system is deeply intertwined with the entire economy, and if a very large bank or other financial institution goes bankrupt, it takes many other firms down with it, threatening the entire economy. Thus, the political reality is that very large financial institutions will not be allowed to go under whether there is Democratic or Republican control of government.

If large banks and other financial institutions will not be allowed to go bankrupt what can be done to reduce the incentives to take on too much risk? One possibility, of course, is to break up existing banks above some maximum size and enact regulations that will make it difficult for others to grow beyond that maximum. Then the much smaller banks can be allowed to fail when they overextend. However, this is an unlikely possibility. Neither political party has been serious about down-sizing over-grown financial institutions. Why? Executives in the financial services industry are major contributors to both parties. The report of the Financial Crisis Inquiry Committee reported that the financial industry spent $2.7 billion on lobbying from 1999 to 2008, while individuals and committees affiliated with it made more than $1 billion in campaign contributions. In addition, government regulators often move back and forth between the private sector and government. As a high-level example, Goldman Sachs paid Larry Summers $135,000 for one speech just before he was appointed to be President Obama's economic adviser. The Citizens United decision by the Supreme Court allowing corporations themselves to make unlimited political contributions has magnified the banks' political clout making it even more unlikely that Congress or the administration will enforce a banking reform that includes breaking up large banks.

If breaking up the very large financial institutions is not on the table, what other policies might be possible to avert another implosion caused by the financial sector taking on excessive risk? What is needed are policies that reduce the incentive for risk taking and/or policies that make it difficult to grow ever larger.

A partial, piecemeal approach would, among other things, establish minimum capital requirements for all large financial institutions above a certain size. But here the reality is that under the administration of President Trump there has been a weakening of the Dodd-Frank legislation that had provisions to set minimum reserve requirements. For a second possibility, a good case can be made for a securities transfer excise tax; it could raise an estimated $100 billion a year in revenue, and it would discourage dubious short-term, speculative practices while fostering a more stable supply of long-run capital funds.[25] Even these proposals were fought by the financial services industry, particularly by the largest institutions. And neither the Congress nor the administration strongly pushed them.

I recognize that there will be opposition to any attempt to re-regulate the financial system. This will be a struggle that will not be won overnight. So, what is a person to do in the meantime? Instead of wringing our hands and saying "woe is me," we do what we can do. First, do everything in our power to keep the issue of financial instability and the promise of reform before the policy makers—write our representatives, donate money to internet groups that are keeping the issue alive, write letters to the editor of our local newspaper, and all the other traditional things. Also push our parish priest and our bishop to join the cause by reminding them that these financial implosions result in damaging effects on the poor. This is the real issue—what happens to people, particularly the poor. For 30 years wages have stagnated, and poverty has worsened as the economy has come more to resemble a casino than a productive system. Second, shift our financial accounts from the big banks to our local community bank or credit union, a version of the 1980s Republican policy of "starve the beast."

As I write during the first half of 2020, the collapse of the economy due to the coronavirus pandemic will test whether the banking system that emerged from the 2008 crisis can survive the stresses of failed mortgages, defaulted loans, and drawn down reserves.

Whether the banking system is successful or not in surviving this new crisis, it may be that political reform will be needed before the power of the financial sector can be restrained and reformed to serve all the people including the poorest and least powerful. That too requires us to do what we can do, letting our representatives know that we will hold them accountable as we expect them to hold the financial services sector accountable.

This chapter has shown how general ethical issues are relevant for analyzing and understanding events. Given the importance of the 2008 global financial crisis and the Great Recession that followed, I have used it as an appropriate event to examine. I have argued that an analysis of ethical considerations that affect norms which influence the behavior of actors in financial markets and other sectors of the economy can increase our understanding of the genesis, spread and continuation of the crisis. I have also examined how the role of greed, which has attracted a fair amount of popular attention, can be given clear analytical foundations. I have also argued that neglect of ethical issues by economists in the study of finance and financial markets, and the economy in general, have created conditions which made the 2008 financial crisis more likely to occur.

NOTES

1. This chapter has drawn heavily on Amitava Krishna Dutt and Charles K. Wilber, *Economic and Ethics: An Introduction*, 2nd edition (London: Palgrave Press, 2013).
2. John Maynard Keynes, *The General Theory of Employment, Interest and Money*, ch. 12 (London: Macmillan, 1936).
3. Off-balance sheet financing is an accounting practice whereby companies record certain assets or liabilities in a way that prevents them from appearing on the balance sheet. It is used to keep debt-to-equity and leverage ratios low, facilitating cheaper borrowing and preventing covenants from being breached.
4. For exceptions, see Ned Dobos, Christian Barry, and Thomas Pogge, *Global Financial Crisis: The Ethical Issues* (Basingstoke, UK, and New York: Palgrave Macmillan, 2011); and Y. V. Reddy, "Ethics and the World of Globalised Finance," in Y. V. Reddy, *Global Crisis, Recession and Uneven Recovery* (Hyderabad: Orient Black Swan, 2011), 31-43. Note, however, that the contributions in the first book are mostly by ethicists and public intellectuals who are not economists, and the second book is by a policymaker rather than an academic economist.
5. Charles P. Kindleberger, *Panics, Manias and Crashes. A History of Financial Crises* (New York: Basic Books, 1978).
6. See Keynes. *The General Theory,* and Hyman Minsky, *Stabilizing an Unstable Economy* (New Haven, CT: Yale University Press, Twentieth Century Fund, 1986).
7. See, for instance, the report in *The Christian Science Monitor*, September 14, 2009.
8. See Phyllis A. Tickle, *Greed* (New York: Oxford University Press, 2004), for a discussion of religious perspectives. For a wide-ranging examination following the crisis, see Alexis Brassey and Stephen Barber, eds., *Greed* (Houndmills, Basingstoke, UK: Palgrave-Macmillan 2009).
9. The full quote is: "The point is, ladies and gentlemen, that greed, for lack of a better word, is good. Greed is right, greed works. Greed clarifies, cuts through, and captures the essence of the evolutionary spirit. Greed, in all of its forms; greed for life, for money, for love, knowledge has marked the upward surge of mankind. And greed, you mark my words, will not only save Teldar Paper, but that other malfunctioning corporation called the USA. Thank you very much."

10. See Reddy, *Ethics*, 2011.

11. Reddy, *Ethics*, 2011.

12. Most economists would deny this characterization. See the research of the American Enterprise Institute. https://www.aei.org/

13. A notable exception is Amartya K. Sen, "Money and Value: On the Economics and Ethics of Finance," *Economics and Philosophy* 9, no. 2 (1993): 203-227, on which this section draws.

14. Aristotle (b350 BC), I, 1258B, p. 49-50, quoted from Sen, "Money and Value." Sen also provides an excellent and wide-ranging discussion of attitudes towards usury and finance in early writers on antiquity, in both the West and the East, and their later critics.

15. Jeremy Bentham, *In Praise of Usury* (London: Payne, 1790).

16. It has been argued, along similar lines, that unlike the purpose of "real" sectors, which provide material goods to people, such as food, housing and clothing, the social purpose of the financial sector is unclear (see, for instance, Dobos et al., *Global Financial Crisis*, 17). This line of argument is problematic both because it ignores the fact that material goods may not necessarily satisfy only social "needs" but at least to some extent "wants" created by the sales promotion efforts of firms, and because it does not take into account the fact that the financial sector may facilitate the real sector's ability to produce goods and services.

17. As spelled out in Chapter 5, ethical theories are sometimes classified into three basic types: consequentialist, deontological, and virtue theories.

18. See Sen, "Money and Value."

19. Adrian Pabst, "Catholic Social Thought and Post-liberal Political Economy," *Radical Orthodoxy Annual Review* (2014): 5-6. https://www.academia.edu/7629696/Catholic_Social_Thought_and_Post-liberal_Political_Economy?email_work_card=title

20. See, for instance, Joseph E. Stiglitz, "Information and Economic Analysis: A Perspective," *Economic Journal* no. 95 (1981): 21-41.

21. Some of these issues are discussed in Charles Ferguson's film, *Inside Job*; see also Charles Ferguson, *Predator Nation: Corporate Criminals, Political Corruption, and the Hijacking of America* (New York: Crown 2012).

22. See https://money.cnn.com/2017/11/21/investing/banks-too-big-to-fail-jpmorgan-bank-of-america/index.html for this and the following statistics.

23. banks-too-big-to-fail

24. banks-too-big-to-fail

25. See more about this in Charles K. Wilber, "Awakening the Giant: Strategies for Restarting the U.S. Economy," *America: The National Catholic Weekly* 203, no. 10 (October 18, 2010): 13-16.

Chapter Eleven

Integral Human Development

Is development more than an economic process? Does economic development itself entail and/or require cultural and political change? Is measuring the impact on human dignity of economic development policies an important criterion of success? Does development raise ethical issues as well as economic ones? Pope Francis answers with an urgent and forceful yes:

> The urgent challenge to protect our common home includes a concern to bring the whole human family together to seek a sustainable and integral development, for we know that things can change. The Creator does not abandon us; he never forsakes his loving plan or repents of having created us. Humanity still has the ability to work together in building our common home.[1]

Is the consumer-driven development of the advanced countries an appropriate model for developing countries in the globalizing world of today? Pope Francis responds in *Laudato Si*: "The economy accepts every advance in technology with a view to profit, without concern for its potentially negative impact on human beings . . . . Yet by itself the market cannot guarantee integral human development and social inclusion." And he goes on to state that we must not allow the invisible forces of the market to regulate the economy, while allowing negative impacts on society and nature, such as economic recessions, environmental pollution and income inequality, to be merely collateral damage.[2] Rather we are called to control the unrestricted pursuit of profit by allowing ethics to guide us as citizens and consumers so that both the planet and all peoples can thrive.

These are among the core issues that Christian economists debate when considering the meaning and purpose of development. For example, see the work of Javier Iguíñiz,[3] Denis Goulet,[4] Pete Danner,[5] James Weaver,[6] Kenneth P. Jameson,[7] Charles K. Wilber.[8]

DEVELOPMENT IN THE WESTERN WORLD

Before exploring the issues facing poor countries today and the proposed development policies, it is worthwhile to briefly review the rise of the modern economy in the Western world that we discussed in Chapter 4. Two facts stand out from an examination of the history of modern capitalist development. First, capitalism has succeeded in producing quantities of goods and services unprecedented in history; second, it has done so in a temporally and spatially uneven manner. The economies of some nations take off into a self-sustaining growth, with other nations eventually catching up. Still others, the loosely called "developing countries," seem to be left hopelessly behind. This pattern occurs across nations as well as across regions within nations.

In both industrial and poor countries, the creative-destructive process of development has created socio-political tensions both because of its uneven nature and because of its challenge to traditional values and ways of life. Today this is true particularly in countries with strong Islamic roots and in countries where readily identifiable minorities control the wealth of the society.

A simple policy of free markets and free elections may not advance the welfare of the poor in the world, and it must be remembered that the Western world did not develop that way itself. Development was slow, its major transformation spread over more than a century.

It was only after centuries of struggle that capitalism established its claim to legitimacy, for it involved a code of economic behavior and a system of human relations sharply at variance with traditional religious customs and values. Originality, self-confidence, and tenacity of purpose were required to initiate and carry on this struggle. This was the role entrepreneurs played. However, economic reasons alone were insufficient to account for the extraordinary power of entrepreneurship and rational profit-seeking in the modern world.

The Modernist Tradition vs. Cultural Values

How does this historical experience of the rise of capitalist economies in the now developed world impact our theory and practice of development today? Mainstream views of development today continue to follow in the Modernization tradition that arose in the aftermath of WW II. On this view the primary measure of development continues to be a self-reinforcing tendency to economic growth and material progress. It is from this basic developmental reality that other positive features of a good society spring, like better health care, improved education, and democratic governance. As Benjamin Friedman says at the close of his moral defense of economic growth, "Only with sustained economic growth, and the sense of confident progress that follows from the advance of living standards for most of its citizens can a nation hope to achieve an open, tolerant, and democratic society."[9]

Over time it has become clear that an equitably growing economy requires financial capital, the adoption of efficient technologies, investment, human capital, entrepreneurship and market-promoting policies and institutions, which begs the question of how to get nations to build and use these necessary attributes. For many theorists, inquiries into this question lead directly to issues of how cultural and social adaptation like that which occurred historically in the West can be facilitated so as to accommodate the needs of modern market economies throughout the world.

On the other hand, many economists believe that socio-cultural attributes are essentially irrelevant to economic development. Instead, the road to development is paved with market-promoting economic policies and institutions. In his treatment of 21st-century development challenges, Jeffrey Sachs calls the importance of culture a myth, saying that cultures often follow rather than lead economic change and that culture-based arguments "are usually made based on prejudice rather than measurable evidence."[10] Summarizing these lines of thought, David Throsby points out that "mainstream texts in economic development have no time for culture; taking three such texts at random, an inquisitive reader can find no reference to culture in the subject indexes of any of them."[11] For such theorists, it is no surprise that nations of greatly diverse cultures, like Ireland, South Korea, France, the United States, and now China and India can all enjoy the fruits of economic progress without seeing culture as either a help or a hinderance in the development process.

However, this dismissal of local culture is rejected by a growing number of social scientists like anthropologist Arturo Escobar. He argues that the discourse dominating development thought and practice today is of Western origin and thus embeds the superiority of its cultural orientations in everything it says and does.[12] When the international development discourse emanates from rich country governments, universities, NGOs and multilateral organizations like the World Bank, all dominated by the institutions of Western and/or Northern culture, is it any surprise that its democratic capitalist ways of life and thought are privileged over others? When international economic, political, and social institutions are structured on the basis of powerful democratic capitalist countries, is it any wonder that other cultures fail to compete successfully? In almost diametrical opposition to cultural modernizers, who believe Western-style cultural reforms are the way to developmental salvation for the poor world, Escobar believes they will bring destruction, for in disrespecting and ultimately undercutting their own cultures, the requisite cultural changes will cause local cultures to lose their identities, meaning systems and control over their own lives, resources and communities. There is in this argument a strong environmental orientation as well, for often people are dispossessed of their property and their livelihoods to make way for dams, agro-export products and mass production techniques that destroy traditional ways of life. Modernizers might think these to be progressive developments, but others believe they lead to domination, dispossession, violence, cultural chaos, and poverty.

Pope Francis has entered this debate by focusing on how the modern development process impacts people's lives and communities:

> It is true that we are children of a culture, at least in the Western world, which has exalted the individual to the point of turning it into an island, as if one can be happy alone. On the other hand, there are ideological views and political powers that have crushed the person, that have standardized it and deprived it of that freedom without which man no longer feels human. This standardization is also due to economic powers that wish to take advantage of globalization, instead of encouraging greater sharing among men, simply to impose a global market of which they themselves set the rules and reap the profits. The self and the community are not in competition with each other, but the self can mature only in the presence of authentic relationships, and the community is generative when its members are, together and individually. This is even more applicable to the family, which is the first cell of society and where we learn to live together. [13]

ECONOMIC DEVELOPMENT IN THE POST-WAR PERIOD

Modern development economics was born after World War II with the acceptance of the inevitability of political, social, and economic change in the non-industrialized countries. The problems of the poor countries of Southeastern Europe were the genesis of much of the initial work, and then the success in rebuilding Europe and Japan emboldened development economists to extend their work to the rest of the world. The break-up of the English and French colonial empires added further emphasis to issues of overcoming poverty. The growing cold war between the United States and its allies against the Soviet Union and its allies helped focus development attention on strategic areas of the so-called Third World. Development thought incorporated an optimism that change could be for the better and that conscious reflection on and control over change, often through national governments and international organizations, could harness change and bring about development.

Thus, the 1950s and 1960s were marked by optimism that world poverty could be conquered by economic growth. Since economists assumed that the question of the nature of a good society was already answered, the issue became one of solving certain practical problems. The good society was simply assumed to be an idealized version of the United States economy, that is, a market economy driven by a consumerist society. The key to a consumer society was growth of per capita income. Thus, the vast bulk of the development literature focused on economic growth rates as a *deus ex machina* to solve all problems.

In the 1970s the hope that underdevelopment would be soon conquered was dashed by growing unemployment and inequality and the intractability of absolute poverty. However, the 1970s also witnessed the birth of a new optimism to replace the old. The pursuit of "growth with equity" or a strategy of targeting "basic human needs" would succeed where economic growth failed.

The 1980s ushered in a period of greater caution. It became widely recognized that world poverty would not be eliminated with simple economic panaceas. Resource shortages (particularly of energy), environmental destruction, rising protectionism in the industrial world, militarism in the Third World, the international arms race, the structure of the world economy all made the design of development strategies a complex problem in political economy rather than a simple technical economic issue.

By the end of the 1990s the Washington Consensus[14] of free markets and free trade began to fall apart. Economists became more aware of the problems created by fast economic growth and slow social change, as well as the difficulty of defining development correctly. Development economics had to learn that "all good things do not go together," that rapid growth and economic development may be accompanied by severe social and political problems such as the loss of deeply felt cultural values, the breakup of community, and the emergence of authoritarian governments.

It is now into the second decade of the 21st century, a time when the old verities are collapsing. The rise of the BRICs—Brazil, Russia, India, China—using a wide variety of development approaches dominates development discussions. The cold war is a distant memory, the Eastern European countries have moved from centrally planned economies of the Soviet type to market-oriented countries. Regional and ethnic conflicts have moved to center stage in the international political arena with the most notable examples being the wars in Iraq, Syria, Afghanistan, the internal conflicts in much of the middle east, in Somalia, Rwanda, much of central Africa.

Despite all this, much has been accomplished since 1945. There has been rapid growth of GDP throughout the world, infant mortality has decreased dramatically, and life expectancy has increased rapidly; and access to education has been extended far beyond what would have been imaginable in 1945.

CST ON DEVELOPMENT

Despite the above noted successes of the post-war development of many poor countries, there remains serious side effects from the process of this development. At the heart of consumerist and profit-driven economic ideologies is a wrong-footed idea of dominion. The result is exploitation, and a throwaway attitude towards nature, culture, and human life itself. In *Evangelii Gaudium*, Pope Francis makes the crucial point that the dominant economic system is economically unsustainable and ethically indefensible:

> Human beings are themselves considered consumer goods to be used and then discarded. We have created a "throw away" culture which is now spreading. It is no longer simply about exploitation and oppression, but something new. Exclusion ultimately has to do with what it means to be a part of the society in which we live; those excluded are no longer society's underside or its fringes or its disenfranchised—they are no longer even a part of it. The excluded are not the "exploited" but the outcast, the "leftovers."[15]

Further, in his encyclical *Laudato Si*, he calls for a bold cultural revolution in our attitude to development and progress. He puts it rather bluntly: "Nobody is suggesting a return to the Stone Age, but we do need to slow down and look at reality in a different way, to appropriate the positive and sustainable progress which has been made, but also to recover the values and the great goals swept away by our unrestrained delusions of grandeur."[16]

While there are several reasons to be concerned with the ethics of the development process, there are three that have become prominent in CST. First, while it is recognized that development helps people by creating jobs, excessive consumption by some individuals and nations while at the same time other individuals and nations suffer from hunger and sickness is judged morally unacceptable. Income spent on luxuries could have been made available to others for their necessities. Typical is Pope Paul VI's statement: "The superfluous wealth of rich countries should be placed at the service of poor nations . . . Otherwise their continued greed will certainly call down upon them the judgment of God and the wrath of the poor." [17] The related problem of consumption spending on products produced under sweatshop conditions is recognized as a serious problem for the rights of workers and the obligations of employers.

Second, excessive development which threatens the earth's environment is morally condemned. Pope John Paul II stated: "Equally worrying is the ecological question which accompanies the problem of consumerism and which is closely connected to it. In his desire to have and to enjoy rather than to be and to grow, man consumes the resources of the earth and his own life in an excessive and distorted way."[18] Pope Francis's encyclical *Laudato Si*, as quoted at the beginning of this chapter, begins with an "urgent challenge to protect our common home . . . to bring the whole human family together to seek a sustainable and integral development, for we know that things can change."[19] Pope Francis calls the earth our "common home," which is like our sister and our mother. But we are damaging this familial relationship as we harm the environment. In so doing, we are damaging our relationship with other humans, particularly those least equipped to defend themselves: the poor and future generations. We are forgetting our interconnectedness with the earth and with all the people in the world now and the generations to come who depend on our good stewardship of the gift of creation. The encyclical firmly posits that a truly ecological approach is also inherently social—an approach that simultaneously hears the cry of the earth and the cry of the poor. Two quotes from Pope Francis highlight CST's view of the importance of the environment to an integral development: "May the relationship between man and nature not be driven by greed, to manipulate and exploit, but may the divine harmony between beings and creation be conserved in the logic of respect and care."[20] "We received this world as an inheritance from past generations, but also as a loan from future generations, to whom we will have to return it!"[21]

Pope John Paul II argues further that there must be social intervention on the international level. To carry out this effort, "it is not enough to draw on the surplus goods which in fact our world abundantly produces: it requires above all a change of life-styles, of models of production and consumption, and of the established structures of power which today govern societies."[22] This strikes at the very heart of a consumption-oriented market system.

Third, treating consumption as the primary goal of development—that is, focusing on *having* instead of *being*—is judged detrimental to human dignity. It is this third concern that I will expand on here. As noted in Chapter 2, the Catholic tradition condemns the materialist view of human welfare. In his 1968 encyclical, *Populorum Progressio*, Pope Paul VI wrote:

> Increased possession is not the ultimate goal of nations or of individuals. All growth is ambivalent. It is essential if man is to develop as a man, but in a way

> it imprisons man if he considers it the supreme good, and it restricts his vision. . . . Both for nations and for individual men, avarice is the most evident form of moral underdevelopment.[23]

Pope Francis has continued and expanded this concern with the development of poor countries. He says in an address during a Dicastery for Promoting Integral Human Development on the fiftieth anniversary of "Populorum Progressio":

> What does full or integral development mean. . . . It means *integrating the different peoples of the earth*. The duty of solidarity requires us to seek fair ways of sharing, so that there is no longer that dramatic inequality between those who have too much and those who have nothing, between those who discard and those who are discarded. Only the path of integration between peoples can permit to humanity a future of peace and hope.[24]

SOCIAL ECONOMICS AND DEVELOPMENT ETHICS

As noted earlier in the chapter, there are several scholars who take ethics, values, and culture seriously. Culture is seen as a vital and, sometimes, revered aspect of a people's identity, and as representing the integral and holistic nature of a society that changes in response to internal and external pressures. Culture is not apart from or outside of economic life but is instead integral to and interactive with it. These scholars, many of them anthropologists and sociologists, are the foxes needed to complement the hedgehog economists.

A well-known Catholic scholar of this view was Denis Goulet, who advocated an understanding of development that respected local cultures while at the same time recognizing the need for cultures to change. Goulet thus tried to find a way out of what he termed "The Cruel Choice," which forced cultures outside the Western mainstream to choose between keeping their local cultural traditions and staying poor or opting to join modernizing trends and losing their identity and sense of meaning.[25] His solution was to work within cultures and to find the "latent dynamisms" that allowed cultural groups to respond constructively to the challenges of modernization.

As we saw in Chapter 1, economists who see themselves as social economists (Christian and other) take ethics, values, and culture seriously while questioning the free market model with its emphasis on fulfilling consumer preferences as the primary criterion of human welfare[26] and as the engine of economic growth and development. The view of human behavior in social economics is much richer than in neo-classical economics, but that very richness of detail causes problems for economic research and policy making. The power of the rational actor model is that its simplicity lends itself to formal modeling and empirical research in a way impossible for the more complex models of social economics. But is there really an advantage? The collapse of the Washington Consensus has opened the debate on best approaches to development. No longer do the prescriptions of free-market economists hold sway without question. More and more policy proposals on development issues recognize the problems of consumerism, sustainability, and human dignity posed by social economists.

As with CST, for social economists, economics and ethics are inherently intertwined.[27] Development ethics, as espoused by social economists, is closely connected with the meaning of development as integral human development. This section briefly examines the main themes of development ethics that are found in the writings of social economists working on development problems.[28]

First, social economists are concerned not so much with economic growth *per se* but with the increase in the material well-being of the poor. But they go beyond that. For instance, they engage in ethical discussions of why one should care about the poor. Goulet, for example, argues that individuals, groups, and nations who are better off have obligations to those who are worse off, calling this "solidarity." One can provide religious and philosophical justifications of absolute respect for the dignity of the human person, regardless of gender, ethnic group, social class, religion, age, or nationality. But Goulet also argues that such obligations follow from some empirical realities; that is, the fact that the rich and poor are involved in one socio-economic unity and that the activities of one group have important effects on the other. For this reason, all groups have a responsibility towards others. Since the rich arguably have a larger influence, they may be held to be especially responsible for the poor. In many cases, this may mean yielding the power to maintain their position at the expense of the poor. These concerns are relevant not only within countries but also between countries, especially in the context of globalization.[29]

Second, there is a stress on the environment, not only because of the contribution that it makes to material well-being—an issue which is often stressed by mainstream economists and that was mentioned above—but mainly because of its intrinsic importance. There is a recognition of the relation of human beings with nature, facilitating responsible use, respectful of biological cycles and the equilibrium of ecosystems—especially those of tropical forests—and in solidarity with future generations.

Third, development is much more than material well-being. It incorporates other changes including, particularly, that of values. Goulet[30] has argued forcefully that development is fundamentally a question of human values and attitudes, goals defined by societies for themselves, and criteria for determining what tolerable costs are to be borne, and by whom, in the course of change. Modernization is not the goal if it is imposed from outside, especially if it destroys values that are of central importance to those who are experiencing development. Social economists also acknowledge the problems of over-consumption. Material goods, of food, housing, medicine and for security, are important because they contribute something essential to human well-being. They also argue against ever-increasing consumption of material goods and consumerism, where the focus is on "having" and not "being."[31] While for many people this view of materialism and consumerism has religious overtones, recent research on subjective well-being also points out that beyond a certain level of income and consumption further increases do not add significantly, or sometimes not at all, to increases in happiness (see further discussion in the section on globalization below).

Fourth, if development is recognized as a means to an end, what is it a means to and how do we find out these ends? Social economists go well beyond the technical focus of much of the literature on the meaning of development by proposing ways in which one can select and weight different ends so they can be included in the concept of development. Some, such as Goulet, focus on religious traditions because of the major hold they have on many societies, but argue for an enlightened and critical borrowing of these traditions such as that espoused by Mahatma Gandhi rather than a fundamentalist one.[32] More importantly, they recommend that development scholars and practitioners examine what people in developing societies, especially the poor who are not trapped by vested interests, want. They argue that authentic development occurs only when people themselves decide what they mean by development.[33]

Not only do mainstream economists and social economists have different views of human nature and the role of ethics but they work out of different conceptions of history—one of historical progress versus one less deterministic, more convoluted.

Modernization vs. Convoluted Development

Mainstream views of development continue to follow in the Modernization tradition that arose in the aftermath of WW II. The social economists' concept of convoluted history is that there is no simple historical march of progress. There are no general paths to development just as there is no general definition of development. Each people must write its own history. As Denis Goulet says regarding the strategy of development pursued by Guinea-Bissau: "Paradoxically, the lesson of greatest importance is that *the best model of development is the one that any society forges for itself on the anvil of its own specific conditions*."[34]

What does this mean for the development economist? There is an interesting parallel in modern medicine in a tension between the "scientific" explanation of a disease and the diagnosis a clinician makes for a particular patient. This is well described by Tolstoy in *War and Peace*:

> Doctors came to see Natasha, both separately and in consultation. They said a great deal in French, German and in Latin. They criticised one another, and prescribed the most diverse remedies for all the diseases they were familiar with. But it never occurred to one of them to make the simple reflection that they could not understand the disease from which Natasha was suffering, as no single disease can be fully understood in a living person; for every living person has his complaints unknown to medicine—not a disease of the lungs, of the kidneys, of the skin, of the heart, and so on, as described in medical books, but a disease that consists of one out of the innumerable combinations of ailments of these organs.[35]

While Tolstoy's depiction of every illness as a unique event may no longer be justified, economic development is even more of an art than medical diagnosis. Economic theorists can scientifically explain the results of underpricing capital regardless of country or time. Development economists, on the other hand, are diagnosticians of the particular illnesses of particular countries at specific points in time. They are forced to transcend a specific scientific paradigm to become artisans of the particular. They are foxes, not hedgehogs.

DEVELOPMENT IN THE AGE OF GLOBALIZATION

The newest challenge to an authentic development is the rapid expansion of the international economy known as globalization. Globalization is largely exogenous to individual companies and countries and inexorable in its spread. Spurred by reduced transport costs and advances in communications and other technologies, globalization has fostered greater interdependence between the countries of the world. The resulting opportunities in international trade and foreign investment have stimulated a large and growing number of countries to liberalize their trade regimes and their domestic economies. Countries that attempt to resist and opt for some form of isolationism risk paying a high price in economic growth. The critical question is how the aggregate gains of globalization can be translated into net benefits for all, particularly the poor in both developed and developing countries.

A good case can be made for being cautious about the headlong rush into globalization taking place in the world today. While the world economy is more closely integrated now than at any time in history, this integration is quite uneven. For example, liberalization of the world economy has proceeded unevenly. Trade liberalization has progressed more slowly in products such as textiles where poor countries are more competitive. In contrast, many more restrictions have been removed on the movement of capital, where industrialized countries have a comparative advantage. Similarly, unskilled labor in which poor countries have a comparative advantage has far fewer transnational employment options than skilled labor.

The result of relying on market forces in combination with asymmetries in liberalization raises real concerns. There are several trends in the world economy suggesting that national economies are polarizing rather than growing closer together. Marginalization and poverty are serious concerns, and the trend toward polarization deeply affects a country's socio-economic fabric.

In both industrial and poor countries, the creative-destructive process of globalization has created socio-political tensions both because of its uneven nature and because of its challenge to traditional values and ways of life. As mentioned earlier, this is true particularly in countries with strong Islamic roots and in countries where readily identifiable minorities control the wealth of the society.

Amy Chua argues that in much of the world ethnic minorities dominate their respective economies—Chinese in South East Asia, East Indians and Europeans in Africa, and Spanish descendants in Latin America. Expanded free markets resulting from globalization exacerbate the ethnic disparities in wealth and income, resulting in increased social and political instability. In this setting, democracy can become the vehicle for a huge ethnic backlash from the dominated majority, led by demagogues preaching revenge.[36]

Professor Chua was writing this book when the 9/11 terrorist attacks occurred in the United States. In explaining the number of people in poor nations who rejoiced, she writes: "The attack on America was an act of revenge directly analogous to the bloody confiscations of white land in Zimbabwe, or the anti-Chinese riots and looting in Indonesia fueled by the same feelings of envy, grievance, inferiority, powerlessness, and humiliation."[37] This is a cautionary tale, though depressing, and should be carefully considered by development policy makers. A simple-minded policy of free markets and free elections may not advance the welfare of the poor in the world.[38]

The reason why economic growth, beyond providing for basic subsistence, may not bring a sense of greater well-being, why the pleasures our new possessions bring melt into thin air, is that beyond a subsistence level what really matters is not one's possessions but one's psychological health, one's richness of human relations and freedom from the conflicts and constrictions that prevent us from enjoying what we have. The consumerist development model leads to a culture in which material goods are seen as an acceptable substitute for these non-material needs. The creative and rewarding use of leisure should be at least as central a concern in the development process as also the need for sustaining and meaningful work.

The key to a humane and sustainable development is to regard economic growth as a means to other things, not as an end in itself. The major change that has occurred over time regarding the meaning of development is the shift from the emphasis on growth of GDP and per capita consumption to one that focuses on income distribution and poverty and on the fulfillment of basic needs. There also has been a shift in emphasis regarding the importance given to environmental issues. However, these do not change the meaning of development in a fundamental way. The focus on distribution and poverty in later years maintains the earlier emphasis on measuring material means of development, although the focus has changed from average per capita income growth to how income is distributed among people, and to how the people at the lower end of the income scale are doing. The focus on non-market production and externalities such as the environment and the role of household production improves the measurement of material production and considers the depletion of resources due to production.

The key problem is that globalization policies have not been carefully prepared, nor have they been fair. In fact, they have been wrong-headed, incorporating an insistence upon free-market ideology resulting in a too rapid implementation of liberalization. The outcome has been increased destitution and social conflict in many poor nations.

Developing solutions is difficult because the world economy differs from any country's domestic economy. In every domestic economy there is a sovereign power, the central government, that establishes the framework and rules for carrying on economic exchange. In the United States the Constitution empowers the federal government to regulate interstate commerce. No state can impose import tariffs on goods produced in other states. The federal government sets minimum wages, environmental regulations, payroll taxes, safety requirements, and so on that are binding on all the states.

This is not the case in the world economy. There is no central government to set the rules. Prior to World War I the hegemonic power of Great Britain set the rules of the international economy. During the inter-war years Great Britain was too weak, and the result was chaos in the international economy. After World War II the Bretton Woods Agreement and the hegemonic power of the United States controlled the world economy. As the Bretton Woods system was abandoned and the relative power of the United States waned since the 1970s, coordination in the international economy was left to unregulated markets, supplemented with Economic Summits and the World Trade Organization, to reestablish international coordination.

These efforts to organize the world economy on pure free-market principles—mainly by preachment—have not been successful. World economic growth has slowed; in many areas of Africa and Latin America, growth became negative during the 1980s and 1990s. Trade imbalances have become extreme. Instability of exchange rates has become endemic in many areas. And the foreign debt borne by many countries, now including the United States, has had a constricting effect on the renewal of economic growth. With the advent of the Trump administration in the United States beginning in 2017, the free trade rules governing the international system have been challenged by his nationalist, America First policies. The result so far has been lose-lose for both the United States and its trading partners.

However, the interdependent nature of international markets and of the various national economies means that individual policies regarding exchange rates, trade, capital flows, and debt issues will be more effective if set within supra-national programs that encourage and coordinate them. Just as it has been necessary for all countries, developed and undeveloped alike, to introduce various measures to control the workings of their domestic economies for the common good, it is time to extend those measures to the international economy. Pope John Paul II argues that there must be social intervention on the international level "to promote development, an effort which also involves sacrificing the positions of income and power enjoyed by the more developed countries."[39] We cannot continue to practice one kind of economics up to our frontiers and another kind beyond them.

SOCIAL POLICIES FOR A HUMANE AND SUSTAINABLE DEVELOPMENT

While there is no single model of development and each country must chart its own path, the reality is that most countries other than the BRICs must conform their policies to the fact that globalization is here to stay and opting out is not possible without great cost—both economic and human. What possible policies are there, given that context?

Good Governance

Achieving the benefits and attenuating the transitional costs of globalization requires good governance in individual countries. This is dependent on the rule of law, democracy, and the provision of basic needs for the population. Without good governance, undesirable side-effects can swamp the benefits of globalization and liberalization. Corruption, organized crime, drug trafficking, and widespread non-compliance can be the result. Good governance must develop from within the poor country itself, but international organizations, NGOs, and countries such as the United States giving aid can provide experience, advice and possibly conditionality on aid, trade, and investment. Unfortunately, during the second decade of the 21st century, nationalist authoritarian governments have grown ever more common and powerful. At the same time, the role of the United States, under the Trump administration, as the guardian of human rights and democracy in the world has declined.

Social Programs

Creating policies to protect people, particularly the poorest, from increased hardships is a major challenge of globalization. Public revenue and expenditure in most of Africa and parts of Latin America have declined since the 1980s. Per capita real expenditure on basic education and health has also fallen. In general, servicing payments on foreign and domestic debt is the primary reason for reduced public expenditures in the social sectors. Increased reliance has been placed on regressive consumption taxes to generate the necessary revenue. Some countries have made major efforts to maintain social expenditures for the poor. The World Bank has been of some help by increasing its lending to basic education and health and by making protection of these sectors a conditionality of structural adjustment loans.

International Governance

While globalization can bring increased productivity to poor countries and improve the condition of their poor, there is no guarantee that it will automatically happen. International flows of finance, investment, and capital goods are notoriously unstable, and as countries liberalize, they become more susceptible to these instabilities. A more effective international institutional framework for oversight, regulation and compensation is necessary to deal with shocks emanating from the volatility of short-term international financial flows. The only way this will work is if countries begin to deal with international capital flows, making them less fluid by regulating them and beginning to tax them. The goal of free capital flows is to move capital to where it can contribute most to production. In fact, however, capital moves as much for speculative and financial reasons that often have little to do with productivity.

Debt Forgiveness, Aid, and Trade

Further debt reduction/forgiveness is necessary to reduce the debt servicing obligations of the least developed countries, particularly in Africa. Such reductions could free up budgetary resources for use elsewhere. As a requirement of debt forgiveness, creditor countries could insist that the released resources be used for basic education, health, and nutrition.

CONCLUSION

An adequate agenda of domestic and international economic policies requires good intentions, clear analysis of the issues, and sustained carry through. All are in short supply in an international economy driven by self-interest, both personal and national. Even more difficult is the problem presented by Professor Chua. The present style of globalization threatens to generate a whirlwind of political backlash. We need to heed the warning given by James Weaver, economist, Church of Christ minister, and social activist, in a talk entitled "Globalization with a Human Face":

> I have wondered about which human face represents the globalization system of the future. There are many candidates. One can see the face of John Maynard Keynes at Bretton Woods, NH in 1944 working to create a new international political economic order that would prevent another Great Depression and world war. One can see the face of a woman in Vietnam who has gotten a job in a Nike shoe factory. One can see the face of Jody Williams and the NGO's, who got most nations in the world to sign a treaty to ban the use of land mines. One can see the face of an auto worker protesting in Seattle because he lost his job when his factory relocated to Mexico. One can see the face of an AIDs patient in South Africa. One can see the face of Osama bin Ladin. (Or in 2020 the face of ISIS!)[40]

NOTES

1. Pope Francis, *Laudato Si*, para. 13
2. Pope Francis, *Laudato Si*, para. 109, 123.
3. Javier Iguíñiz. "Freedom in Amartya Sen and Gustavo Gutiérrez: Religious and Secular Common Grounds," in James Boyd White editor, *How Should We Talk About Religion? Perspectives, Contexts, Particularities* (Notre Dame, IN: University of Notre Dame Press, 2006). Also see his "Ethical Dilemmas of Theory or Reality? Three Approaches to the Inevitability of Sacrifices in Economic Development," in Charles K. Wilber and Amitava Krishna Dutt, editors, *New Directions in Development Ethics* (Notre Dame, IN: University of Notre Dame Press, 2010).

4. Denis Goulet, *Looking at Guinea-Bissau: A New Nation's Development Strategy*, Occasional Paper no. 9 (Washington, DC: Overseas Development Council, March 1978), p. 52; and Denis Goulet, *Development Ethics at Work: Explorations 1960-2002* (New York: Routledge, 2006).

5. Peter Danner, *The Economic Person* (London: Rowman and Littlefield Publishers, 2002).

6. James H. Weaver, "Globalization with a Human Face." Paper delivered to the Association for Social Economics, ASSA Convention, 2004, San Diego, CA.

7. Kenneth P Jameson., James H. Weaver, and Charles K. Wilber, "Strategies of Development: A Survey," in *Development Economics: Theory, Practice, and Prospects*, ed. Thomas R. DeGregori (Kluwer Academic Publishers, 1989), 137-177.

8. Charles K. Wilber, "Sustainable Development, Consumerism, & Catholic Social Thought." In *Looking beyond the Individualism & Homo Economicus of Neo-classical Economics*, ed. Edward J. O'Boyle (Milwaukee, WI: Marquette University Press, 2011), 129-43.

9. Benjamin M. Friedman, *The Moral Consequences of Economic Growth* (New York: Vintage Books, 2005).

10. Jeffrey Sachs, *The End of Poverty: Economic Possibilities for Our Time* (New York: Penguin Press, 2005).

11. David Throsby, *Economics and Culture* (Cambridge: Cambridge University Press, 2001).

12. Arturo Escobar, *Encountering Development* (Princeton: Princeton University Press 1994). See also Arturo Escobar, "Environmental Social Movements and the Politics of Place," *Development* 45 (March 1, 2002), 28-36 and Arturo Escobar, "Development, Violence and the New Imperial Order," *Development* 47 (March 2004): 15-21.

13. Francis, Audience with the participants in the Convention organized by the Dicastery for Promoting Integral Human Development on the fiftieth anniversary of "Populorum Progressio" (2018). http://press.vatican.va/content/salastampa/en/bollettino/pubblico/2017/04/04/170404a.html

14. The term was coined in 1989 by John Williamson, of the Institute for International Economics, to describe the conventional wisdom at the U.S. Treasury Department, the World Bank, and the International Monetary Fund on policy reforms that would aid development in Latin America. Over time the term took hold in public debate, where the Washington Consensus became synonymous with market fundamentalism, globally applied. A short-hand term was "get your prices right."

15. Pope Francis, *Evangelii Gaudium*, apostolic exhortation, Vatican website, November 24, 2013, chapter 2. http://w2.vatican.va/content/francesco/en/apost_exhortations/documents/papa-francesco_esortazioneap_20131124_evangelii-gaudium.html

16. Francis, *Laudato Si*, para. 114.

17. Paul VI, *Populorum*, para. 49.

18. John Paul II, *Centesimus*, para. 37.

19. Francis, *Laudato Si*, para. 13.

20. Francis, General audience, Vatican City, April 22, 2015. http://www.vatican.va/content/francesco/en/audiences/2015/documents/papa-francesco_20150422_udienza-generale.html

21. Francis, Remarks, meeting with political, business and community leaders, Quito, Ecuador, July 7, 2015. http://www.vatican.va/content/francesco/en/speeches/2015/july/documents/papa-francesco_20150707_ecuador-societa-civile.html

22. John Paul II, *Centesimus*, para. 58.

23. Paul VI, *Populorum*, para. 19.

24. Francis, Audience with the Dicastery for Promoting Integral Human Development.

25. Denis Goulet. *The Cruel Choice: A New Concept in the Theory of Development* (New York: Atheneum, 1971); and Goulet, Denis, 'Development Experts: The One-Eyed Giants,' *World Development*, 8, no. 7/8, (July/August 1980), 481-489.

26. Like anthropologists, social economists are akin to the fox, adding to and correcting the neoclassical hedgehog.

27. Amitava Krishna Dutt and Charles K. Wilber, *Economics and Ethics: An Introduction* (New York and London: Palgrave Press, 2010). Revised paperback edition, 2013.

28. See Charles K. Wilber and Amitava Krishna Dutt. *New Directions in Development Ethics: Essays in Honor of Denis Goulet* (Notre Dame, IN: University of Notre Dame Press, 2010).

29. Denis Goulet, "Inequalities in the Light of Globalization", in Louis Sabourin, ed., *Globalisation and Inequalities* (Vatican City: Pontifical Academy of Social Sciences, 2002), 3-29.

30. Goulet, *Development Ethics at Work.*

31. Wilber, "Sustainable Development," 129-43.

32. Denis Goulet, "On Culture, Religion, and Development," in *Reclaiming Democracy*, ed. Marguerite Mendell (Montreal & Kingston, London, Ithaca: McGill-Queen's University Press, 2005), 21-32.

33. Wilber, "Sustainable Development," and Goulet. *Development Ethics at Work.*

34. Goulet, *Looking at Guinea-Bissau*, 52.

35. Quoted from Stanley Hauerwas, David Burrell, and Richard Bondi, *Truthfulness and Tragedy: A Further Investigation in Christian Ethics* (Notre Dame, IN: University of Notre Dame Press, 1977).

36. Amy Chua, *World on Fire: How Exporting Free Market Democracy Breeds Ethnic Hatred and Global Instability* (New York: Doubleday, 2002).

37. Chua, *World on Fire*, 207.

38. Another note of caution regarding globalization is the disenchantment by a number of developed countries, particularly the United States under the Trump administration. Concern about lost jobs to Mexico, China, India, et al, exacerbated by the coronavirus pandemic, has led to a renewal of trade barriers and restrictions on emigration.

39. John Paul II, *Centesimus*, para. 52.

40. Weaver,"Globalization with a Human Face."

Part III

WHITHER THE FUTURE

Chapter Twelve

The Economy, the Family, and Mediating Institutions

David Brooks, columnist for the *New York Times*, writes: "A society is healthy when its culture counterbalances its economics. That is to say, when you have a capitalist economic system that emphasizes competition, dynamism and individual self-interest, you need a culture that celebrates cooperation, stability and committed relationships. We don't have that. We have a culture that takes the disruptive and dehumanizing aspects of capitalism and makes them worse."[1] He concludes with a statement that "The lone wolf man has had his day; the weaving man is what we need, the one strong enough to bind himself into a community."[2] The problem is that those communities, what I call mediating institutions, such as the family, the church, the neighborhood are all in decline. The CST response is clearly seen in the preface to the United States Catholic bishops' pastoral letter *Economic Justice for All*:

> With what care, human kindness and justice do I conduct myself at work? How will my economic decisions to buy, sell, invest, divest, hire, or fire serve human dignity and the common good? In what career can I best exercise my talents so as to fill the world with the Spirit of Christ? How do my economic choices contribute to the strength of my family and community, to the values of my children, to a sensitivity to those in need? In this consumer society, how can I develop a healthy detachment from things and avoid the temptation to assess who I am by what I have? How do I strike a balance between labor and leisure that enlarges my capacity for friendships, for family life, for community? What government policies should I support to attain the well-being of all, especially the poor and vulnerable?[3]

As we saw earlier, CST sees society as made up of a dense network of relations among individuals, families, churches, neighborhood associations, business firms, labor unions, and different levels of government. Thus, every level of society has a role to play in ensuring basic human rights and the common good. This is expressed as the "principle of subsidiarity." This principle provides for a pluralism of social actors. Each, from the individual person to the federal government, has obligations. Higher levels should not usurp the authority of lower levels except when necessary. In this chapter I want to focus on the family and its role in society as a mediating institution.

MEGA-INSTITUTIONS AND THE DECLINE OF MEDIATING INSTITUTIONS

The United States economy is characterized by largeness of firms, unions, and government institutions. To cite just a few examples: General Motors, Exxon, AT&T, Ford Motor Company, Amazon, Apple, and Microsoft each had net sales larger than the GDP of over 120 different countries. Apple employs around 125,000 workers, General Motors 180,000, Ford over 200,000. Walmart is the world's largest company, measured by sales volume, at $500 billion and 2,300,000 employees. And this is not all. Despite their decline over the past 30 years, unions such as the Teamsters, UAW, the Carpenters Union, Service Employees, et al. are all mega-institutions. Government agencies such as the Department of Defense are even larger. The Russian and Chinese economies share this same characteristic. Their economic institutions are even larger and more bureaucratized than ours.

The development of the U.S. economy (and most other industrialized economies) has created a fundamental dichotomization of social, political, and economic life.[4] Put most simply, the dichotomy is between the mega-institutions and the private life of the individual. These two divisions of our society are experienced and apprehended by the individual in quite different ways. The GMs, UAWs, DODs, UCLAs, AMAs are "remote, often hard to understand or downright unreal, impersonal, and ipso facto unsatisfactory as sources for individual meaning and identity. . . . By contrast, private life is experienced as the single most important area for the discovery and actualization of meaning and identity."[5]

People could cope with these mega-institutions if the dichotomization process had not so deinstitutionalized the private life of individuals. People have always found their identity and, in turn, impressed their values on the mega-institutions through what Berger calls "mediating structures." However, this interlocking network of mediating institutions—family, church, voluntary association, neighborhood, and subculture—has been severely weakened by the growth of the mega-institutions that have taken over many of the traditional functions of the mediating institutions.

In the face of this dichotomization of modern life the concept of Christian responsibility or stewardship falls on infertile soil. There are a number of reasons why this is true. People feel helpless in the face of these mega-institutions. Their sheer size is so alienating that the individual retreats to private life believing that nothing can be done about THEM OUT THERE. However, private life is becoming less of a refuge as mediating institutions continue to decay in the face of the expansion of the mega-institutions. As Berger says, "The situation becomes intolerable . . . when, say, my wife leaves me, my children take on life styles that are strange and unacceptable to me, my church becomes incomprehensible, my neighborhood becomes a place of danger, and so on."[6] The result is a turn to hedonism and mefirstism at the worst and quietism at the best. And, of course, this further weakens the mediating institutions of private life.

Not only do people feel helpless to change things but in fact they are helpless as individuals to make any difference. With the mega-institutions "taking-care" of the hungry, the thirsty, the stranger, the naked, the ill, and the prisoner; and with the family, church, voluntary association, neighborhood, and subculture weakened and defensive; the individual finds it difficult if not impossible to carry out his or her Christian responsibilities for social justice.

A third factor is vital in understanding why the environment of modern life is alien to the practice of Christian stewardship and deserves extended treatment. As Berger says, "No society, modern or otherwise, can survive without what Durkheim called a 'collective conscience,' that is without moral values that have general authority."[7] Most economists have forgotten (if they ever knew) that Adam Smith said the same thing. While in *The Wealth of Nations* he stressed the importance of competition (and assumed the small scale of institutions), in *The Theory of Moral Sentiments*, he argued, as we saw in an earlier chapter, that widespread acceptance of a "general moral law" was a prerequisite for the proper functioning of the economy and society.

The assumption that individual self-interest in a competitive environment is enough to yield the common good is an illusion. An economy, capitalist or socialist, where everyone—buyers, sellers, workers, managers, consumers, firms—constantly lied, stole, committed fraud and violence, etc., would neither yield the common good nor would it be stable. Yet pushed to its logical extreme, individual self-interest suggests that it is usually in the interest of an individual to evade the rules by which others are guided. Similarly, the "free-rider" concept suggests that it is in an individual's interest not to cooperate in a situation of social interdependence if others do cooperate, for he/she will obtain the same benefits without any sacrifice. Therefore, why do individuals in societies usually not operate in this fashion? The answer is not primarily fear of the police power of the state but rather that our basic selfishness is inhibited by a deeply ingrained moral sense, one usually based on religious convictions.

The Erosion of the Inherited Moral Base

Fred Hirsch reintroduced the idea of moral law into economic analysis: "Truth, trust, acceptance, restraint, obligation—these are among the social virtues grounded in religious belief which . . . play a central role in the functioning of an individualistic, contractual economy. . . . The point is that conventional, mutual standards of honesty and trust are public goods that are necessary inputs for much of economic output."[8]

The major source of this collective conscience or moral law has been the religious heritage of the pre-capitalist and preindustrial past as embodied in the mediating institutions of private life. The legacy of religious values has diminished over time because of a twofold change: (1) the repudiation of the social character and responsibility of religion meant its banishment to a purely private matter[9] and (2) the elevation of selfinterest as a praiseworthy virtue in turn undermined that privatized religious ethic.

The erosion of this preindustrial, pre-capitalist moral legacy has proceeded slowly for two reasons: (1) economic growth was spread over a very long time period and (2) that growth relied on decentralized decision making for the most part. This slow and seemingly natural process allowed popular acceptance of the social changes as well as permitting adjustment in the moral base of society. However, the limits to this process may now be starting to be reached in the United States.

Capitalist development was far from conflict-free in the past. But one of its advantages was the absence of an identifiable villain behind the disruptions which occurred. Such changes resulted from the independent decisions of thousands of persons. Few could rig the rules to his or her benefit, so inequalities appeared legitimate and the undermining of religious values had no identifiable cause. The centrality of government in most developed countries today, however, provides a target for dissatisfaction. In such circumstances the legitimacy of inequalities and changes in values are open to question and to challenge. The gradual disappearance of the moral base of society forces government to attempt to act as a substitute and to provide a context which will encourage principled action among the elite while at the same time ensuring acceptance of the outcome by the majority. Thus, government must create or in some sense embody a "civil religion."

Let me summarize the argument this far. The erosion of the inherited moral base under the onslaught of continuous growth and spread of individualism creates the following condition: The entrepreneurial elite and many other groups have been freed of the old religious and moral values, but the individualistic growth process has not provided any ready substitute social morality. Thus, the previously effective inhibitions on lying, cheating, and stealing have lost their power, and the functioning of the private sector is suffering as a result.

A second problem arises in the central role played by the state in managing the economy. There is a central flaw in the current approach of planned capitalist growth. It calls for the pursuit of self-interest by individuals in the private sector but forbids it in the public sector. The expectation that public servants will not promote their private interests at the expense of the public interest reinforces the argument that the economy rests as importantly on moral behavior as self-interested behavior. "The more a market economy is subjected to state intervention and correction, the more dependent its functioning becomes on restriction of the individualistic calculus in certain spheres, as well as on certain elemental moral standards among both the controllers and the controlled. The most important of these are standards of truth, honesty, physical restraint, and respect for law."[10] But the more that self-interest progresses and the more that the original moral base of society is undercut, the less likely are these conditions to be met.

Attempts to rely solely on material incentives in the private sector and more particularly in the public sector suffer from two defects: First, a policeman on every corner to prevent cheating simply does not work. Regulators have a disadvantage in relevant information compared to those whose behavior they are trying to regulate. In addition, who regulates the regulators? Thus, there is no substitute for an internalized moral law that directs persons to seek their self-interest only in "fair" ways.[11] Second, a reliance on external sanctions further undermines the remaining aspects of an internalized moral law. Thus, the erosion of society's moral base under the onslaught of self-interest has important practical results.

Because of their remoteness and sheer size, the mega-institutions are "consumers" not "producers" of such a general morality. "Bureaucrats are the poorest of moralists."[12] A general moral code cannot rest on the activities of individuals either. The experiments with "lifestyles" of "consenting adults" is a too unstable and unreliable basis for the generation and maintenance of a collective conscience. However, without it, the ethic of Christian stewardship must languish.

From Personal to Institutional Sin in Moral Theology

The dichotomization of modern life has been paralleled by developments in moral theology.[13] Two opposite but complementary phenomena are important in this context.

First is the shift of emphasis from personal to institutional sinfulness. It is true that the previous focus on personal sins of commission obscured the nature of systemic evil and that the analogy of putting band-aids on cancers is powerful. However, the present focus on institutional and systemic evil undermines personal responsibility. Given the earlier point that mediating institutions have been weakened severely and faced with the systemic evil of the mega-institutions, a feeling of impotence overwhelms the individual. Since there are few avenues for exercising personal responsibility, the conscientious individual ends up feeling guilty. And unrelieved guilt leads to apathy or cynicism which reinforces the dichotomization of life and further undermines the prospects for Christian responsibility.

A second development in religious thought is the neglect of traditional Catholic social teaching with its emphasis on subsidiarity; that is, the principle that tasks should be performed at the lowest possible level, beginning with the individual, and moving upward through intermediate institutions to the national or global level as required. Instead contemporary Catholic social thought, for example the United States Catholic Bishops' *Economic Justice for All*, has mirrored the secular worlds neglect of mediating institutions in favor of state action or individual social ministry. Thus, the family, parish, neighborhood have been on the defensive even within religious social thought.

None of the above is meant to deny the importance of recognizing institutional and systemic evil. It is quite clear that racism in the United States is a systemic evil that will require not only personal conversion of white peoples' thoughts and actions, but must be rooted out root and branch from policing practices, bank lending, hiring, and every aspect of the social system. Rather it is a call to see the importance of mediating institutions—particularly the family—in providing the base for Christian stewardship to flourish and function as a means for reforming societal structures.

WHAT ROLE MIGHT THE FAMILY PLAY AS A MEDIATING INSTITUTION?

Our modern political philosophies—liberalism, conservatism, socialism—have failed precisely because they have not understood the importance of mediating institutions. Liberalism has constantly turned to the state and conservatism to the market and corporate sector for solutions to social problems. Neither recognizes the destructiveness to the social fabric caused by relying on mega-institutions. Socialism also suffers from this myopia. Even though it places its faith in renewed community it fails to see that socialist mega-institutions are just as destructive as capitalist ones.

If we accept the importance of mediating institutions, there are two areas of concern. The first is that of public policy. For our present purposes I merely will cite my agreement with Peter Berger's two points: "One: Public policy should protect and foster mediating structures. Two: Wherever possible, public policy should utilize the mediating structures as its agents."[14]

More importantly ways must be found to revitalize mediating institutions from the bottom up. For the rest of this chapter I will focus on the family as a key mediating institution.

The American family has been in crisis for many years; first came the family breakdown with rising divorce rates and now the trend is the lack of family formation. In 1960, 82 percent of those between 25 and 34 were married; in 2000, 55 percent were; and in 2013 less than 50 percent were; and the downward trend shows no sign of ending. Marriage may have become less popular because of what Senator Elizabeth Warren calls the "two-income trap."[15] Lagging wages during the past 20 years plus the inflation of key purchases of families—houses, education, health care—have driven both parents into the workforce to try and make ends meet. However, for the less well off the cost of childcare comes close to cancelling out the increased income. And the flexibility of the family unit is dramatically reduced. If a child gets sick a parent has to take off work and the family loses income. If one of the parents get sick the family income is reduced and there is no one to care for the children.

The response to Warren's theory is that this is what women want. They want to be free to choose to be in the workforce and not have to stay at home to raise children. However, there is substantial evidence from the American Community Survey data by the Institute for Family Studies that only 17 percent of mothers with children three years or younger say they prefer to work full time. The other 83 percent feel they have to work full time either because their income is needed or by more affluent women because they fear their careers will be side-tracked.

The serious problem of childcare has led to proposals to provide subsidizes to less affluent families. If we are willing to pay for childcare for working families at, say, $400 a week, why not pay one of the parents that same $400 to stay home and take care of their own children? Rebuilding family structures may be the most important and most difficult task in making the family a functioning mediating institution in the United States today.

Thus, the modern United States economy with its high level of occupational and geographic mobility, its sharp division of work life from home life, and its transfer of education, welfare, and old age security functions to mega-institutions has transformed the nature of the family. The "two-income trap" has weakened the family's ability to reach beyond itself. As a result, individual families have difficulty coping with the dichotomization of modern life. Families can be a powerful force for Christian stewardship, but they need help. Somehow individual families must band together in groups that can provide their members with an understanding of the social world, a mechanism for acting as Christians, and a faith that will permeate the other institutions of society.[16] It is worthwhile quoting from Pope John Paul II's encyclical *Familiaris Consortio*:

> Society should never fail in its fundamental task of respecting and fostering the family. The family and society have complementary functions in defending and fostering the good of each and every human being. But society—more specifically the state—must recognize that "the family is a society in its own original right," and so society is under a grave obligation in its relations with the family to adhere to the principle of subsidiarity.[17]

In Latin America, the Comunidades de Base[18] are functioning as mediating institutions for individuals and families. In Sri Lanka the Sarvodaya Shramadana movement is based on groups of families at the village level. Both the United States and Europe lack equivalent movements. The closest type of institution has been those built on Catholic action—Young Christian Students, Young Christian Workers, and Christian Family Movement. All three are past their peak but the basic philosophy has potential for revitalization in new structures. This is what the Sarvodaya Shramadana movement did with Buddhist values in Sri Lanka.

The Family as a Mediating Institution

In this section, I want to focus on the potential role of the Christian family as a mediating institution in the United States, now and in the future—with "its own special gift, its own special grace, its own special duty."[19]

The Second Vatican Council sets out a social role for the Christian family which is extremely demanding. In addition to the raising of children as Christians, it calls for: "the adoption of abandoned infants, hospitality to strangers, assistance in the operation of schools, advise and help for adolescents, help to engaged couples, catechetical work, support of married couples and families in material or moral crises, help for the aged."[20] And that is not all: "It is of the highest importance that families should devote themselves directly and by common agreement to transforming the very structure of society."[21] I agree that the family, as the key "mediating institution" in society, is needed as a prime agent of social justice in the economy, but that is easier said than done.

It is appropriate that this challenge to live as Christians is laid before us while large state agencies have taken over the provision of these needs. Christian families cannot replace these welfare structures, but they can provide real, loving care for the oppressed and afflicted while working to change the structures of oppression and affliction. Rosemary Haughton sums up the importance of families:

> In this time of upheaval when so many innocent people are being hurt, there is an almost prophetic quality about that passage from the Council's document which firmly, almost ruthlessly, sets the Christian family at the heart of the church's mission of compassion for the world which God loves so much. That, then, is the vocation of the family in the Church—to discover its identity, to fulfill its needs, to grow in unity and loyalty by responding—each in its own way—to the Christian vocation of loving service. In each age, the church has called on special kinds of people to carry out its work. There is always a need for the religious congregation and other dedicated single people who can devote their lives to work beyond the scope and skill of an ordinary family. But it does seem that the church has a need at this particular historical moment for what a family can best provide: the sense of intimacy, the personal touch, a human environment of ordinary warmth and friendliness and lovingness. Very many people have pointed to the impersonality of the big cities, the big organizations, and to the loneliness and despair of those who feel rejected and depersonalized in their misery. Families, just because they have a continuous, ordinary, every-day life of their own and don't exist just to provide help, can give the sense of belonging, a feeling of positive, future-facing life.[22]

One of the primary functions of the family is to educate its members by precept and example to see their duties and responsibilities as Christians. As the Second Vatican Council stated: "In the family, parents have the task of training their children from childhood to recognize God's love for all men. Especially by example they should teach them little by little to show concern for the material and spiritual needs of their neighbor. The whole of family life, then, would become a sort of apprenticeship for the apostolate."[23]

This process of formation is not a one-way street. Parents learn from their children and from the very process of family life. What do they learn? "First of all, forgiveness." Children do not necessarily accept the beliefs of their parents. "Parents can't dismiss what has happened by blaming it entirely on others. Parents find that they made mistakes." Thus, they need to forgive and to be forgiven. Second, Compassion. "I see only two ways to compassion. The natural way is through family life, through the vulnerability of loving, through the kind of commitment of loved ones that ends in suffering with others their miseries and griefs. . . . In our confused and convoluted, twisted and fragmented world, we are confronted daily with those who are in need of our compassion. It is necessary only to be aware and capable of compassion."[24]

The inward focus on education naturally leads to an outward role for the family. This outward focus takes several forms. First, teaching children by example requires that the family reach outside of itself. Second, when and if the children become filled with an understanding of stewardship, they will take on as part of their life's work the alleviation of suffering.

As should be clear, the family must be seen as more than an end in itself. It must be seen also as a path leading into the larger world of society. As Christians we are called to go out from the family as individuals and by way of united effort with others.

Some new structures are necessary to channel this effort. Unfortunately, little attention has been given to the family as a mediating institution. One thought is to revitalize the Catholic action groups such as the Christian Family Movement that my wife and I were formed by, as I noted in Chapter 1. They were built upon a very traditional Catholic methodology—the observe-judge-act approach—first developed by Cardinal Joseph Cardijn when he was a parish priest in Belgium before World War II.

Typically, a small group meets every two weeks and discusses a different topic, i.e., unemployment, racism, etc. The meeting is structured into sections—scriptural reflection, social inquiry, and action. See my little book for details.[25]

The meeting begins by reflecting together on a relevant scripture passage that then leads into the social inquiry. The social inquiry part of each session utilizes the observe-judge-act approach. It works in the following way. Members *observe* a situation from daily life, *judge* whether or not the situation needs to be changed and agree to *act* in order to help bring about the desired change. Observations are most often gleaned from information obtained by consulting various sources. These observations are *events*, such as the county wanting to raise property taxes; *statistics*, such as the percentage unemployed in the county increased to 10 percent; *opinions of others*, such as five out of seven neighbors talked with think more funds need to be spent on the local high school; or a person's *own experiences*, such as men get promoted ahead of women at your place of employment, even when the women are clearly more qualified.

The sources of information are important, of course. Information from several different places, with varying points of view, will usually give a better view of reality than will be gleaned from a single source. So, for example, one should read both the *New York Times* and the *Washington Times*, watch both Fox News and MSNBC. It is not enough to simply gather facts from sources with whom one tends to agree. Listening to a variety of presentations and interpretations of the event, statistic, or opinion being observed before one begins to evaluate or judge it is essential. While it is never possible to be completely objective about an observation, it is important to do what one can as an individual and as a group to get close.

While the observe section tries to answer the question, "What is really going on here?" the judge section uses one's Christian faith to evaluate the reality observed and answer the question, "How can we make it better?" We make it better when we are able to advance human dignity.

Answering, "How can we make it better?" leads to the act section of the process. The best actions are those that grow out of the group's discussion of the observations and the judgments reached by applying Catholic social teaching to those observations. The actions suggested are just that—suggestions. The group will have ideas of its own, some far better suited to the situation than what a national group such as CFM might suggest in its annual guide.

The above is just one example of how Catholic action can be generated. In addition, by incorporating some of the aspects of the Comunidades de Base,[26] family-based Catholic action groups can be strengthened. These communities are the basic unity of the Church where deeper prayer and shared values are lived, where personal and group objectives merge to question, discuss and act; and where ordinary people are given a sense of being the Church as a leaven in society and the world. Members of these small groups of Christians have a sense of responsibility for themselves as they celebrate the faith together. They form the Church as God's People rather than God's building.

Individual families need help in fulfilling their role as training grounds for the Christian apostolate. Parishes, groups of families, etc. must function as a network of mediating institutions. If this help is not forthcoming, family life will turn inward to escape the helplessness generated by the mega-institutions.

To conclude, my argument is that the growth of mega-institutions, both corporate and governmental, has undermined society's mediating institutions; in particular, the family has been undermined also by economic conditions. It is the mediating institutions which always have given meaning to people's lives and through which, in turn, they have impressed their values on society. We must find ways to revitalize the mediating institutions, particularly the family, if we are to successfully cope with the problems facing us now and in the future.

In his classic book, *After Virtue*, Alasdair MacIntyre anticipated my argument concluding with the statement that in the period in which the Roman empire gave way to the so-called dark ages:

> A crucial turning point . . . occurred when men and women of good will turned aside from the task of shoring up the Roman imperium and ceased to identify the continuation of civility and moral community with the maintenance of that imperium. What they set themselves to achieve instead—often not recognizing fully what they were doing—was the construction of new forms of community

within which the moral life could be sustained so that both morality and civility might survive the coming ages of barbarism and darkness. If my account of our moral condition is correct, we ought also to conclude that for some time now we too have reached that turning point. What matters at this stage is the construction of local forms of community within which civility and the intellectual and moral life can be sustained through the new dark ages which are already upon us. And if the tradition of the virtues was able to survive the horrors of the last dark ages, we are not entirely without grounds for hope. This time however the barbarians are not waiting beyond the frontiers; they have already been governing us for quite some time. And it is our lack of consciousness of this that constitutes part of our predicament.[27]

In the next chapter I will present a version of CST, the Catholic Worker movement, that is centered on local community action as one way to build a new society within the shell of the old.

NOTES

1. David Brooks, "The Rise of the Haphazard Self," *New York Times*, May 14, 2019.
2. Brooks, "The Rise."
3. "Pastoral Message," *Economic Justice for All*, para. 23.
4. Peter Berger, "In Praise of Particularity: The Concept of Mediating Structures," *The Review of Politics* (July, 1976); reprinted in Walter Nicgorski and Ronald Weber eds., *An Almost Chosen People* (Notre Dame, IN: University of Notre Dame Press, 1976).
5. Berger, "In Praise," 133.
6. Berger, "In Praise," 133.
7. Berger, "In Praise," 134.
8. Fred Hirsch, *Social Limits to Growth* (Cambridge, MA: Harvard University Press, 1978), 141.
9. See R. H. Tawney, *Religion and the Rise of Capitalism* (New York: Harcourt, Brace and World, Inc., 1926), and Charles K. Wilber, "The New Economic History Reexamined: R.H. Tawney on the Origins of Capitalism," *The American Journal of Economics and Sociology* 33, no. 3 (July 1974): 249-258.
10. Hirsch, *Social Limits*, 128-129.
11. This casts new light on the recent attempts to construct theories of justice that are acceptable to all. See John Rawls, *A Theory of Justice* (Cambridge, MA: Harvard University Press, 1971), and the literature spawned by that work. The whole endeavor can be seen as an attempt to create a substitute moral law based on rationality rather than religion.
12. Berger, "In Praise," 134.

13. These observations are based on the Roman Catholic tradition with which I am familiar.

14. Berger, "In Praise," 138.

15. Elizabeth Warren and Amelia Warren Tyagi, *The Two-Income Trap: Why Middle-Class Parents Are (Still) Going Broke* (New York: Basic Books, revised, updated edition, 2016).

16. Charles K. Wilber, *Catholics Spending and Acting Justly* (Notre Dame, IN: Ave Maria Press, 2011).

17. Pope John Paul II, *Familiaris Consortio* (Washington, DC: United States Catholic Conference, 1981), 43.

18. See *Proceedings of the Latin American Bishops Conference*, Puebla, Mexico (Notre Dame, IN: CCUM, 1979).

19. "Toward the Synod of 1980: The Role of the Christian Family in Modern Society: Preliminary Paper of the Vatican Synod Secretariat," *Origins: NC Documentary Service* 9, no. 8 (July 19, 1979): 115.

20. "Decree on the Apostolate of the Laity," *The Documents of Vatican II* (New York: Guild Press, 1966), 503.

21. "Toward the Synod of 1980," 127.

22. Rosemary Haughton, "Testimony on the Family," *Liberty and Justice for All: Atlanta Hearing* (National Conference of Catholic Bishops, Committee for the Bicentennial, August 9, 1975), 67.

23. "Decree on the Apostolate of the Laity," 518.

24. Eugene S. Geissler, "Our Children Our Greatest Teachers," in *Marriage among Christians*, ed. by James T. Burtchaell, C.S.C. (Notre Dame, IN: Ave Maria Press, 1977), 58, 61-62.

25. See Wilber, *Catholics Spending.*

26. See http://smallchristiancommunities.org/; https://www.cfm.org/; Charles K. Wilber, *Catholics Spending.*

27. Alasdair MacIntyre, *After Virtue*, (Notre Dame, IN: University of Notre Dame Press, 1984), 263.

Chapter Thirteen

Distributism and the Catholic Worker Movement

AMERICANIST AND RADICALIST CATHOLIC TRADITIONS

The United States Catholic Bishops' Committee on Christianity and Economics, which prepared the pastoral letter *Economic Justice for All: Pastoral Letter on Catholic Social Teaching and the U.S. Economy*, were convinced that the letter had to address two audiences, the people in the pews *and the policy-making community*. They believed this was necessary because the bishops would not be listened to otherwise. The result was a document filled with biblical, theological, philosophic, and economic argument. It was certainly listened to by policy makers if not acted upon. But it appears to have had little effect on people in the pews despite a bishop-led five-year-long implementation office. In contrast, Pope Francis directed his words to the people in the pews and to their families, unions, and parishes:

> The Lord promises refreshment and freedom to all the oppressed of our world, but he needs us to fulfill his promise. He needs our eyes to see the needs of our brothers and sisters. He needs our hands to offer them help. He needs our voice to protest the injustices committed thanks to the silence, often complicit, of so many. I should really speak of many silences: the silence of common sense; the silence that thinks, 'it's always been done this way;' the silence of 'us' as opposed to 'you.' Above all, the Lord needs our hearts to show his merciful love towards the least, the outcast, the abandoned, the marginalized. (Pope Francis, *Homily*, Holy Mass for Migrants, July 6, 2018)

This experience with the bishops' committee plus my work with the Catholic Worker movement have made me look beyond the dominant American

Catholic approach, developed over the past fifty years or so, that appears to assume a fundamental compatibility between Catholicism (and CST) and American political and economic institutions and traditions. This assumption underlies the work of both neo-liberal and neo-conservative Catholics alike.

A different application of CST, what Michael Baxter has called the "Evangelical Catholic" or "Catholic radicalist" tradition, is rooted in the ideas of G. K. Chesterton, Dorothy Day, Peter Maurin, Paul Hanley Furfey, and others associated with the Catholic Worker Movement.

The difference between the two traditions is found in the understanding of the *polis* embodied in each one's social theory. In the Americanist tradition, the *polis* is identified with the modern state and in particular with the American state, with the result that the state is seen as the primary mechanism for attaining justice. Thus, it is not surprising that the bishops' pastoral letter ended being most useful to public policy makers. "In the radicalist tradition, however, the *polis* is identified with Christ and the Church, and with smaller, practice-based communities whose forms of life are closely patterned after the body of Christ and the Church."[1]

In a religiously pluralistic country, a theology geared to speak to policy makers has to be stripped of substantive theological content to gain currency in the nation at large. The central philosophical claim underlying this theology is that reality discloses a divine plan in the form of natural law. Because this natural law is imprinted on the human mind, people are capable of grasping the law through direct intuition combined with discursive reason. Revelation and the Gospel are not required.

A fundamental criticism of this tradition is that there is no role for the Church as the representative of divine revelation to speak "truth to power." Baxter argues that the more fundamental Catholic position is that it is theology not philosophy that must interact with economic and political theory because philosophic reason becomes too easily distorted when it is not elevated and corrected by the truths of revelation.[2] A morality based on natural law quickly degenerates into a minimalism that promotes conformity to the status quo. A morality rooted in Jesus's love as revealed in scripture, on the other hand, and nourished by the life of the church, calls on Christians to live heroic lives patterned after the example of Christ and the saints.

Let me look in turn at biblical teaching and modern CST to understand the position of the Catholic radicals. Since the Bible originated in a completely different culture and historical setting than our own, it is questionable practice to directly transport specific Scriptural rules into the modern world. God's will was mediated to the Israelites in their concrete historical situation and can only be mediated to us in our concrete historical situation. And it is true that in our world the state must act to correct those injustices that individuals or small groups cannot cope with. But we as individuals are still called to feed the hungry, visit those sick and in prison, and clothe the naked *ourselves* not just as citizens paying taxes. And we must never accept political and economic institutions as God-given as long as the least of our brothers and sisters are in want. As the Catholic Worker Movement has striven to do, "we must fight to build a new society within the ruins of the old," a society in which it is easier for people to love God and their neighbors.

We should certainly attempt to discern basic ethical principles in Scripture and apply them to our economic situation, but this is different from finding exact blueprints. CST is an attempt to use Scripture and Tradition to address the problems of the modern economy. As we have seen, CST is rooted in a commitment to certain fundamental values—the right to human dignity, the need for human freedom and participation, the importance of community, and the nature of the common good. These values are drawn from the belief that each person is called to be a co-creator with God, participating in the redemption of the world and the furthering of the Kingdom. This requires social and human development where the religious and temporal aspects of life are not separated and opposed to each other.

The right to private property and the principle of subsidiarity limit the role of the state, while the principle of solidarity requires that society and the state intervene in markets to protect human rights, particularly of the poorest. The thrust of CST, therefore, has been to repudiate both state socialism and free-market capitalism. What economic system does it endorse? Explicitly, none. As Pope John Paul II says: "The Church has no models to present"[3] of the best economic system; that is for history to decide in each individual case.

However, the neo-liberal version of the Americanist tradition would argue that CST prefers a regulated market economy that protects the poor, defends human rights, allows all to participate in social groups such as trade unions, and controls market failures such as environmental pollution. The neo-conservative version would argue for much less regulation and for more individual solutions.

THE CATHOLIC WORKER MOVEMENT

The Catholic radicalist tradition, as exemplified by the Catholic Worker movement, criticizes both capitalist domination of the market and the collusive role of the state. Dorothy Day was fond of saying she did not worship what she called "Holy Mother the State." The Catholic Worker criticizes monopoly capitalism, where a few wealthy capitalists own the capital and the majority, the masses, work each day in monotonous jobs. The Catholic

Worker insists that all people are created in the image and likeness of God, and should not be treated like cogs in a machine or made to work long hours every day in back-breaking work as wage slaves, while large corporations and their directors become fabulously wealthy.

The Catholic Worker philosophy is best described as personalism. Pope Francis's *Speech at World Meeting of Popular Movements*[4] captures that spirit of personalism:

> This ability to see yourselves in the faces of others, this daily proximity to their share of troubles and their little acts of heroism: this is what enables you to practice the commandment of love, not on the basis of ideas or concepts, but rather on the basis of genuine interpersonal encounter. We do not love concepts or ideas; we love people. . . . Commitment, true commitment, is born of the love of men and women, of children and the elderly, of peoples and communities . . . of names and faces which fill our hearts. From those seeds of hope patiently sown in the forgotten fringes of our planet, from those seedlings of a tenderness which struggles to grow amid the shadows of exclusion, great trees will spring up, great groves of hope to give oxygen to our world.

The *economic philosophy* of the Catholic Worker is best described as distributism, and the focus of distributism is on private property. The word comes from the idea that a just social order can be best achieved through a widespread distribution of property. Distributism means that property should belong to the many rather than the few. It is derived from the idea of subsidiarity, emphasized in all papal social encyclicals, particularly since Pope Pius XI's 1931 encyclical *Quadragesimo Anno*.

Dorothy Day described it this way: "The aim of distributism is family ownership of land, workshops, stores, transport, trades, professions, and so on. Family ownership in the means of production so widely distributed as to be the mark of the economic life of the community—this is the Distributist's desire. It is also the world's desire."[5] G. K. Chesterton said: "If capitalism means private property, I am capitalist. If capitalism means capital, everybody is capitalist. But if capitalism means this particular condition of capital, only paid out to the mass in the form of wages, then it does mean something, even if it ought to mean something else. The truth is that what we call Capitalism ought to be called Proletarianism."[6]

When Chesterton wrote about the enormous discrepancies in income and wealth of the haves and have nots, it sounded as if he were speaking of today's world: "To say that I do not like the present state of wealth and poverty is merely to say that I am not the devil in human form. No one but Satan or Beelzebub could like the present state of wealth and poverty."[7]

The Catholic radicalist approach does not lend itself to easy policy prescriptions. Rather, its focus is on creating a new society within the old. In her memoir, *The Long Loneliness*, Dorothy Day said: "Ours was a long-range program, looking for ownership by the workers of the means of production, the abolition of the assembly line, decentralized factories, the restoration of crafts and ownership of property."[8]

In *The Outline of Sanity*, making the case for distributism, Chesterton argued:

> They say it is Utopian; and they are right. They say it is idealistic; and they are right. They say it is quixotic; and they are right. It deserves every name that will indicate how completely they have driven justice out of the world; every name that will measure how remote from them and their sort is the standard of honourable living; every name that will emphasize and repeat the fact that property and liberty are sundered from them and theirs, by an abyss between heaven and hell.
>
> Distributism may be a dream; three acres and a cow may be a joke; cows may be fabulous animals; liberty may be a name; private enterprise may be a wild goose chase on which the world can go no further. But as for the people who talk as if property and private enterprise were the principles now in operation—those people are so blind and deaf and dead to all the realities of their own daily existence, that they can be dismissed from the debate.[9]

In responding to charges that the Catholic Worker was communist, Dorothy Day replied, "Our insistence on worker-ownership, on the right of private property, on the need to de-proletarize the worker, all points which had been emphasized by the Popes in their social encyclicals, made many Catholics think we were Communists in disguise, wolves in sheep's clothing."[10]

In more concrete terms, what is the Catholic Worker and what does it do? The Catholic Worker movement was founded in 1933, in the depths of the Great Depression, by Peter Maurin and Dorothy Day in New York City to implement the teachings of the Gospels and Catholic social teaching, especially as presented in the social encyclicals. Their first project was the creation of the Catholic Worker newspaper which started with a first issue of twenty-five hundred copies. Dorothy Day and a few others sold the paper in Union Square, New York City, for a penny a copy (still the price) to passersby.

A basic concept of their movement was hospitality, and Dorothy, Peter, and a few others began to house the homeless immediately. The movement grew, and many other houses of hospitality began across the United States. Today, about 200 Catholic Worker communities remain committed to hospitality for the homeless, exiled, hungry, and forsaken. Catholic Workers embrace nonviolence, voluntary poverty, prayer, and continue to protest injustice, war, racism, and violence of all forms. Their basic aim is, in Peter's words, to build "the kind of society where it would be easier to be good."

There is wide variability among Catholic Worker communities.[11] For example, the Dorothy Day Catholic Worker House in Berkeley, California, serves over one thousand meals per day, and offers no residential services. Houston's Casa Juan Diego Catholic Worker community has ten houses, a social services center, and a medical clinic. Both are living examples of the Catholic Worker and are much more than these few phrases convey.

Personalism, the focus on the human person made in the image and likeness of God, is the primary motivation. Inspired by Emmanuel Mounier and Jacques Maritain and others, it is based on the implementation of Matthew 25, "What you did for the least of the brethren you did for me." Each person is to be received as Jesus.

Sociologist Harry Murray[12] was a participant observer in a number of Catholic Worker communities, studying what "personalism" meant in behavioral terms. He concluded that most Catholic Workers would identify the term *personalist* with their work in the same way as most nurses, social workers, et al. would link the term *professional* with theirs.[13] Murray identified five ways that staff workers in Houses of Hospitality embody personalism, all of which distinguish the Catholic Worker from professional social service workers.

First, he says that Catholic Worker staff people place the inherent dignity and worth of the individual as more important than any other consideration, more important than, for example, welfare policies, the police, or any government entity. Considerations such as eligibility requirements or immigration status would never be given priority over an individual's need.

Second, staff speak and act with appreciation for the reality that both guests and they are simultaneously wounded and healers. Guests and staff are both teachers and learners.

Third, there are few written rules in a Worker house other than those required to ensure safety. The worker's responsibility is determined not by written rules or job descriptions, but by each one's sense of personal responsibility to the community.

Fourth, the personalist philosophy leads to a living out of Martin Buber's nonhierarchical I-Thou spirit of relationships.[14] These relationships are present-oriented rather than past history. Since Houses of Hospitality are not social agencies and do not receive government funds, they do not maintain written records. Everyone works together face-to-face every day. Hence, communication about guests is all conversational, leading to a norm of discussion balanced between positive and negative dimensions of behavior.

Fifth, every Worker assumes personal responsibility to promote social change, and most identify that as a key factor in their decision to enter a

House of Hospitality. Constant close contact with the poor and vulnerable combined with weekly roundtable discussions challenge the cultural assumption that blames guests for their circumstances. The unbreakable connection between practical works of mercy, critical group reflection, and social activism is the heart of the Catholic Worker movement.[15]

Staff reflections frequently express the constant tension inherent in trying to live up to the personalist norm. Whether by humorous or serious spiritual reflections, these provide convincing evidence of the transformational impact of living out the Gospel demands in a world that encourages self-advancement.[16]

In a column entitled "Aims and Purposes of the Catholic Worker Movement," Dorothy Day tried to explain what the movement is all about:

> Together with the Works of Mercy, feeding, clothing and sheltering our brothers and sisters, we must indoctrinate. We must "give reason for the faith that is in us." Otherwise we are scattered members of the Body of Christ, we are not "all members one of another." Otherwise our religion is an opiate, for ourselves alone, for our comfort or for our individual safety or indifferent custom.
>
> We believe that all people are brothers and sisters in the Fatherhood of God. This teaching, the doctrine of the Mystical Body of Christ, involves today the issue of unions (where people call each other brothers and sisters); it involves the racial question; it involves cooperatives, credit unions, crafts; it involves Houses of Hospitality and Farming Communes. It is with all these means that we can live as though we believed indeed that we are all members one of another, knowing that when "the health of one member suffers, the health of the whole body is lowered."
>
> What we do is very little. But it is like the little boy with a few loaves and fishes. Christ took that little and increased it. He will do the rest. What we do is so little we may seem to be constantly failing. But so did He fail. He met with apparent failure on the Cross. But unless the seed fall into the earth and die, there is no harvest.
>
> And why must we see results? Our work is to sow. Another generation will be reaping the harvest.[17]

The Holy Family Catholic Worker House

My wife and I joined with three other couples in 1985 to start the Holy Family Catholic Worker House in South Bend, Indiana. It housed homeless families until they could get back on their feet. It ran for 20 years before we finally had to close and sell the house. The stimulus for starting the house was the national crisis of homelessness. The recession of the early 1980s combined with the anti-welfare policies of the newly elected national administration led to a dramatic increase in homeless people, particularly families. In South Bend, at that time, there were no places for homeless families. Instead, the city gave families one-way bus tickets to Chicago where there were beds for families.

Our group of four couples including friends Ralph and Reggie Weissert, Steve and Cathy Moriarty, Michael and Margaret Garvey and ourselves met and discussed what could be done. We knew our Christian faith called us to do something and CST emphasized subsidiarity. Thus, this was our problem, not someone else's. One of the couples had experience running a Catholic Worker House in Davenport, Iowa. Margaret Garvey had started it and Michael Garvey worked there until they got married, had children, and came to Notre Dame for work. Almost like a *sign,* Sally Schlipmann, a worker from the Davenport house showed up in South Bend and said she would run one here if we got a house. So, we decided to raise the money to buy a house near Notre Dame so we could tap into student volunteers.

Our initial fund-raising drive took place around a kitchen table one winter night after a very good dinner and in the glow of much wine. We pooled our ideas and address books and began writing to like-minded and generous friends, asking their assistance in the purchase of a house about a mile south of the Notre Dame campus. Before very long, personal checks began to arrive in the mail and began to pile up in a wicker basket over which a plaster statue of St. Joseph the Worker presided. Our development program did not really grow much more sophisticated than that over the years.

Before too long, we'd raised $19,000, but we went ahead and agreed to purchase the house for $22,000. We didn't worry too much about starting out $3,000 in the hole, because we knew people would be kind, and a few of us remembered how Dorothy Day used to quote (with dubious accuracy) Pope Pius XII about how one should never hesitate "to run up bills for the poor." People were kind. Guests came, and we began to argue among ourselves about the quality of hospitality we could provide them. That is pretty much what went on right to the end. Our annual budget rarely exceeded $12,000, and our house was staffed entirely by unpaid volunteers who lived with the people they served.

Our small size enabled us to provide a form of hospitality more personal than what larger, and sometimes more efficient, local shelters are able to offer. The precarity of our finances, the idiosyncrasy of our community, and the fallibility of our administration invited us to regard our guests as ambassadors of Christ. We were the first to admit that we far too often declined that invitation, but we all knew that it is a standing invitation, and we all shared a conviction that it was the central treasure of our work.

At the beginning of Advent and at the beginning of Lent we sent out a fund-raising appeal written by Michael Garvey, that usually concluded with this paragraph:

> We want to share with you the invitation which Christ has extended to us. We ask for your help in finding and greeting the Risen Christ in the suffering families who are our guests. We ask for your money, your labor, your friendship and your prayers. And we pray that the One Who rose from the dead, even as He said He would, will bless you and your family and friends.
>
> Yours in Christ the Worker.

The four couples plus others over time functioned as a "board" that handled finances, repairs, insurance, taxes, public relations, etc. The director, Sally, and many successors, lived in the house keeping order and directing daily operations. The board and a growing list of volunteers helped out. The four bedrooms were continually full, with whole families in each bedroom. At one time we numbered 17 guests living there. We housed and fed people; we searched for jobs, apartments, and financial assistance ranging from food stamps to disability insurance.

In addition, we held a Mass at the house on the first and third Sundays of the month. They started at 11:00 a.m. and were followed by juice, coffee, rolls, and lots of talk and fun. We tried hard to bring together the guests with volunteers and supporters to form a community of support. We also held a once a month Friday night discussion (what Peter Maurin called "clarification of thought"); such topics as "Saints for Today," "Teenage Pregnancies," "Irish Music," and "Mideast Crisis." Every Thursday a potluck dinner was held at the house with volunteers and anyone interested invited to share food and companionship with each other and with the guests.

Not all things went well. There were many challenges that tested both our dedication, and our good humor. One family set fire to the curtains in their bedroom, and before it could be put out the fire marshal estimated it caused $23,000 in damages. Fortunately, our insurance company honored their policy despite our inadvertently not paying the premium that year. Also, fortunately, we did the repairs much cheaper because we got free labor, not only our usual volunteers but the university provided students who had to do service for misbehavior. We got mainly football players who caught the spirit of the Catholic Worker and did great work.

We also struggled with the parents of some of the families who believed that corporal punishment was the answer to any misbehavior. We insisted no hitting your kids as long as you lived with us. We lost a few families because of this.

During our last years of operation, we had ever greater difficulty finding live-in directors. Attempts to run the house with just a board that did not live with the guests simply did not work. At the time we finally decided to close the Holy Family Catholic Worker House, the proceeds from the sale were given to Michael Baxter and Margie Pfeil who had recently started a new Catholic Worker called Peter Claver House.

The Peter Claver Catholic Worker House

Their focus was more traditional in that they catered to single men and women. The Peter Claver House has gone on to do wonderful things. They operate a house for men, another for women, and Our Lady of the Road Café and Drop-in Center. These all serve the homeless population of the area. They feed and house the homeless, provide showers, clothes, laundry services, and general hospitality. They operate a food co-op that brings together local farmers and under-served populations. They hold monthly Friday night "clarification sessions" based on those started in the 1930s by Peter Maurin. These cover a wide range of issues and often lead to action by the Catholic Worker staff or by friends of the movement. They have a chapel where both Catholic Masses and ecumenical services are held. The inner-city block where they located their men's and women's houses has been renovated by both ex-guests and ex-staff buying homes and remodeling them. They have made the neighborhood attractive without pushing out the low-income residents. They have set up a shop to make coffins for the homeless. And as of 2020, Our lady of the Road, with financial assistance from the city, is providing daytime shelter from the hard winter weather of South Bend. They are living the Catholic Worker motto: "To build a new society within the ruins of the old."

Casa Juan Diego Catholic Worker House

Probably the most thriving Catholic Worker house, of the 200 in existence, is in Houston, Texas. Casa Juan Diego was founded in 1980, following the Catholic Worker model of Dorothy Day and Peter Maurin, to serve immigrants and refugees and the poor. From one small house it has grown to ten houses. Casa Juan Diego publishes a newspaper, the *Houston Catholic Worker*, six times a year to share the values of the Catholic Worker movement and the stories of the immigrants and refugees uprooted by the realities of the global economy.[18] They provide many services, particularly to immigrants, and spread the Catholic Worker message through their newspaper and their work. For example, these are some of their activities:

- Women's House of Hospitality: Hospitality and services for immigrant women and children, especially serving pregnant or physically battered women and their children or those whose husbands have been deported.
- Assistance to paralyzed or seriously ill immigrants living in the community.
- Casa Don Marcos men's house: Hospitality for immigrant men new to the country.

- Casa Don Bosco for sick and wounded men.
- English classes for guests of the houses.
- Casa Maria Social Service Center and Medical Clinic; food is distributed at Holy Ghost Church.
- Casa Juan Diego Medical Clinic.
- Food Center: serves 300 people each week.
- Liturgy in Spanish Wednesdays at 7:00 p.m.

Pope Francis's writings indicate a strong affinity for the Catholic Worker position. In a *Letter Sent by the Holy Father for the Event "Economy of Francesco,"* he starts this way:

> I am writing to invite you to take part in an initiative very close to my heart An event that will allow me to encounter young men and women studying economics and interested in a different kind of economy: one that brings life not death, one that is inclusive and not exclusive, humane and not dehumanizing, one that cares for the environment and does not despoil it. An event that will help bring us together and allow us to meet one another and eventually enter into a "covenant" to change today's economy and to give a soul to the economy of tomorrow.[19]

The event is to meet in Assisi, and Pope Francis goes on to say:

> For me, it is also a fitting place to inspire a new economy. There Francis stripped himself of all worldliness in order to choose God as the compass of his life, becoming poor with the poor, a brother to all. His decision to embrace poverty also gave rise to a vision of economics that remains most timely. A vision that can give hope to our future and benefit not only the poorest of the poor, but our entire human family. A vision that is also necessary for the fate of the entire planet, our common home, "our sister Mother Earth", in the words of Saint Francis in his Canticle of the Sun.
>
> The name of this event—Economy of Francesco—clearly evokes the Holy Man of Assisi and the Gospel that he lived in complete consistency, also on the social and economic level. Saint Francis offers us an ideal and, in some sense, a programme. For me, who took his name, he is a constant source of inspiration.[20]

CONCLUSION

Finally, the Catholic radicalist tradition would argue that we must remember that we are but short-term sojourners in this world. It is a temporary dwelling place, where Christians reside not as citizens with full rights but as aliens or pilgrims whose true home is in a city to come. The Church's tendency to provide religious legitimation to the debilitating and sometimes lethal workings of the market and/or the state must be resisted. Is this setting the Church over and against the world? Yes and no! Yes, if by the world we mean autonomous individualism, mass culture, economic oppression, and the rule of secular power. No, if this means rejecting in principle all social activity outside the Church. What is needed is an alternative space from which the Church (the members of Christ's body) can mount a critique of the iniquities of both the market and the state. And from which they might carry out their obligation to love God and their neighbor.

NOTES

1. Michael J. Baxter, "Notes on Catholic Americanism and Catholic Radicalism: Toward a Counter-Tradition of Catholic Social Ethics," in *American Catholic Traditions: Resources for Renewal*, eds. Sandra Yowm Mize and William L. Portier (Maryknoll, NY: Orbis Books, 1997), 54.
2. Baxter, "Notes." 61.
3. John Paul II, *Centesimus Annus*, para. 43.
4. Francis, "Address at Expo Fair," Santa Cruz de la Sierra, July 9, 2015. http://www.archivioradiovaticana.va/storico/2015/07/10/pope_francis_speech_at_world_meeting_of_popular_movements/en-1157291
5. Dorothy Day, *The Catholic Worker*, June 1948.
6. G. K. Chesterton, *The Outline of Sanity* (London: Methuen and Co., 1926), 108, 151.
7. Chesterton, *Outline*, 148.
8. Dorothy Day, *The Long Loneliness* (New York: Harper, 1952), 224.
9. Chesterton, *Outline*.
10. William Miller, *Dorothy Day: A Biography* (Harper and Row, 1982), 428.
11. See http://www.cjd.org/whatis.html.
12. Harry Murray, *Do Not Neglect Hospitality: The Catholic Worker and the Homeless* (Philadelphia: Temple University Press, 1990).
13. Murray, *Hospitality*, 212.
14. Martin Buber, *I and Thou* (New York: Free Press, 1971).
15. See Helen Deines, "The Catholic Worker Movement: Communities of Personal Hospitality and Justice." https://www.academia.edu/8962828/The_Catholic_Worker_Movement_Communities_of_Personal_Hospitality_and_Justice
16. See R. R. Troester, *Voices from the Catholic Worker* (Philadelphia: Temple University Press, 1993); Michael O. Garvey, *Confessions of a Catholic Worker* (Notre Dame, IN: Ave Maria Press, 1978); M. H. Ellis, *A Year in the Catholic Worker: A Spiritual Journey with the Poor* (New York: Paulist Press, 2000).
17. Dorothy Day, "Aims and Purposes of the Catholic Worker Movement," *The Catholic Worker*, February 1940.

18. See https://cjd.org/.

19. Pope Francis, *LETTER SENT BY THE HOLY FATHER FOR THE EVENT "ECONOMY OF FRANCESCO"*, Vatican City, May 1, 2019. http://www.vatican.va/content/francesco/en/letters/2019/documents/papa-francesco_20190501_giovani-imprenditori.html

20. Francis, *Economy of Francesco*.

Chapter Fourteen

Wisdom and the Christian Economist

Or: Was the Good Samaritan a Bad Economist?

As I worked on this book I constantly prayed for guidance and for wisdom—to be guided by scripture and CST, to try to see both sides of an argument, to put myself in the shoes of the marginalized, to not ignore inconvenient facts, to recognize my limitations, and always to listen:

> Give me Wisdom, the consort at your throne, and do not reject me from among your children; For I am your servant . . . a man weak and short-lived and lacking in comprehension of judgment and of laws. Indeed, though one be perfect among mortals, if Wisdom, who comes from you, be lacking, that one will count for nothing. (Wisdom 9: 4-6)

In his paper, "Reflections of an (Unreflecting) Christian Economist," Professor John Lunn says: "I don't think there is a uniquely 'Christian economics.' Instead, there are Christians who do economics."[1] He goes on to say that he believes that economics is simply a social science that attempts to explain and predict certain types of human behavior. Thus, the task of the economist, Christian or otherwise, is rational inquiry into the ways that societies coordinate the economic activities of their members. Christians, as economists, are not called to build a better economic system.

In the body of the paper, Professor Lunn discusses three research projects that he has worked on. He concludes from this discussion: "My faith has not had a noticeable impact on the approach I take when engaging in research."[2]

He concludes the paper with an appeal to Luther's Two Kingdoms to justify this way of approaching economics. According to Luther, there are two ways that God works in the world—through the Gospel and through the law. The first is given to us by the person of Jesus Christ. The second is from the order of creation and has legitimacy independent of the Gospel. That is, those without the Gospel can create good social, political, and economic systems. The Gospel rules in our relations to God and the law in our relations with other people and society. The economy is a special covenantal structure, as are the family, educational institutions, and legitimate government. Another one is vocations including occupations. "Vocation is directed towards this life, and towards one's neighbor rather than toward God."[3] He goes on to argue that "economics is a legitimate vocation."[4] Economists do not have the wisdom to determine goals; rather, they help determine the most efficient means of attaining the posited goals. In Professor Judith Deane's words, they are merely good physicians.[5] I find their use of vocation to be unduly limited. Rather it can be seen as the underlying motivation for "the calling or destiny we have in this life and the hereafter. . . . The vocation of the laity consists in seeking the Kingdom of God by engaging in temporal affairs and directing them according to God's will."[6]

There are three specific reasons why I am unconvinced by Professor Lunn's defense of an economics uninfluenced by faith. First, Luther, in fact, argued that even in their vocations Christians serve Christ, are bound by his moral law, and are to do everything that they do in service to him. Lunn writes as if faith and Scripture have little to say about life in this world.

Second, as we saw in Chapter 2, unlike natural sciences, economics is prescriptive as well as descriptive. Values are built into the core of economic theory. Therefore, efficiency itself is value based. I am unable to accept the values embedded in economic theory, particularly the elevation of self-interest that supposedly leads to efficiency, the neglect of income distribution, and the attempts to export these values into studies of the family, the role of the state and so on. Christian thought and biblical tradition make self-interest a central aspect of *fallen* human nature which as Christian believers we are bound to strive to counter with prayer, good works, and the cultivation of virtue.

The most extreme of the free-market economists and utilitarians, Ludwig von Mises, rejected the notion that faith and its call for love of neighbor, could have anything to do with economic order:

> Neither love nor charity nor any other sympathetic sentiments but rightly understood selfishness is what originally impelled man to adjust himself to the requirements of society, to respect the rights and freedoms of his fellow men and to substitute peaceful collaboration for enmity and conflict.[7]

Mises goes on to make it clear that there really can be no sentiment beyond selfishness: "The man who gives alms to hungry children does it, either because he values his own satisfaction expected from this gift higher than any other satisfaction he could buy by spending this amount of money, or because he hopes to be rewarded in the beyond."[8]

What Mises did not realize is the god-like ability of people to include the good of others within the notion of their own good. The father and mother labor long hours to support each other and their children because they are able to see their own good in the good of those they love. When as Christians we reflect that all men and women are made in the image and likeness of God and deserving of our love, then the notion of a common good becomes intuitively obvious. "Mises rejected the notion of God, and hence was forced to reject the notion of love, so that the only thing left was naked self-interest, pure selfishness. But on the foundation of selfishness, we can build neither a peaceable kingdom nor a rational economy."[9]

Third, in my opinion the Two Kingdoms thesis (and its counterpart in Roman Catholicism) runs the danger in a pluralistic society of leading to a marginalization of Gospel demands to bring the Good News of Jesus to all we encounter. For both reasons, the Christian economist needs that wisdom of the heart to know when the Gospel is being compromised in the name of "value-free" science.

Kathryn Tanner, Professor of Theology at Princeton, argues that serving God and Mammon is an impossibility. The reality is, we cannot do so because both God and Mammon demand priority, and only one can be first. In the language of Scripture, both are jealous gods. Christian life should be marked by a commitment to God above all: "One should never be wholeheartedly committed to any ordinary pursuit in the way one is to be committed to God," Tanner writes.[10]

Yes, we have a fallen nature, but grace allows us to constrain that self-interest and be loving and cooperative; at least some of the time. But as Pope Francis points out:

> Time, my brothers and sisters, seems to be running out; we are not yet tearing one another apart, but we are tearing apart our common home. . . . The earth, entire peoples and individual persons are being brutally punished. And behind all this pain, death and destruction there is the stench of what Basil of Caesarea called "the dung of the devil". An unfettered pursuit of money rules. The service of the common good is left behind. Once capital becomes an idol and guides people's decisions, once greed for money presides over the entire socioeconomic system, it ruins society, it condemns and enslaves men and women, it destroys human fraternity, it sets people against one another and, as we clearly see, it even puts at risk our common home.[11]

We need to be reminded that we live in a world where the strong all too often exploit the weak and befoul the nest we call Earth and that we live in a society imbued with a mindless materialism which corrodes the spirit through its banality and aimless distractions. Underneath the pervasive presence of the external world is an inner reality that reflects the mystery of life. Hopefully, faith will allow us to see that at profound, often unperceived levels "everything connects"—even apparent opposites such as hope and despair and that despair contains hope and hope is always poised to be overcome by despair. The clash of hope and despair calls us to pause and reflect on the meaning of life and the nature of that power, we call God, which is its source.

As noted in the previous chapter, in May 2019, Pope Francis wrote a letter to "Young Economists and Entrepreneurs" to invite them to an event "close to his heart" in Assisi, March 2020. In the letter he says this will allow him to encounter:

> "Young men and women studying economics and interested in a different kind of economy: one that brings life not death, one that is inclusive and not exclusive, humane and not dehumanizing, one that cares for the environment and does not despoil it. An event that will . . . allow us to . . . enter into a *"covenant" to change today's economy and to give a soul to the economy of tomorrow*."[12]

Pope Francis goes on to say: "I invite each of you to work for this covenant, committing yourselves individually and in groups to cultivate together the dream of a new humanism responsive to the expectations of men and women and to the plan of God."[13]

As we just saw in the previous chapter, Roman Catholic thought in the United States has developed a tradition analogous to the Two Kingdoms thesis, what theologian Michael Baxter calls the "Catholic Americanist Tradition."[14] Those traditions that separate the Gospel and the natural law dominate the academic world. The controlling assumption of scholarship in the university is that true, authentic scholarship can flourish only in an environment of "academic freedom" of intellectual inquiry from all prior assumptions about nature, the world, human society, human destiny, and especially God.[15] The result is an increasing irrelevance of religious faith for higher education qua education and for the practice of science, natural and social sciences.

I have spent my academic life trying to bring my Christian faith, and specifically CST, to bear on my work. But in doing so, I have had to water down Christianity, moving from the theological to the philosophic, from Christ's love to human values. I remember a dinner party of faculty soon after being hired at my first job following graduate school. A faculty member, who later became well known in the profession, asked me upon hearing I was a believing Christian, "Do you really believe all that s___!" Later at Notre Dame several PhD students wanted to do dissertations that openly called upon their

Christian beliefs. I said, "No, if you want the profession to listen, your work must be cast in secular terms."

How can a committed Christian economist respond to Pope Francis's call "to give a soul to the economy of tomorrow"? A nonstarter is to keep your Christian intellectual tradition to yourself as I did in much of my work. But this carries with it a terrible disadvantage—it reduces Christianity to an extracurricular activity. That is, it presumes that Christianity "has no real part to play when it comes to genuine, authentic, hard-core, nuts-and-bolts academic . . . scholarship."[16]

Economists must be careful from unwittingly accepting the so-called "subtraction story"—the myth that all the goods of modernity are the result of subtracting religion from all domains of life. Charles Taylor, in *A Secular Age,* argues that lying at the root of the Modern Moral Order is what he labels exclusive humanism mainly arising in the 18th century.[17] This moral order conceives of the person in overly individualistic or atomistic terms, readily accepts the epistemological turn, opposes reason and science to "religion," imposes a system of impersonal forces (i.e., "the market") and thus marginalizes a traditional Christian worldview replete with grace, mystery, exorbitant love, sanctity and sin. Traditional Christianity (and historical religion more broadly) now becomes associated with the irrational, superstitious, fanatical and, of course, always potentially violent. One result is that any self-respecting scientist, including economists, must disavow that their religious faith, if any, has anything to do with their scientific work.

The alternative is difficult for us secular-trained academic economists to even begin to visualize and I do not have any secret answers. While accurate description of empirical reality is crucial for any economic analysis, it is equally important to locate these descriptions within a broader theological vision of the final destiny of those human beings we call producers and consumers. Here is where Christian wisdom must play a role.

What is that Christian wisdom? I have had to grapple with the question: "Was the Good Samaritan a bad economist?" As we saw in Chapter 1, Dickens's character, Thomas Gradgrind, in his novel, *Hard Times*, is: "A man of realities. A man of facts and calculations . . . proving something no doubt—probably . . . that the Good Samaritan was a Bad Economist."[18] He was a person who understood the wisdom of the head but knew nothing of the wisdom of the heart.

What is that wisdom of the heart and where is it found? To use Isaiah Berlin's words, as we saw in Chapter 2, we need to be foxes not hedgehogs. Hedgehogs distill the world's complexity into a simple and universal theory. Foxes do the opposite and are skeptical of simple theories about complex systems such as national economies. Wisdom of the head is found in the hedgehog, but wisdom of the heart is the possession of the fox.

Economics needs the humanities, particularly Christian wisdom, to be the fox that makes their theories both accurate and more humane. As economists, a place to start might be with the criteria for a richer research agenda that Donald Hay derived from his biblical analysis in *Economics Today: A Christian Critique*:

i. How far do economic institutions allow human beings to exercise responsible stewardship?
ii. Is the use of natural resources characterized by care for the created order?
iii. Does the economy create opportunities for satisfying work?
iv. What are the causes of poverty and are there societal mechanisms to prevent destitution?
v. Has the pursuit of wealth, for its own sake, become detrimental to other values in society e.g. family life?
vi. How effective are the authorities at promoting justice in the economic sphere?[19]

However, people need their material needs met *and* they need meaning in their lives. For the Christian, this means they need the love of Christ in their lives. Liberals with their focus on the role of the state to help the poor and conservatives with their worship of liberty and the free market both err. While it is true that the economy is not the cause of all problems and cannot solve all of them either, attention must be paid to where the economy helps or hinders people to lead a life with meaning.

Minimally this forces me to evaluate every economic policy and economic institution on how they affect "these least ones"—materially and spiritually. There is great room for debate on how best to help the poor and disadvantaged but that must always be the goal. It is most important to recognize that the poor and disadvantaged are God's beloved children with a dignity and importance second to none. Policies need to work *with* them not *for* them.

I also realize that there are very smart and moral people who disagree with my positions. Additionally, I must not forget that I as a member of the body of Christ am the one called to feed, clothe, house, visit, and bring the Good News of Christian redemption. I cannot delegate all this duty to the state. Much I must do on my own, with others in the family, in civic groups, and through the Church.

Though I have been disillusioned about the results of both free markets and economic policy since the 1980s, I realize that there is no alternative to finding better macroeconomic policies that prioritize full employment and greater equality. At the same time policies need to be designed to utilize and strengthen the mediating institutions, particularly families and unions.

As an economist *qua* economist, I must continually search for how my belief in Jesus Christ makes a difference in how I do economics. Economic theory abstracts men and women into rational calculators of pleasure and pain. Christianity teaches us the stories of the Good Samaritan[20] and the Sermon on the Mount. We need an economics that accounts for and approves of people following the beatitudes and being Good Samaritans. This book has been my attempt, however inadequate, to create such an economics.

I close with Pope Francis's reflection on the Good Samaritan from his latest encyclical, *Fratelli Tutti*,[21] which he offers in the mode of St. Ignatius's *Spiritual Exercises*. Rather than focus on abstract moralizing or a social and ethical message, Francis invites us to enter into the Gospel parable. Christ's words to the scholar of the law are directed to us: "*Which of these three, do you think, was a neighbor to the man who fell into the hands of the robbers?*"[22] Among the priest, the Levite, the Samaritan, "Which of these persons do you identify with? . . . Which of these characters do you resemble?"[23] We face a fundamental choice. "Here, all our distinctions, labels and masks fall away: it is the moment of truth. Will we bend down to touch and heal the wounds of others? Will we bend down and help another to get up?"[24]

> The parable eloquently presents the basic decision we need to make in order to rebuild our wounded world. In the face of so much pain and suffering, our only course is to imitate the Good Samaritan. Any other decision would make us either one of the robbers or one of those who walked by without showing compassion for the sufferings of the man on the roadside. The parable shows us how a community can be rebuilt by men and women who identify with the vulnerability of others, who reject the creation of a society of exclusion, and act instead as neighbors, lifting up and rehabilitating the fallen for the sake of the common good. At the same time, it warns us about the attitude of those who think only of themselves and fail to shoulder the inevitable responsibilities of life as it is.[25]

Pope Francis's reflections on the Good Samaritan show that he refuses to accept the private/public or charity/justice dichotomies. Francis refuses to separate love from politics. He sees the future of politics to be at the local level with personal interactions and the revitalization of families, parishes, and other mediating institutions. Francis writes:

> We should not expect everything from those who govern us, for that would be childish. We have the space we need for co-responsibility in creating and putting into place new processes and changes . . . [we] can start from below and, case by case, act at the most concrete and local levels, and then expand to the

farthest reaches of our countries and our world, with the same care and concern that the Samaritan showed for each of the wounded man's injuries.[26]

Thus, my answer to the question, "Was the Good Samaritan a Bad Economist?" is no!

NOTES

1. John Lunn, "Reflections of an (Unreflecting) Christian Economist," paper prepared for the Conference on Christian Economists Doing Economics: A View from the Trenches, Association for Christian Economists, Chicago, January 5, 1998, pp. 2-3.

2. Lunn, "Reflections," 16.

3. Lunn, "Reflections," 18.

4. Lunn, "Reflections," 19.

5. Judith M. Deane, "Being a Good Physician: Reflections on Christianity and Economic Research," paper prepared for the Conference on Christian Economists Doing Economics: A View from the Trenches, Association for Christian Economists, Chicago, January 5, 1998.

6. "Vocation," in *Catechism of the Catholic Church* 906. https://www.usccb.org/sites/default/files/flipbooks/catechism/905/#zoom=z

7. Ludwig von Mises, *Human Action: A Treatise on Economics*, vol. 4, revised (San Francisco: Fox & Wilkes, 1963), 165.

8. von Mises, *Human Action,* 35.

9. John Medaille, "Three Mistakes about Economics, and One Serious Error about Man." https://www.academia.edu/35862530/Three_Mistakes_about_Economics.docx

10. Kathryn Tanner, *Christianity and the New Spirit of Capitalism* (New Haven: Yale University Press, 2019). Also see the excellent review, "Grace over Greed," in *Commonweal* (September 24, 2019) by Meghan J. Clark.

11. Francis, Address at Expo Fair, Santa Cruz de la Sierra, July 9, 2015. http://www.archivioradiovaticana.va/storico/2015/07/10/pope_francis_speech_at_world_meeting_of_popular_movements/en-1157291

12. Francis, "Letter Sent by the Holy Father for the Event 'Economy of Francesco,'" Vatican City, 2019. The coronavirus pandemic of 2020 forced cancellation of the June meeting and its rescheduling as a virtual gathering in November 2020.

13. Francis, "Letter."

14. Michael J. Baxter, "Notes on Catholic Americanism and Catholic Radicalism: Toward a Counter-Tradition of Catholic Social Ethics," in *American Catholic Traditions: Resources for Renewal*, eds. Sandra Yowm Mize and William L. Portier (Maryknoll, NY: Orbis Books, 1997), 53-71.

15. This view has been ridiculed by Bernard Lonergan as "the principle of the empty head." Quoted in Michael J. Baxter and Frederick C. Bauerschmidt, "*Eruditio*

without *Religio*?: The Dilemma of Catholics in the Academy," *Communio* 22 (Summer 1995), 285.

16. Baxter and Bauerschmidt, "*Eruditio* without *Religio,*" 287.

17. Charles Taylor, *A Secular Age* (Cambridge: Harvard University Press, 2018).

18. Charles Dickens, *Hard Times*, Book 1, Chapter 2.

19. Donald A. Hay, *Economics Today: A Christian Critique* (Grand Rapids, MI: Eerdmans, 1989), 2.

20. See Donald E. Frey, "The Good Samaritan as Bad Economist," *Cross Currents* 46, no. 3 (Fall 1996).

21. Francis, *Fratelli Tutti*, encyclical letter, Vatican website, October 3, 2020, Vatican website, 2020. http://www.vatican.va/content/francesco/en/encyclicals/documents/papa-francesco_20201003_enciclica-fratelli-tutti.html

22. Francis, *Fratelli Tutti*, para. 56.

23. Francis, *Fratelli Tutti*, para. 64.

24. Francis, *Fratelli Tutti*, para. 70.

25. Francis, *Fratelli Tutti*, para. 67.

26. Francis, *Fratelli Tutti*, para. 77-78.

Bibliography

Akerlof, George A., and Robert J. Shiller. *Animal Spirits.* Princeton, NJ: Princeton University Press, 2009.

Anderson, Elizabeth. "The Ethical Limitations of the Market." *Economics and Philosophy* 6, no. 2 (1990): 179-205.

Aristotle. *Nicomachean Ethics*, 1103b.

Aristotle. *The Politics.* Trans. Carnes Lord. Chicago: University of Chicago Press, 1984.

Arrow, Kenneth. "Gifts and Exchange." *Philosophy and Public Affairs* I, no. 4 (Summer 1972): 343-362.

Barry, Brian M. *Treatise on Social Justice.* Vol. 1, *Theories of Justice.* Berkeley: University of California Press, 1989.

Baxter, Michael J. "Notes on Catholic Americanism and Catholic Radicalism: Toward a Counter-Tradition of Catholic Social Ethics." In *American Catholic Traditions: Resources for Renewal*, edited by Sandra Yowm Mize and William L. Portier, 53-71. Maryknoll, NY: Orbis Books, 1997.

Baxter, Michael J., and Frederick C. Bauerschmidt. "*Eruditio* without *Religio*?: The Dilemma of Catholics in the Academy." *Communio* 22 (Summer 1995).

Bazen, Stephen. "Minimum Wages and Low-wage Employment." In *Labour Market Inequalities*, edited by Mary Gregory, Wiemer Salvedra, and Stephen Bazen, 124-130. Oxford: Oxford University Press, 2000.

Becker, Gary S., and Guity Nashat Becker. *The Economics of Life: From Baseball to Affirmative Action to Immigration, How Real-world Issues Affect Our Everyday Life.* New York: McGraw-Hill, 1996.

Benedict XVI, *Deus Caritas Est*, encyclical letter, Vatican website, 205. http://www.vatican.va/content/benedict-xvi/en/encyclicals/documents/hf_ben-xvi_enc_20051225_deus-caritas-est.html

Benedict XVI. *Caritas in Veritate*, encyclical letter, Vatican website, para. 34. http://www.vatican.va/content/benedict-xvi/en/encyclicals/documents/hf_ben-xvi_enc_20090629_caritas-in-veritate.html

Bentham, Jeremy. *In Praise of Usury.* London: Payne, 1790.

Berger, Peter. "In Praise of Particularity: The Concept of Mediating Structures." *Review of Politics* 38, no. 3 (July 1976): 134.

Berlin, Isaiah. "The Hedgehog and the Fox: An Essay of Tolstoy's View of History." In *Russian Thinkers,* edited by H. Hardy. Princeton, NJ: Princeton University Press, 2013.

Bernhardt, Annette, et al. "Broken Laws, Unprotected Workers: Violations of Employment and Labor Laws in America." *A Report of the National Employment Law Project.* Available at http://www.nelp.org/content/uploads/2015/03/Broken LawsReport2009.pdf?nocdn=1, 2-6.

Beyer, Gerald J. "The Principle of Mercy in the World of Work Today." In *Ekonomia a chrześcijaństwo: świat biznesu przez pryzmat encyklik św. Jana Pawła II Centesimus annus i Laborem Exercens*, edited by Agnieszka Lekka-Kowalik, 141-168. Warszawa: Instytut Papieża Jana Pawła II, 2017.

Boland, Lawrence. "On the Futility of Criticizing the Neo-classical Maximization Hypothesis." *American Economic Review* 71, no. 5 (December 1981): 1031-1036.

Boland, Lawrence. *The Foundations of Economic Method.* London: Allen & Unwin, 1982.

Boulding, Kenneth E. *The Economy of Love and Fear.* Belmont, CA: Wadsworth Publishing Co., 1973.

Bradshaw, Ted K. "Theories of Poverty and Anti-Poverty Programs in Community Development," Oregon State University, Rural Poverty Research Center, Working Paper No. 06-05 (February 2006).

Brassey, Alexis, and Stephen Barber, eds. *Greed.* Basingstoke, UK: Palgrave-Macmillan 2009.

Brooks, David. "The Rise of the Haphazard Self." *New York Times*, May 14, 2019.

Brooks, David. "I Was Once a Socialist. That Changed." *New York Times*, December 6, 2019.

Buber, Martin. *I and Thou.* New York: Free Press, 1971.

Buchanan, James M. *Liberty, Market and State: Political Economy in the 1980s.* New York: New York University Press, 1986.

Card, David, and Alan Krueger. *Myth and Measurement.* Princeton, NJ: Princeton University Press, 1995.

Catechism of the Catholic Church. https://www.usccb.org/sites/default/files/flipbooks/catechism/905/#zoom=z

Chesterton, G. K. *The Outline of Sanity.* London: Methuen and Co., 1926.

Chua, Amy. *World on Fire: How Exporting Free Market Democracy Breeds Ethnic Hatred and Global Instability.* New York: Doubleday, 2002.

Clark, Meghan J. "Grace over Greed." *Commonweal,* September 24, 2019.

Cohen, Patricia. "Ivory Tower Unswayed by Crashing Economy." *New York Times*, March 4, 2009.

Cohn, Alain, et al. "Civic Honesty around the Globe." *Science* 20 (June 2019). https://science.sciencemag.org/content/early/2019/06/19/science.aau8712

Colander, David. *The Making of an Economist, Redux.* Princeton: Princeton University Press, 2007.

Covino, William, and D. Jolliffe. *Rhetoric: Concepts, Definitions, Boundaries.* Boston: Allyn and Bacon, 1995.

Cowan, Tyler. "The Scope and Limits of Preference Sovereignty." *Economics and Philosophy* 9, no. 2 (1993): 253-269.

Crowley, Sharon. *Ancient Rhetorics for Contemporary Students.* New York: MacMillan College Publishing Company, 1994.

Daly, Herman E., and John B. Cobb Jr. *For the Common Good: Redirecting the Economy toward Community, the Environment, and a Sustainable Future*, 2nd ed. Boston: Beacon Press, 1994.

Danner, P. *The Economic Person.* London: Rowman and Littlefield Publishers, 2002.

Day, Dorothy. "Aims and Purposes of the Catholic Worker Movement," *The Catholic Worker*, February 1940.

Day, Dorothy. *The Catholic Worker.* June 1948.

Day, Dorothy. *The Long Loneliness.* New York: Harper, 1952.

Deane, Judith M. "Being a Good Physician: Reflections on Christianity and Economic Research," paper prepared for the Conference on Christian Economists Doing Economics: A View from the Trenches, Association for Christian Economists, Chicago, January 5, 1998.

Deines, Helen. "The Catholic Worker Movement: Communities of Personal Hospitality and Justice." https://www.academia.edu/8962828/The_Catholic_Worker_Movement_Communities_of_Personal_Hospitality_and_Justice

Dempsey, B. *The Functional Economy: The Bases of Economic Organization.* Englewood Cliffs, NJ: Prentice-Hall, Inc.

Desmond, Matthew. "Americans Want to Believe Jobs Are the Solution to Poverty, They're Not." *New York Times*, September 11, 2018. https://www.nytimes.com/2018/09/11/magazine/americans-jobs-poverty-homeless.html

Dickens, Charles. *Hard Times.* New York: Random House, 2001.

Dobos, Ned, Christian Barry, and Thomas Pogge. *Global Financial Crisis: The Ethical Issues.* Basingstoke, UK, and New York: Palgrave Macmillan, 2011.

Dutt, Amitava Krishna, and Charles K. Wilber. *Economics and Ethics: An Introduction.* New York and London: Palgrave Press, 2010; revised paperback edition, 2013.

Easterlin, Richard A. "Does Economic Growth Improve the Human Lot? Some Empirical Evidence." In *Nations and Households in Economic Growth: Essays in Honor of Moses Abramovitz,* edited by Paul A. David and Melvin W. Reder, 89-126. New York: Academic Press, 1974.

Ellis, M. H. *A Year in the Catholic Worker: A Spiritual Journey with the Poor.* New York: Paulist Press, 2000.

Escobar, Arturo. *Encountering Development.* Princeton: Princeton University Press 1994.

Escobar, Arturo. "Development, Violence and the New Imperial Order." *Development* 47 (March 2004): 15-21.

Escobar, Arturo, "Environmental Social Movements and the Politics of Place." *Development* 45 (March 1, 2002): 28-36.

Etzioni, Amitai. "Toward a Kantian Socio-Economics." *Review of Social Economy* 45, no. 1 (April 1987): 37-47.

Evensky, Jerry. "Ethics and the Invisible Hand." *Journal of Economic Perspectives* 7, Vol. 2 (Spring 1993): 197-205.

Falk, Armin, and Michael Kosfeld. "The Hidden Costs of Control." Working Paper No. 250, 2005, Institute for Empirical Research in Economics, University of Zurich.

Fehr, Ernst, and Simon Gächter. "Do Incentive Contracts Undermine Voluntary Cooperation?" Working Paper No. 34, 2002, Institute for Empirical Research in Economics, University of Zurich.

Fehr, Ernst, and Simon Gachter. "Fairness in the Labour Market: A Survey of Experimental Results." Working Paper No. 114, 2002, Institute for Empirical Research in Economics, University of Zurich.

Fehr, Ernst, and John A. List. "The Hidden Costs and Returns of Incentives: Trust and Trustworthiness among CEOs." *Journal of the European Economic Association* 2, no. 5 (2004): 743-771.

Fehr, Ernst, and Bettina Rockenbach. "Detrimental Effects of Sanctions on Human Altruism." *Nature* 422 (2003), 137-140.

Ferguson, Charles. *Predator Nation: Corporate Criminals, Political Corruption, and the Hijacking of America.* New York: Crown 2012.

Folbre, Nancy. "Shared Capitalism." *Economix: New York Times Blog*, May 30, 2011. http://economix.blogs.nytimes.com/2011/05/30/shared-capitalism

Francis. Letter from Pope Francis to Prime Minister David Cameron for the G8 Meeting, June 17-18, 2013. http://w2.vatican.va/content/francesco/en/letters/2013/documents/papa-francesco_20130615_lettera-cameron-g8.html

Francis. *Evangelii Gaudium*, apostolic exhortation, Vatican website, November 24, 2013, chapter 2. http://w2.vatican.va/content/francesco/en/apost_exhortations/documents/papa-francesco_esortazioneap_20131124_evangelii-gaudium.html

Francis. General audience, Vatican City, April 22, 2015. http://www.vatican.va/content/francesco/en/audiences/2015/documents/papa-francesco_20150422_udienza-generale.html

Francis. Remarks, meeting with political, business and community leaders, Quito, Ecuador, July 7, 2015. http://www.vatican.va/content/francesco/en/speeches/2015/july/documents/papa-francesco_20150707_ecuador-societa-civile.html

Francis. Address at Expo Fair, Santa Cruz de la Sierra, July 9, 2015. http://www.archivioradiovaticana.va/storico/2015/07/10/pope_francis_speech_at_world_meeting_of_popular_movements/en-1157291

Francis. *Laudato Si*, encyclical letter, Vatican website. http://w2.vatican.va/content/francesco/en/encyclicals/documents/papa-francesco_20150524_enciclica-laudato-si.html

Francis. Audience with the participants in the Convention organized by the Dicastery for Promoting Integral Human Development on the fiftieth anniversary of "Populorum Progressio" (2018). http://press.vatican.va/content/salastampa/en/bollettino/pubblico/2017/04/04/170404a.html

Francis. "Letter Sent by the Holy Father for the Event 'Economy of Francesco,'" Vatican City, 2019. The coronavirus pandemic of 2020 forced cancellation of the June meeting and its rescheduling as a virtual gathering in November 2020.

Francis. *Fratelli Tutti*, encyclical letter, Vatican website, October 3, 2020, Vatican website, 2020. http://www.vatican.va/content/francesco/en/encyclicals/documents/papa-francesco_20201003_enciclica-fratelli-tutti.html

Francis. "Letter Sent by the Holy Father for the Event 'Economy of Francesco," Vatican City, May 1, 2019. http://www.vatican.va/content/francesco/en/letters/2019/documents/papa-francesco_20190501_giovani-imprenditori.html

Frank, Robert H., Thomas Gilovich, and Dennis T. Regan. "Does Studying Economics Inhibit Cooperation." *Journal of Economic Perspectives* 7, no. 2 (Spring 1993): 159-171.

Freeman, Richard B., Joseph R. Blasi, and Douglas L. Kruse. "Inclusive Capitalism for the American Workforce: Reaping the Rewards of Economic Growth through Broad-based Employee Ownership and Profit Sharing." *Center for American Progress* (March 2011). http://www.americanprogress.org/issues/2011/03/pdf/worker_productivity.pdf

Frey, Bruno S. "Institutions and Morale: The Crowding-out Effect." In *Economics, Values and Organizations*, edited by Avner Ben-Ner and Louis Putterman, 437-460. Cambridge: Cambridge University Press, 1998.

Frey, Bruno S., and Felix Oberholzer–Gee. "The Cost of Price Incentives: An Empirical Analysis of Motivation Crowding-Out." *American Economic Review* 87, no. 4 (1987): 746-755.

Frey, Donald E. "The Good Samaritan as Bad Economist." *Cross Currents* 46, no. 3 (Fall 1996).

Friedman, Benjamin M. *The Moral Consequences of Economic Growth.* New York: Vintage Books, 2005.

Friedman, Milton. *Capitalism and Freedom.* Chicago: University of Chicago Press, 1962.

Fuchs, Victor. "Economics, Values, and Health Care Reform." *The American Economic Review* 86, no. 1 (March 1996): 1-24.

Galbraith, James K. "The Populist." Interview by Debra Solomon. *New York Times Magazine,* November 2, 2008. https://www.nytimes.com/2008/11/02/magazine/02wwln-Q4-t.html?partner=permalink&exprod=permalink

Galbraith, John Kenneth. *American Capitalism. The Concept of Countervailing Power.* New York: Houghton Mifflin Company, 1952.

Garvey, Michael O. *Confessions of a Catholic Worker.* Notre Dame, IN: Ave Maria Press, 1978.

Geissler, Eugene S. "Our Children Our Greatest Teachers." In *Marriage among Christians,* edited by James T. Burtchaell, C.S.C., 58, 61-62. Notre Dame, IN: Ave Maria Press, 1977.

Gneezy, Uri, and Aldo Rustichini, "A Fine Is a Price." *Journal of Legal Studies* 29, no. 1 (2000): 1-17.

Gneezy, Uri, and Aldo Rustichini. "Pay Enough or Don't Pay at All." *Quarterly Journal of Economics* 115, no. 2 (2000): 791-810.

Goodin, Robert E. "Making Moral Incentives Pay." *Policy Sciences* 12 (1980): 131-145.

Goulet, Denis. *The Cruel Choice: A New Concept in the Theory of Development.* New York: Atheneum, 1971.

Goulet, Denis. *Looking at Guinea-Bissau: A New Nation's Development Strategy.* Occasional Paper no. 9. Washington, DC: Overseas Development Council, March 1978.

Goulet, Denis. "Development Experts: The One-Eyed Giants." *World Development* 8, no. 7/8 (July/August 1980): 481-489.

Goulet, Denis. "Inequalities in the Light of Globalization." In *Globalisation and Inequalities,* edited by Louis Sabourin, 3-29. Vatican City: Pontifical Academy of Social Sciences, 2002.

Goulet, Denis. "On Culture, Religion, and Development." In *Reclaiming Democracy,* edited by Marguerite Mendell, 21-32. Montreal & Kingston, London, Ithaca: McGill-Queen's University Press, 2005.

Goulet, Denis. *Development Ethics at Work: Explorations 1960-2002.* New York: Routledge, 2006.

Greenspan, Alan. Testimony before the U.S. House of Representatives' Committee on Oversight and Government Reform in late October. https://www.congress.gov/congressional-report/110th-congress/house-report/930/1

Gross, James A. *A Shameful Business: The Case for Human Rights in the American Workplace.* Ithaca: ILR Press/Cornell University Press, 2010.

Gula, Richard M., PSS. "Moving Hearts." *Give Us This Day* 10, no. 9 (July 2019): 104-5.

Haskins, Ron, and Isabel V. Sawhill. *Creating an Opportunity Society.* Washington, DC: Brookings Institution Press, 2009.

Hauerwas, Stanley, David Burrell, and Richard Bondi. *Truthfulness and Tragedy: A Further Investigation in Christian Ethics.* Notre Dame, IN: University of Notre Dame Press, 1977.

Hauerwas, Stanley. *A Community of Character.* Notre Dame, IN: University of Notre Dame Press, 1981.

Haughton, Rosemary. "Testimony on the Family." *Liberty and Justice for All: Atlanta Hearing.* National Conference of Catholic Bishops, Committee for the Bicentennial, August 9, 1975.

Hausman, Daniel M., and Michael S. McPherson. *Economic Analysis and Moral Philosophy,* 2nd edition. Cambridge: Cambridge University Press, 2006.

Hay, Donald A. *Economics Today: A Christian Critique.* Grand Rapids, MI: Eerdmans, 1989.

Heckman, James J. *Giving Kids a Fair Chance.* Boston: The MIT Press, 2013.

Hirsch, Fred. *Social Limits to Growth.* Cambridge, MA: Harvard University Press, 1978.

Hirschman, Albert O. *Exit, Voice, and Loyalty.* Cambridge, MA: Harvard University Press, 1970.

Hirschman, Albert O. *Rival Views of Market Society.* New York: Viking, 1986.

Hollenbach, David. *Claims in Conflict: Retrieving and Renewing the Catholic Human Rights Tradition.* New York: Paulist Press, 1979.

Hunt, H. L. *Alpaca.* Dallas, TX: H. L. Hunt Press, 1960.

Iguíñiz, Javier. "Freedom in Amartya Sen and Gustavo Gutiérrez: Religious and Secular Common Grounds." In *How Should We Talk about Religion? Perspectives, Contexts, Particularities*, edited by James Boyd White. Notre Dame, IN: University of Notre Dame Press, 2006.

Iguíñiz, Javier. "Ethical Dilemmas of Theory or Reality? Three Approaches to the Inevitability of Sacrifices in Economic Development." In *New Directions in Development Ethics*, edited by Charles K. Wilber and Amitava Krishna Dutt. Notre Dame, IN: University of Notre Dame Press, 2010.

Ireland, Thomas R., and James V. Koch. "Blood and American Social Attitudes." In *The Economics of Charity*, 145-155. London: Institute of Economic Affairs, 1973.

Jameson, Kenneth P. "Data and Social Science Rhetoric: Policy and Instruction." Presented at joint IASSIST/Computing in the Social Sciences Conference, Minneapolis, MN, May 15, 1996.

Jameson, Kenneth P., James H. Weaver, and Charles K. Wilber. "Strategies of Development: A Survey." In *Development Economics: Theory, Practice, and Prospects*, edited by Thomas R. DeGregori, 137-177. Kluwer Academic Publishers, 1989.

Jayachandran, Seema. "A Raise for Workers Can Be a Win for All." *New York Times*, June 21, 2020.

John Paul II. *Familiaris Consortio*. Washington, DC: United States Catholic Conference, 1981.

John Paul II. *Sollicitudo Rei Socialis*, encyclical letter, Vatican website, 1987. http://www.vatican.va/content/john-paul-ii/en/encyclicals/documents/hf_jp-ii_enc_30121987_sollicitudo-rei-socialis.html

John Paul II. *Centesimus Annus*, encyclical letter, Vatican website, 1991. http://www.vatican.va/content/john-paul-ii/en/encyclicals/documents/hf_jp-ii_enc_01051991_centesimus-annus.html

John XXIII. *Pacem in Terris*, encyclical letter, Vatican website, April 11, 1963. http://www.vatican.va/content/john-xxiii/en/encyclicals/documents/hf_j-xxiii_enc_11041963_pacem.html.

Johnson, Allan G. Why Is There Poverty? Excerpt from Allan G. Johnson, *The Forest and the Trees: Sociology as Life, Practice, and Promise*. Temple University Press; 3rd edition (September 12, 2014). https://www.agjohnson.us/essays/poverty/

Kahrl, Andrew W. "Black People's Land Was Stolen." *New York Times*, June 21, 2019.

Kay, John. "How Economics Lost Sight of Real World." *Financial Times*, April 21, 2009. https://www.ft.com/content/35301d06-2eaa-11de-b7d3-00144feabdc0

Kelman, Steven. *What Price Incentives? Economists and the Environment*. Boston, MA: Auburn House Publishing Company, 1981.

Keynes, John Maynard. *The General Theory of Employment, Interest and Money*. London: Macmillan,1936.

Kindleberger, Charles P. *Panics, Manias and Crashes. A History of Financial Crises*. New York: Basic Books, 1978.

Knox, F. "The Doctrine of Consumer Sovereignty." *Review of Social Economy* 18, no. 2 (1960): 138-149.

Kristof, Nicholas. "'We're No. 28! And Dropping!'" *New York Times*, September 9, 2020. https://www.nytimes.com/2020/09/09/opinion/united-states-social-progress.html

Krugman, Paul. "Inequality Is a Drag." *New York Times*, August 7, 2014. http://www.nytimes.com/2014/08/08/opinion/paul-krugman-inequality-is-a-drag.html?emc=edit_th_20140808&nl=todaysheadlines&nlid=41712839

Kruse, Douglas L., Richard B. Freeman, and Joseph R. Blasi, eds. *Shared Capitalism at Work: Employee Ownership, Profit and Gain Sharing, and Broad-based Stock Options.* Chicago: University of Chicago Press, 2010.

Kuhn, Thomas S. "Reflections on My Critics." In *Criticism and the Growth of Knowledge*, edited by Imre Lakatos and Alan Musgrave. Cambridge: Cambridge University Press, 1970.

Kuhn, Thomas S. *The Structure of Scientific Revolutions*, 2nd ed. Chicago: University of Chicago Press, 1970.

Kymlicka, Will. "The Social Contract Tradition." In *A Companion to Ethics*, edited by Peter Singer, 186-96. Oxford: Blackwell, 1991.

Lanchester, John. "Can Economists and Humanists Ever Be Friends?" *New Yorker,* July 16, 2018. https://www.newyorker.com/magazine/2018/07/23/can-economists-and-humanists-ever-be-friends.

Latin American Bishops Conference. *Proceedings of the Latin American Bishops Conference.* Puebla, Mexico. Notre Dame, IN: CCUM, 1979.

Lebergott, Stanley. *Pursuing Happiness: American Consumers in the Twentieth Century.* Princeton, NJ: Princeton University Press, 1993.

Leo XIII. *Rerum Novarum*, encyclical letter, Vatican website, May 15, 1891. http://www.vatican.va/content/leo-xiii/en/encyclicals/documents/hf_l-xiii_enc_15051891_rerum-novarum.html

Loury, Glenn C. "God and the Ghetto." *Wall Street Journal*, February 25, 1993.

Luce, Stephanie. *Labor Movements: Global Perspectives.* Chichester, Great Britain: Polity, 2011.

Lunn, John. "Reflections of an (Unreflecting) Christian Economist." Paper prepared for the Conference on Christian Economists Doing Economics: A View from the Trenches, Association for Christian Economists, Chicago, January 5, 1998.

MacIntyre, Alasdair. *After Virtue: A Study in Moral Theory,* 2nd ed. Notre Dame, IN: University of Notre Dame Press, 1984.

MacIntyre, Alasdair. *Dependent Rational Animals: Why Human Beings Need the Virtues.* Chicago: Open Court Publishing Co., 2001.

Maki, Uskali. "Diagnosing McCloskey." *The Journal of Economic Literature* 33 (September 1995): 1300-1318.

McCloskey, Donald. "The Rhetoric of Economics." *The Journal of Economic Literature* 21 (June 1983): 481-517.

Medaille, John. "Three Mistakes about Economics, and One Serious Error about Man." https://www.academia.edu/35862530/Three_Mistakes_about_Economics.docx.

Mellstrom, Carl, and Magnus Johannesson. "Crowding Out in Blood Donation: Was Titmuss Right?" Working Papers in Economics #180, Department of Economics. Goteborg University, 2005.

Miller, William. *Dorothy Day: A Biography.* Harper and Row, 1982.

Minsky, Hyman. *Stabilizing an Unstable Economy.* New Haven, CT: Yale University Press, Twentieth Century Fund, 1986.

Morson, Gary Saul, and Morton Schapiro. *Cents and Sensibility: What Economics Can Learn from the Humanities.* Princeton, NJ: Princeton University Press, 2017. Cited by Jeffrey R. Bloem in a review in *Faith & Economics*, No. 71 (Spring 2018), 75.

Murray, Charles. *Losing Ground: American Social Policy 1950-1980.* New York, NY: Basic Books, 1984.

Murray, Harry. *Do Not Neglect Hospitality: The Catholic Worker and the Homeless.* Philadelphia: Temple University Press, 1990.

Neuhaus, Richard John. *Doing Well and Doing Good: The Challenge to the Christian Capitalist.* New York: Doubleday Religious Publishing Group, 1992.

Nielsen, Richard P. "Arendt's Action Philosophy and the Manager as Eichman, Richard III, Faust, or Institution Citizen." *California Management Review* 26, no. 3 (Spring 1984): 191-201.

Nordhaus, William, and James Tobin. *Is Growth Obsolete?* Washington, DC: National Bureau of Economic Research, 1972.

Novak, Michael. *The Spirit of Democratic Capitalism.* New York: Simon & Schuster, 1982.

Nozick, Robert. *Anarchy, State and Utopia.* New York: Basic Books, 1974.

O'Boyle, Edward J. *Personalist Economics: Unorthodox and Counter-Cultural*, Presidential Address, Association for Social Economics, January 6, 2001, New Orleans, Louisiana. Revised. August 15, 2001

O'Boyle, Edward. "Requiem for Homo Economicus." *Markets and Morality* 10, no. 2 (2007): 321-338.

Okun, Arthur M. *Equality and Efficiency: The Big Tradeoff.* Washington, DC: The Brookings Institution, 1975.

Ostry, Jonathan D., and Andrew Berg. "Treating Inequality with Redistribution: Is the Cure Worse Than the Disease?" *IMFdirect: The International Monetary Fund's Global Economy Forum*, posted February 26, 2014. http://blog-imfdirect.imf.org/2014/02/26/treating-inequality-with-redistribution-is-the-cure-worse-than-the-disease/

Pabst, Adrian. "Catholic Social Thought and Post-liberal Political Economy." *Radical Orthodoxy Annual Review* (2014). https://www.academia.edu/7629696/Catholic_Social_Thought_and_Post-liberal_Political_Economy?email_work_card=title

Paul VI. *Populorum Progressio*, encyclical letter, Vatican website, March 26, 1967, para. 23. http://www.vatican.va/content/paul-vi/en/encyclicals/documents/hf_p-vi_enc_26031967_populorum.html

Pearce, D. W., and C. A. Nash. *The Social Appraisal of Projects*. New York: John Wiley & Sons, 1981.

Piketty, Thomas. *Capital in the Twenty-First Century.* Cambridge: Belknap Press, 2014.

Piketty, Thomas. *Capital and Ideology.* Belknap Press: An Imprint of Harvard University Press, 2020.

Pius XI. *Quadragesimo Anno*, encyclical letter, Vatican website, 1931. http://www.vatican.va/content/pius-xi/en/encyclicals/documents/hf_p-xi_enc_19310515_quadragesimo-anno.html

Polanyi, Karl. *The Great Transformation.* New York: Farrar and Rinehart, 1944.

Posner, Richard. "The Financial Crisis: Why Were Warnings Ignored?" *The Becker-Posner Blog*, October 12, 2008. https://www.becker-posner-blog.com/2008/10/the-financial-crisis-why-were-warnings-ignored—posner.html

Putnam, Robert D. *Our Kids: The American Dream in Crisis.* New York: Simon & Schuster, 2015.

Rabin, Matthew. "Behavioral Economics." In *New Frontiers in Economics*, edited by Michael Szenberg and Lall Ramrattan. Cambridge, UK: Cambridge University Press, 2004.

Randazzo, Anthony, and Jonathan Haidi. "The Moral Narratives of Economists." *Economic Journal Watch* 12, no. 1 (January 2015): 49-57.

Reddy, Y. V. *Global Crisis, Recession and Uneven Recovery.* Hyderabad: Orient Black Swan, 2011.

Rodgers, H. R. *American Poverty in a New Era of Reform.* New York: M. E. Sharpe, 2000.

Rorty, Richard. "Science as Solidarity." In *The Rhetoric of the Human Sciences: Language and Argument in Scholarship in Public Affairs*, edited by John Nelson, et al. Madison: The University of Wisconsin Press, 1987.

Ross, Martha and Nicole Bateman. "Low-Wage Work Is More Pervasive Than You Think, and There Aren't Enough 'Good Jobs' to Go Around." Brookings, Thursday, November 21, 2019.

Rothenberg, Jerome. "Cost-Benefit Analysis: A Methodological Exposition." In *Handbook of Evaluation Research*, Vol. II, edited by M. Guttentag and S. Strueninge. Beverly Hills: Sage Publications, 1975.

Rowe, Jonathan, and David Bollier. "The Missing Sector: Enlarging Our Sense of the Economy." http://jonathanrowe.org/the-missing-sector

Sachs, Jeffrey. *The End of Poverty: Economic Possibilities for Our Time.* New York: Penguin Press, 2005.

Sandel, Michael. *Liberalism and the Limits of Justice*. Cambridge: Cambridge University Press, 1982.

Sandel, Michael J. "What Money Can't Buy: The Moral Limits of Markets." *The Tanner Lectures on Human Values.* Delivered at Brasenose College, Oxford, May 11 and 12, 1998, 89-122.

Schmid, A. Allan. *Property, Power, and Public Choice.* New York: Praeger, 1978.

Schotter, Andrew. *Free Market Economics: A Critical Appraisal.* New York: Palgrave Macmillan, 1984.

Schumpeter, Joseph A. *Capitalism, Socialism, and Democracy,* 3rd ed. New York: Harper & Brothers, 1950.

Schwartz, Barry. "The Dark Side of Incentives." *Business Week,* November 23, 2009.

Scitovsky, Tibor. *The Joyless Economy: An Inquiry into Human Satisfaction and Consumer Dissatisfaction.* New York: Oxford University Press, 1976.

Sen, Amartya K. "The Moral Standing of the Market." In *Ethics and Economics*, edited by Ellen Frankel Paul, Fred D. Miller Jr., and Jeffrey Paul, 1-20. Oxford: Blackwell, 1985.

Sen, Amartya K. "Money and Value: On the Economics and Ethics of Finance." *Economics and Philosophy* 9, no. 2 (1993): 203-227.

Sen, Amartya K. *On Economic Inequality*, Oxford, UK: Oxford University Press, 1973, expanded edition, 1997.

Shearer, Chad, and Isha Shah. "Exploring the Industries That Concentrate Good and Promising Jobs in Metropolitan America." Brookings. December 18, 2018. https://www.brookings.edu/research/opportunity-industries/

Smith, Adam. *An Inquiry into the Nature and Causes of the Wealth of Nations*, ed. W. B. Todd, Vol. 2 of *The Glasgow Edition of the Works and Correspondences of Adam Smith*, general editors, D. D. Raphael and A. Skinner. Oxford: Clarendon Press, 1976.

Smith, Adam. *The theory of moral sentiments*, ed. D. D. Raphael and A. L. Macfie, Vol. 1 of *The Glasgow edition of the works and correspondences of Adam Smith*, general editors, D. D. Raphael and A. Skinner, Oxford: Clarendon Press, 1976.

Solomon, W. David. "Normative Ethical Theories." In *Economics, Ethics, and Public Policy*, edited by Charles K. Wilber, 119-38. Lanham, MD: Rowman & Littlefield, 1998.

Sterba, James. "Social Justice." in *Economics, Ethics and Public Policy*, edited by Charles K Wilber, 187-215. London: Rowman and Littlefield, 1999.

Stewart, David. *Business Ethics.* New York: McGraw-Hill, 1995.

Stiglitz, Joseph E. "Information and Economic Analysis: A Perspective." *Economic Journal*, no. 95 (1981): 21-41.

Streeten, Paul. "What Do We Owe the Future?" *Resources Policy* (March 1986): 4-16.

Tanner, Kathryn. *Christianity and the New Spirit of Capitalism.* New Haven: Yale University Press, 2019.

Tawney, R. H. *Religion and the Rise of Capitalism.* New York: Harcourt, Brace and World, Inc., 1926.

Tawney, Richard. *R. H. Tawney's Commonplace Book*. Cambridge: Cambridge University Press, 1972, 2006.

Taylor, Charles. *A Secular Age.* Cambridge: Harvard University Press, 2018.

Throsby, David. *Economics and Culture*. Cambridge: Cambridge University Press, 2001.

Tickle, Phyllis A. *Greed.* New York: Oxford University Press, 2004.

Titmuss, Richard M. *The Gift Relationship: From Human Blood to Social Policy.* London: Allen and Unwin, 1970.

Troester, R. R. *Voices from the Catholic Worker.* Philadelphia: Temple University Press, 1993.

Trzeciak, Stephen, and Anthony Mazzarelli. *Compassionomics: The Revolutionary Scientific*

United States Catholic Bishops. *Economic Justice for All: Pastoral Letter on Catholic Social Teaching and the U.S. Economy*. U.S. National Catholic Conference of

Bishops: Washington, DC, November 18, 1986. http://usccb.org/upload/economic_justice_for_all.pdf

United States Census Bureau. "Income and Poverty in the United States: 2018." September 10, 2019. https://www.census.gov/library/publications/2019/demo/p60-266.html

Vatican II. "Decree on the Apostolate of the Laity." *The Documents of Vatican II.* New York: Guild Press, 1966.

Vatican Synod Secretariat. "Toward the Synod of 1980: The Role of the Christian Family in Modern Society: Preliminary Paper of the Vatican Synod Secretariat." *Origins: NC Documentary Service* 9, no. 8 (July 19, 1979).

von Mises, Ludwig. *Human Action: A Treatise on Economics*, vol. 4, revised. San Francisco: Fox & Wilkes, 1963.

Wachtel, Paul L. *The Poverty of Affluence: A Psychological Portrait of the American Way of Life.* New York: Free Press, 1983.

Warren, Elizabeth, and Amelia Warren Tyagi. *The Two-Income Trap: Why Middle-Class Parents Are (Still) Going Broke.* New York: Basic Books, revised, updated edition, 2016.

Weaver, James H. "Globalization with a Human Face." Paper delivered to the Association for Social Economics, ASSA Convention, 2004, San Diego, CA.

Whitaker, Morgan. "Most Republicans Think Poverty Caused by Laziness, New Poll Finds." January 23, 2014. http://www.msnbc.com/politicsnation/gop-blames-poverty-laziness#49786

Wicksell, Dustin. "Warren Buffett: Poverty Is the 'American Nightmare.'" Inquisitr. May 9, 2015. https://www.inquisitr.com/2077281/warren-buffett-poverty-is-the-american-nightmare/

Wilber, Charles K. "Awakening the Giant: Strategies for Restarting the U.S. Economy." *America: The National Catholic Weekly* 203, no. 10 (October 18, 2010): 13-16.

Wilber, Charles K. *Catholics Spending and Acting Justly.* Notre Dame, IN: Ave Maria Press, 2011.

Wilber, Charles K. "Empirical Verification and Theory Selection: The Keynesian-Monetarist Debate." *Journal of Economic Issues* XIII, no. 4 (December 1979): 973-982.

Wilber, Charles K. "The New Economic History Reexamined: R.H. Tawney on the Origins of Capitalism." *The American Journal of Economics and Sociology* 33, no. 3 (July 1974): 249-258.

Wilber, Charles K. "Sustainable Development, Consumerism, & Catholic Social Thought." In *Looking beyond the Individualism & Homo Economicus of Neoclassical Economics*, edited by Edward J. O'Boyle, 129-143. Milwaukee, WI: Marquette University Press, 2011.

Wilber, Charles K. "Thomas Aquinas." In *The SAGE Encyclopedia of World Poverty*, Second Edition, edited by Mehmet Odekon, Vol. 1, 74-76. Los Angeles, CA: SAGE Reference, 2015.

Wilber, Charles K., and Amitava Krishna Dutt. *New Directions in Development Ethics: Essays in Honor of Denis Goulet.* Notre Dame, IN: University of Notre Dame Press, 2010.

Wilber, Charles K., and Roland Hoksbergen. "Ethical Values and Economic Theory: A Survey," *Religious Studies Review* 12, no. 3/4 (July/October 1986): 211-212.

Wilkinson, T. M. "The Ethics and Economics of the Minimum Wage." *Economics and Philosophy* 20 (2004): 351-374.

Woodfield, G. "Road Blocks in Achieving a 100% Voluntary Blood Donation Rate in the South Asian Region." *Asian J Transfus Sci,* serial online, 1:33-38 (2007). Cited March 23, 2007. Available from: http://www.ajts.org/article.asp?issn=0973-6247;year=2007;volume=1;issue=1;spage=33;epage=38;aulast=Woodfield

Index

About the Author

Charles K. Wilber is Emeritus Professor of Economics and Fellow, Joan B. Kroc Institute for International Peace Studies at the University of Notre Dame. He is the author of 15 books and over 100 articles in both professional journals and more popular venues. His research and writing have focused on issues of economic development, ethics and economics, Social Economics. The present work pulls together my journey as a Christian and an economist. How has my faith impacted my view of economics and how has my work as an economist challenged my faith?

www.ingramcontent.com/pod-product-compliance
Ingram Content Group UK Ltd.
Pitfield, Milton Keynes, MK11 3LW, UK
UKHW041841031026
15587UKWH00002B/941

9 781793 637000